ROUTLEDGE LIBRARY EDITIONS: THE GULF

Volume 16

THE YEMEN ARAB REPUBLIC

THE YEMEN ARAB REPUBLIC
The Politics of Development, 1962–1986

ROBERT D. BURROWES

LONDON AND NEW YORK

First published in 1987 in Great Britain by Croom Helm Ltd.
First published in 1987 in the United States of America by Westview Press, Inc.

This edition first published in 2016
by Routledge
2 Park Square, Milton Park, Abingdon, Oxon OX14 4RN

and by Routledge
711 Third Avenue, New York, NY 10017

Routledge is an imprint of the Taylor & Francis Group, an informa business

© 1987 Robert D. Burrowes

All rights reserved. No part of this book may be reprinted or reproduced or utilised in any form or by any electronic, mechanical, or other means, now known or hereafter invented, including photocopying and recording, or in any information storage or retrieval system, without permission in writing from the publishers.

Trademark notice: Product or corporate names may be trademarks or registered trademarks, and are used only for identification and explanation without intent to infringe.

British Library Cataloguing in Publication Data
A catalogue record for this book is available from the British Library

ISBN: 978-1-138-11959-8 (Set)
ISBN: 978-1-315-64190-4 (Set) (ebk)
ISBN: 978-1-138-18312-4 (Volume 16) (hbk)
ISBN: 978-1-138-18433-6 (Volume 16) (pbk)
ISBN: 978-1-315-64530-8 (Volume 16) (ebk)

Publisher's Note
The publisher has gone to great lengths to ensure the quality of this reprint but points out that some imperfections in the original copies may be apparent.

Disclaimer
The publisher has made every effort to trace copyright holders and would welcome correspondence from those they have been unable to trace.

The Yemen Arab Republic

The Politics of Development, 1962–1986

Robert D. Burrowes

Westview Press • Boulder, Colorado

Croom Helm • London and Sydney

This volume is included in Westview's Special Studies on the Middle East.

All rights reserved. No part of this publication may be reproduced or transmitted in any form or by any means, electronic or mechanical, including photocopy, recording, or any information storage and retrieval system, without permission in writing from Westview Press.

Copyright © 1987 by Westview Press, Inc.

Published in 1987 in the United States of America by Westview Press, Inc.; Frederick A. Praeger, Publisher; 5500 Central Avenue, Boulder, Colorado 80301

Published in 1987 in Great Britain by Croom Helm Ltd., Provident House, Burrell Row, Beckenham, Kent, BR3 1AT

Library of Congress Cataloging-in-Publication Data
Burrowes, Robert D.
  The Yemen Arab Republic.
  (Westview special studies on the Middle East)
  Bibliography: p.
  Includes index.
  1. Yemen—Politics and government. I. Title.
II. Series.
DS247.Y48B87 1987   953'.32   86-15832
ISBN 0-8133-0435-0

British Library Cataloguing-in-Publication Data
Burrowes, Robert D.
The Yemen Arab Republic: the politics of development, 1962-1986.
(Westview special studies on the Middle East)
1. Yemen—social conditions
I. Title
953'.32053   HN564.A8
ISBN 0-7099-5024-1

Printed and bound in the United States of America

∞ The paper used in this publication meets the requirements of the American National Standard for Permanence of Paper for Printed Library Materials Z39.48-1984.

10   9   8   7   6   5   4   3   2   1

To

Ron Hart, a young anthropologist and friend
who died before he could write about the
Yemenis he knew and loved so well

and to

Leigh Douglas, a young and dedicated student
of Yemeni political history
who was killed by terrorists in Lebanon

and to

Four of the Yemenis who freely taught me so well
of the history, culture, and politics of
their beloved Yemen

Dr. Abd al-Karim al-Iryani

Muhammad Anaam Ghaleb

Muhammad Abdullah al-Shami

Amin Abd al-Wahid

Contents

List of Maps xi
Preface xiii
List of Abbreviations and Acronyms xvii

1 Yemen and the Yemenis: An Introduction 1

   Terrain and Climate 1
   Settlements and Communications 6
   People and Society 7
   History and the Yemeni Nation 12

2 From Imamate to Republic: 1904–1967 15

   The Time of Imams Yahya and Ahmad 15
   The 1962 Revolution, the YAR, and the al-Sallal Era 22

3 National Reconciliation and the al-Iryani Era:
   1967–1971 28

   Conservative Republicanism and Its Constraints 28
   Security Needs and Economic Constraints 34
   Economic and Financial Institution Building 38

4 Contradictions in the al-Iryani Regime: 1971–1974 43

   Improved Prospects 44
   Manifest Political Constraints 49
   The Coalition Strained 52

5 Political Adjustment and Socioeconomic Development
   Under al-Hamdi: 1974–1976 57

   Political Adjustment Under al-Hamdi 58
   State Building and Modernization Under al-Hamdi 62
   The al-Hamdi Regime and Political Construction 67

6	Domestic Stalemate and Fast-evolving External Politics: 1975–1977	75
	The Domestic Stalemate	75
	Foreign Policy and External Relations	78
7	The al-Ghashmi Interlude: 1977–1978	86
	The Death and Legacy of al-Hamdi	86
	The Accession and Rule of al-Ghashmi	88
	Al-Ghashmi's Demise	92
8	The Salih Regime: Bleak Prospects and Faint Hopes, 1978–1981	94
	The Salih Regime Hits Bottom: Spring 1979	94
	Attempts to Stem and Turn the Political Tide: 1979–1981	98
9	Political Pieces Put into Place: 1982–1984	118
	The NDF and the PDRY	119
	Completion and Promotion of the Second Five-Year Plan	122
	The National Dialogue and the General People's Congress	124
	Economic Troubles and Political Order: 1983–1984	125
10	Yemen and Petroleum: The Mid-1980s and Beyond	133
	The Search for Oil in Yemen	134
	Yemeni Oil: Current Effects and Implications for the Future	140
	Conclusion	151
	Postscript: December 1986	153

Notes 157
Bibliographical Essay 161
Index 163

Maps

1 Regional setting 2
2 The Yemen Arab Republic 3
3 The two Yemens 13

Preface

From my notebook on Christmas Day 1975, in the city of Taiz, the Yemen Arab Republic: "I want to keep my story about the politics of development in Yemen current, to bring it down as close to today as I can. The general reading public in the USA is not exactly waiting with bated breath for a book on Yemen. I want to snare a few readers who are not Middle East specialists or blood relatives, and I think my chances will be better if I can lay claim to the latest word on a place that, if I'm lucky, may be somewhat in the news." I finally finished the book in late spring 1986, and I was lucky. Hunt Oil Company struck oil in the Yemen Arab Republic (YAR) in 1984, and newspaper and magazine coverage picked up after that. The YAR president opened the first Yemeni oil refinery in April 1986, an occasion attended by U.S. Vice President George Bush and, among others, executives from Hunt Oil and Exxon Corporation. Three months earlier, the ruling Marxist party in the People's Democratic Republic of Yemen, the other Yemen, was convulsed by a very bloody and public struggle for power, an event of considerable interest to corporate and government leaders in the United States.

Why a book on North Yemen or, more properly, the Yemen Arab Republic? This book is my equivalent of Hillary's climbing Everest because it was there: I wrote about North Yemen because that's where I ended up. I went to the YAR for the first time and in complete ignorance to visit with friends when I fled Lebanon and my teaching job at the American University of Beirut during the fighting in late 1975. The "short visit until things settled down in Beirut" turned into a year's stay, lasting through most of 1976, and a decision to learn from scratch about the politics of development in the YAR. A year in New York and Beirut was followed by a four-year stay in the YAR, from 1978 through 1981. During my time in the YAR, while residing in Taiz, Sanaa, and a bit in rural al-Mahwit, I built furniture for expatriates, helped bring up and teach soccer to a fine young man, did consulting and a couple of studies for development agencies, and directed a USAID-funded rural-development project for American Save the Children. Mostly, though, I spent my five years in the YAR poking around and studying the Yemenis and their politics. Largely by chance, I became friends with several very knowledgeable Yemenis in high posts, and I have had the good luck of being able to maintain some of these contacts since leaving the YAR.

One peevish reason for writing about the YAR is to counter the Saudi-centered view of the Arabian Peninsula that prevails in the United States, one in which the Peninsula is seen as big, rich Saudi Arabia surrounded by a handful of tiny, weak, and artificial Arab oil states and an uncertainly located place or places called Yemen. ("Is there more than one of them?" "It's Communist, isn't it?") I have come to care greatly for this place called Yemen. It has been of real importance from time to time in human history and is just now again becoming an important country on the Arabian Peninsula. Indeed, I have my own metaphor for the Peninsula, one that reveals my bias in favor of Yemen. Yemen is comparable to the lowest corner of a giant, mostly empty, rectangular pants pocket—the Arabian Peninsula. Over the millennia, this corner has collected most of the pocket's mountains, rainfall, vegetation, people, history, monuments, and other cultural artifacts. Seemingly not included, alas, was the oil of Arabia and the new cities, industries, and wealth spawned by that oil. It is in combination with these other resources that the recent discovery of oil is about to make a big difference for the YAR.

Another reason for this book is my long intellectual and emotional involvement in politics, nation-state building, and socioeconomic change in the Third World. North Yemen informs the student of the history of modernity. Almost totally isolated and insulated from the modern world and modern politics until the 1962 Revolution, it is still for the most part a living museum—one of the last extant examples of a large and complex traditional social system—and a nearly unique historical laboratory for students of political and socioeconomic change. These processes, now moving very rapidly in the YAR, are still in their early stages, and many of the leaders who initiated modern nation-state building, political construction, and socioeconomic change are still active in Yemeni government and politics— and willing to talk about it. Having grown to young adulthood in a profoundly traditional society, they are now, in their mid-40s to early-50s, contemporary equivalents of the men who launched the process of state building in fifteenth- or sixteenth-century England and France. They will not be found in the YAR, nor will their likes be found elsewhere in the world, for many more years.

This study focuses on the events and issues of nation-state building and socioeconomic change in North Yemen in the years just before the 1962 Revolution and, in much greater detail, during the quarter century since the YAR was founded. The material is presented chronologically and by regime. An introductory chapter on Yemen and the Yemenis is followed by a chapter on the traditional political system of North Yemen, the Zaydi imamate, particularly during the first six decades of the twentieth century, and on the al-Sallal regime that founded the YAR and ruled from the 1962 Revolution until 1967. Chapters 3 and 4 deal at length with the regime headed by President Abd al-Rahman al-Iryani and with efforts to end a long civil war and to proceed with the tasks of state building and modernization between 1967 and 1974. Chapters 5 and 6 explore the efforts of

President Ibrahim al-Hamdi to renovate the political system and to establish the YAR in the regional system during the years between his assumption of power in 1974 and his assassination in 1977. After a short chapter on the brief tenure of President Ahmad al-Ghashmi, chapters 8 and 9 discuss the long rule of President Ali Abdullah Salih and his relatively successful effort since 1978 to reconstitute the political system and to generate support and legitimacy for himself and the system over which he presides. Chapter 10, the final chapter, deals with the politics of development during the period 1984–1986, particularly as it relates to the discovery and initial development of oil in the YAR, and with the domestic and external implications of this oil for the future.

I regard it a great privilege to have lived and worked in the YAR during this exciting and crucial period of its history. It would take a full page just to list all of the Yemenis, other than the four in the dedication, who helped make this study possible. Let me offer them a collective but nonetheless heartfelt thanks, a thanks for being, in addition to kind and generous, so open to and trusting of the questioning American in their midst. I don't like to call my friends "my informants," but my friends did inform me so well and freely. I also want to thank my many non-Yemeni friends, American and otherwise, who supported my efforts in Yemen and New York with free lodging, little jobs, facts, ideas, and kind encouragement. My thanks also to the Social Science Research Council and the American Council of Learned Societies for funds for research in the YAR in 1978 and to my colleagues at New York University's Hagop Kevorkian Center for Near Eastern Studies, especially R. Bayly Winder, Farhad Kazemi, Alexander Melamid, and Peter Chelkowski, for their support and encouragement since 1982. Finally, I want to thank JoAnn Stevens, my wife, who put up with four years of groans, long silences, and tiresome threats of suicide. "Do it or don't do it, but stop whining," she said—often. And she also got us both to quit smoking well before I finished my fitful scribbling.

Robert D. Burrowes
Hagop Kevorkian Center for Near Eastern Studies
New York University

Abbreviations and Acronyms

ANM	Arab Nationalist Movement
BP	British Petroleum
CPO	Central Planning Organization
CYDA	Confederation of Yemeni Development Associations
FLOSY	Front for the Liberation of Occupied South Yemen
GPC	General People's Congress
IFC	International Finance Corporation
IMF	International Monetary Fund
LCCD	local council for cooperative development
LDA	local development association
NLF	National Liberation Front
NIPA	National Institute for Public Administration
NDF	National Democratic Front
NDC	National Dialogue Committee
OPIC	(United States') Overseas Private Investment Corporation
PDRY	People's Democratic Republic of Yemen
PRF	Popular Resistance Forces
PLO	Palestine Liberation Organization
PCA	People's Constituent Assembly
UNDP	United Nations Development Program
YAR	Yemen Arab Republic
YBRD	Yemen Bank for Reconstruction and Development
YHOC	Yemen Hunt Oil Company
Yomico	Yemen Oil and Mines Industry Company
Yominco	Yemen Oil and Mineral Company
YSP	Yemeni Socialist party

1

Yemen and the Yemenis: An Introduction

North Yemen, or, more properly, the Yemen Arab Republic (YAR), is located on the margins of the Arab world, on the southwest corner of the Arabian Peninsula, the corner that is formed by the Red Sea and the Gulf of Aden, pointed toward Ethiopia and Djibouti, and separated from the African continent by the narrow Bab al-Mandab Straits. (See Map 1.) It shares this corner of Arabia with South Yemen, the People's Democratic Republic of Yemen (PDRY), which is less to its south than to its southeast and east. The YAR is bounded unambiguously on the west by the waters of the Red Sea and less precisely on the north and northeast by the Kingdom of Saudi Arabia. The YAR's long eastern border with the PDRY and its shorter northeastern one with Saudi Arabia are still undemarcated; the YAR and its two neighbors converge at an uncertain point on the edge of the inhospitable desert known as the al-Rub al-Khali, the Empty Quarter. Dwarfed by Saudi Arabia, which is eleven times its size, the YAR occupies a tiny portion of the land mass of the Arabian Peninsula. Although its exact size is made uncertain by undemarcated borders, it is roughly the size of the state of Nebraska or South Dakota. In this small area reside, according to the 1986 census, approximately nine million people, a bit fewer than in Ohio but more than in Michigan. The YAR's population is larger than that of the Kingdom of Saudi Arabia and slightly more than half the total for the entire peninsula. Its number of people may be four times that of the PDRY, even though the YAR has less than two-thirds the area of this neighbor. Together, the two Yemens contain a clear majority of the total population of the Arabian Peninsula.

Terrain and Climate

Much of North Yemen consists of ruggedly mountainous terrain, belying notions that the Arabian Peninsula consists of only flat or gently rolling expanses of sand desert and otherwise arid land. The steep, jagged mountains run roughly north and south the full length of the country, parallel to the Red Sea coast. (See Map 2.) The mountain peaks rise higher as one moves

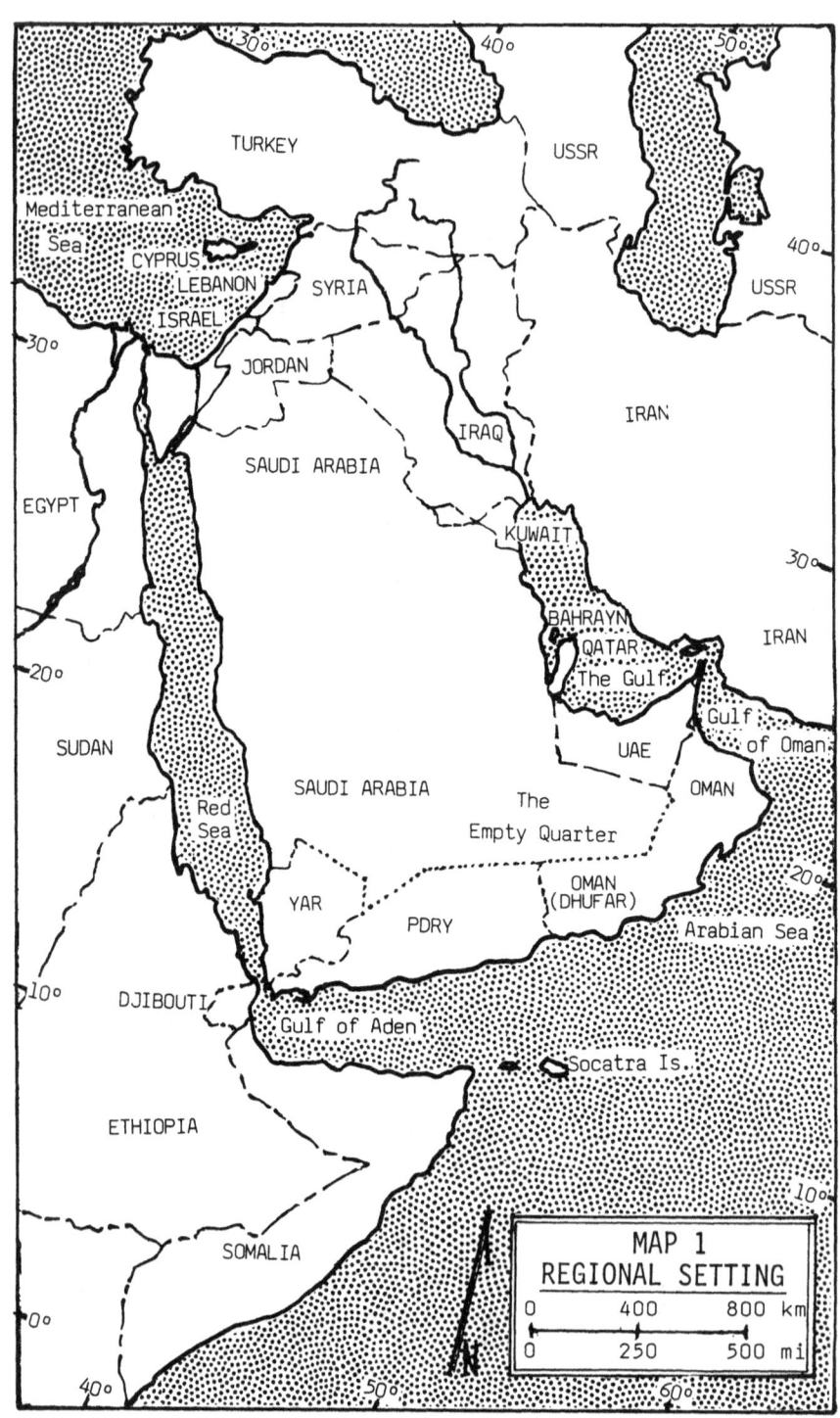

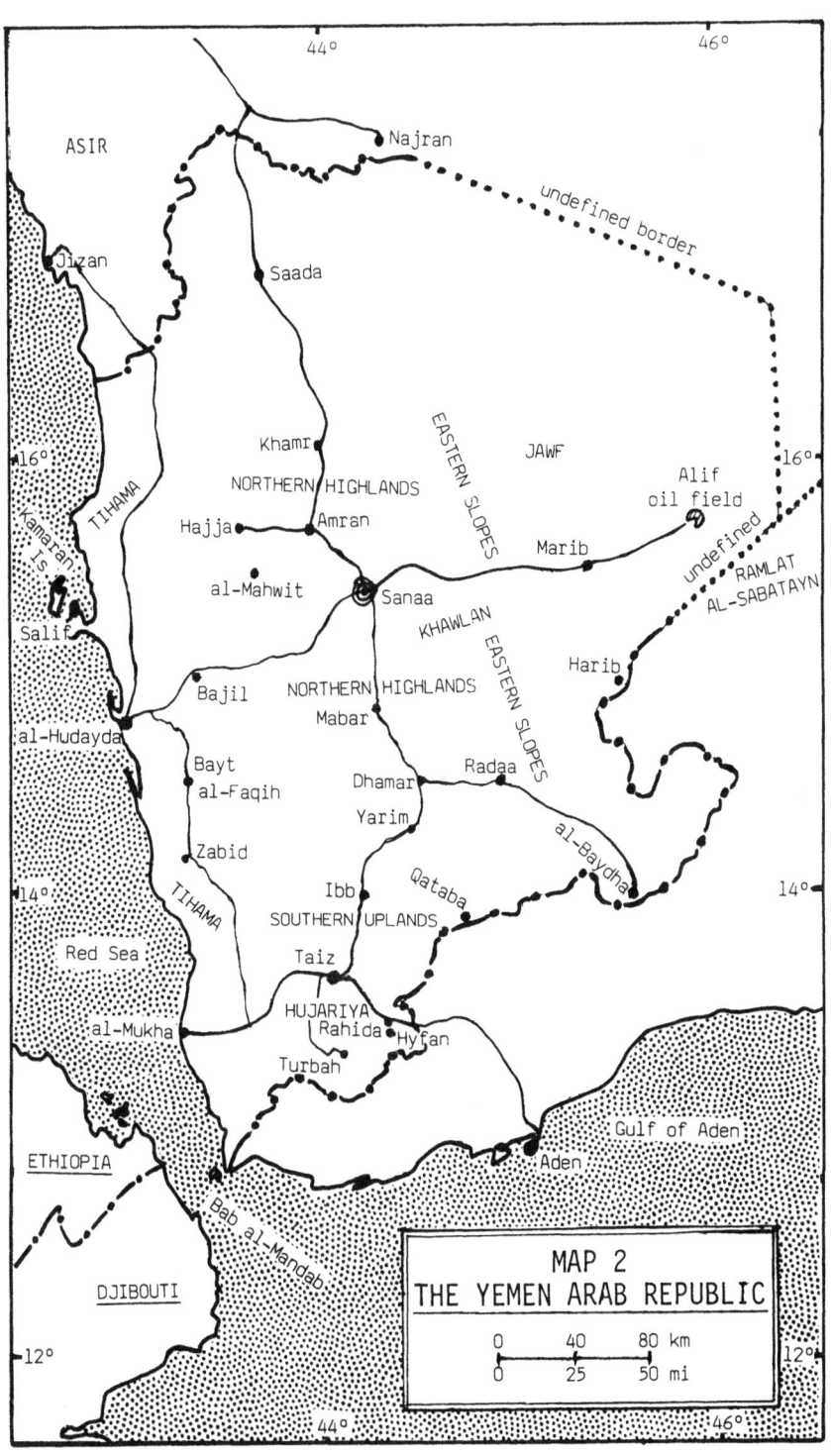

south from the border with Saudi Arabia and attain their greatest height west of Sanaa, the YAR's capital city. The summit of Jabal Nabi Shuayb, at more than 12,000 feet (3,700 meters), is the highest point on the Arabian Peninsula. Though still formidable, the mountains gradually diminish in height as one moves south from Sanaa toward the PDRY. They turn nearly 90° to the east near the border between the two Yemens, and their southern face drops off precipitously several thousand feet to lowlands that then slope south toward Aden, the capital of the PDRY, and the Gulf of Aden.

North Yemen is located between the equator and the Tropic of Cancer, at about the same latitude as the northern half of Central America from Nicaragua to southern Mexico. Proximity to the equator means that the length of days and nights varies little from season to season and that periods of light and dark are roughly of equal length throughout the year. This, in combination with high elevations, results in a climate for much of the country that is pleasantly temperate year-round. Sanaa, at about 7,500 feet (2,300 meters [m]) and 15° North, boasts fine weather marred only by lip-cracking dryness and dust-laden winds during part of the year. A key to the pleasant weather of Sanaa and most of those areas of the country at altitudes from 4,500 to 9,000 feet (1,400 to 2,800 m) is the speed with which the earth's surface heats and cools in the often cloudless sky and thin atmosphere. Summer days, typically very warm and sometimes quite hot, are usually tempered by cool evenings and nights. Midwinter nights can be quite cold, and temperatures occasionally drop a bit below freezing during the early morning hours. Winter days, however, are generally warm, owing to the sunny, clear skies that usually prevail. The weather at low elevations, on the Red Sea coast and in the interior to the east and northeast, is far less benign.

Although more abundant in North Yemen than elsewhere on the Arabian Peninsula, the rainfall in most of the country is sparse and erratic at best. The country is on the edge of the Indian Ocean monsoon system. In years when the warm, moist winds from the southwest blow strong, the rain falls as the cooling air is forced up and over the mountains; but when the winds fail, the rain does not come and the land is subject to drought, sometimes for two or more years in succession. Ordinarily there are two rainy seasons, one in the spring and the bigger, more reliable one in the summer and early fall. Hailstorms occur in summer, but few Yemenis have ever seen snow, even from a distance. The rainfall in the Sanaa region, the geographic center of the country, ranges from 8 to 20 inches (20 to 50 centimeters) per year. Greater at the higher elevations to the west and in the uplands south of Sanaa, which are positioned to benefit first and most from the moist winds, the rainfall drops off markedly to the north, northeast, and east of Sanaa. By the time the winds reach these areas, if they reach them at all, they have been stripped of moisture.

The mountain spine of North Yemen helps divide it into four major geographic regions. The heart of the country is in and just to the east of this spine and is divided nearly 85 miles (135 kilometers [km]) south of

Sanaa by the major north-south pass, the Samarra Pass, into two regions, the northern highlands and the southern uplands. The less extensive southern uplands, also known as Lower Yemen, are somewhat lower in elevation and less rugged than the much larger northern highlands, or Upper Yemen. A disproportionately large part of the population of North Yemen is concentrated on the plateaus and terraced hillsides as well as in the valleys and stream beds of the northern highlands and especially the southern uplands. It is in these two regions of higher elevation and cooler temperatures that most of the country's small amount of rain falls, making possible the cultivation of life-sustaining crops of sorghum and some wheat, barley, and alfalfa. Also grown here are coffee and *qat*, the privet-like shrub whose tender leaves are chewed regularly by many Yemeni men and women for their mildly stimulative effect. The rain and the wild vegetation and cultivated crops in streambeds and on the fine system of dry-well terraces of these regions provide sharp contrast to the forbidding aridity of most of the rest of the Arabian Peninsula, earning Yemen in ancient times the name Arabia Felix. Ibb province, in the southern uplands just below the Samarra Pass, is called the Green Province and, along with Taiz province farther to the south, supports the most intensive cultivation and the highest population density in the country. The climatic change is sudden and pronounced travelling south from Samarra—warmer, moister air as well as more abundant and different vegetation, including cacti and yuccas that do not thrive in the harsher, more austere climate in the northern highlands.

The Tihama, or coastal plain, is the third and the most clearly defined region of North Yemen. Varying in width from 20 to 40 miles (32 to 64 km), the Tihama runs the full length of the country, squeezed between the Red Sea and the mountains that rise abruptly to the east. Near sea level and very flat, the Tihama receives no appreciable rainfall and is extremely hot, hazy, and humid much of the year. The heat and humidity, especially during the summer sandstorms, are enervating and make work, and even living, difficult. At present, the Red Sea provides a livelihood for some fishermen, and its beaches and breezes afford relief and pleasure for a small number of others, mostly foreigners. Although most of it is extremely arid, and some of it is sand desert, the Tihama is cut east-west by several major stream beds, or wadis, each fed by the runoff from large catchment areas that begin high in the mountains to the east. Filled with water for only short periods during and after the rainy seasons, these wadis contain considerable amounts of water below the surface that bubble up at springs or can be tapped by shallow wells. Even the ports, fishing villages, and palm groves on the edge of the sea are sustained by the water that flows underground after falling as rain far inland on the mountains. The relatively small population of the Tihama is densely concentrated in places where this groundwater is readily accessible—at the base of the foothills and along the major wadis and their tributaries. In those few places where water is available in abundance, the Tihama is lush and tropical, dotted with irrigated fields of cotton, millet, bananas, papayas, melons, and vegetables. Indeed, modern technology and the sizable aquifer at the foot of the mountains make the wadis on the Tihama places of significant agricultural potential, more so than anywhere else in the YAR.

The fourth geographic region lies to the east and northeast of the peaks and plateaus of the northern highlands. In contrast to the sharp drop down to the Tihama, the mountains gently slope eastward toward the interior of the Arabian Peninsula and the forbidding Empty Quarter. The farther one moves east, the more the land looks like either a moonscape or a Hollywood desert. This large region is by far the most sparsely populated in all of North Yemen and contains no town of any size or consequence. The only bedouins in the country are found on the region's eastern edge, living a nomadic or semi-nomadic existence. Nevertheless, the runoff eastward for many miles from the mountains provides abundant groundwater to some places—for example, in Wadi Jawf and around the town of Marib. Modern pumps and irrigation works, the latter epitomized by the recent construction of a new version of the fabled Marib Dam, the engineering marvel of the Sabean Kingdom more than two millennia ago, hold out the promise of agricultural development in parts of the region. And more than agricultural change is in the offing. It is here that oil was discovered in 1984, and the new refinery and oil wells will surely rival the Marib Dam as symbols of the YAR's progress.

Settlements and Communications

Historic Yemen was, and today's YAR to a surprising degree still is, a country of a few small cities, many towns, and a vast number of small villages and tiny hamlets. The combined population of the YAR's three cities—Sanaa, with about 425,000 persons, and the much smaller Taiz (175,000) and al-Hudayda (250,000)—still comprise less than 10 percent of the total population of the country. By comparison, greater Beirut alone contained a third of the entire population of Lebanon in 1975. North Yemen's thousands of towns, villages, and hamlets are widely distributed over much of the country. Rooted firmly in the distant past, this settlement pattern persists today both because Yemen is still in the early stages of development and because the recent flow of workers from the countryside has been abroad rather than to the cities within the country. As a consequence, the YAR has thus far been largely spared the urban problems that have plagued most late-developing countries. On the other side of the ledger, the difficulty of delivering services and the inability of the state to exercise much control over the citizenry have been costs of the widely dispersed population. A land of rugged terrain in which settlement areas were linked, if at all, by tenuous and limited means of transportation and communications, North Yemen was and still remains marked by areas of isolation and great diversity from place to place, a sharp contrast to societies on deltas and in river valleys where populations are more homogeneous and accessible.

The vital center of North Yemen in recent decades has been the misnamed, misshapen "triangle," the area traced by the three roads that connect Sanaa,

Taiz, and al-Hudayda. Each side of this triangle is roughly 150 miles (250 km) long, and the area enclosed is the southwestern third of the country. The state in modern times has rarely had effective control over more than the area of the triangle, and often the reach of the government has fallen well short of that. Much of what little modernization has come to North Yemen has taken place on and near the three roads that trace the triangle. In addition to the cities of Sanaa, Taiz, and al-Hudayda, four of the country's five largest towns—Ibb, Dhamar, Zabid, and Bayt al-Faqi—lie on these roads. Only Saada, far to the north, falls well outside the triangle.

The history of the YAR since 1962 is largely the history of its new roads as agents of integration and change. The asphalted, two-lane roads connecting the three cities, which roughly follow centuries-old footpaths and caravan ways, are the YAR's three main roads. The construction and paving of these modern roads was begun about 1960 and not finished until well into the mid-1970s. Spreading from this core, paved roads have been completed since the late 1970s from Sanaa to Saada in the far north, south from Taiz to Turbah, east from Sanaa to Marib, east from Dhamar to Radaa and al-Baydha, west from Sanaa to Hajja via Amran, north from al-Hudayda to the Saudi border and southeast from Taiz to the PDRY border. When completed, a second road between Sanaa and al-Hudayda, arcing south of the one built in the early 1960s, will ease traffic on the YAR's most heavily travelled artery. As significant as the paved roads has been the rapid construction of thousands of miles of dirt and stone feeder roads, making thousands of villages and hamlets reachable by four-wheel drive vehicles for the first time. Roadheads, advancing slowly behind bulldozers and blasting crews toward remote villages, are foci of change and sites of makeshift shops with imported canned goods, taxis to carry people to the cities, and drums of gasoline to fuel electrical generators and four-wheel drive vehicles. The new feeder roads mean new opportunities, and many Yemenis with money earned working abroad have been quick to buy the vehicles that will help them take advantage of these new opportunities.

People and Society

The peoples indigenous to the northern highlands, the southern uplands, and the eastern slopes are racially Arab Semites. They are small-boned and of diminutive stature—indeed, they are among the smallest people of the world. The people of the southern uplands, and of the PDRY to the south, tend to have slightly darker complexions and rounder facial features than those of the north and east, suggesting a greater mixing of the Semites of Arabia with other racial groups. The people of the Tihama, very different from those of the other regions, evidence strong influence of nearby Africa. Here are found the stature, color, and facial features of both Ethiopians and negroidal Africans.

Many persons familiar with both North Yemen and Afghanistan maintain that each of these late-developing countries is more like the other than like any other country in the world. The resemblance is as much or more a matter of culture and social organization than of geography and settlement pattern. North Yemen, like Afghanistan, is a pervasively Islamic country. Except for a small Ismaili Muslim population and a tiny Jewish community, both of which are now much smaller than in past generations, the people of North Yemen are divided between two Islamic groups, the Zaydis and the Shafais, and this sectarian division has had a profound effect, political and otherwise, on historic and modern Yemen. The two communities established themselves in Yemen early in the Islamic era, at least a thousand years ago, and have been the dominant groups in most generations since that time. The old myth of numerical parity notwithstanding, the Shafai community is and probably has been for a long time considerably larger than the Zaydi community. Over the centuries, the Zaydis came to reside in the mountainous highlands as well as in the far north and northeast, whereas the Shafais populated the southern uplands and the Tihama. The rough dividing line between the two communities is the same Samarra Pass that separates Upper Yemen from Lower Yemen, and the Iryan, an area to the west of Samarra, has been described as part of the DMZ—the demilitarized zone—separating the Zaydis and the Shafais. Ibb and Taiz provinces as well as al-Hudayda province are Shafai areas, whereas Dhamar province and the provinces to its north are Zaydi. South Yemen, the PDRY, is wholly Shafai.

Although the Zaydis are Shii Muslims and the Shafais are Sunni, the Zaydi branch of Shiism is more similar to the rationalist schools of Sunnism than to the mystical, millenarian sects that are typical of Shiism. Like Sunnism generally, Zaydi Shiism is an establishment religion, not one born of defeat and dissent. As a result, the very real differences between the two communities in Yemen have been and are less religious—less matters of dogma and ritual—than cultural, social, and political. The Zaydis of the northern highlands and the Shafais of the southern uplands constitute separate subcultures, the main features of which were forged in the history of the past four or five centuries. Each community has viewed its relationship to the other in "us-them" terms. Segregated socially as well as geographically, the members of each community have tended to feel more comfortable with and more easily understood by their own kind.

The differences between the Zaydis and the Shafais are partly matters of oppressors and oppressed, of warrior-rulers and subject peasants and merchants. The Zaydis have ruled the Shafais more often than not over recent centuries, and Zaydi jurists and theologians developed an elaborate political theory that justified the rule of the Zaydi ruler, the imam, over fellow Zaydis as well as non-Zaydi subjects. Almost all the imams' counselors, judges, and administrators were drawn from the upper ranks of the Zaydi community, and it was the Zaydi tribes in the north that supported the Zaydi imams with their armed tribal irregulars. The Zaydi imamate patronized culture, learning, and the arts, albeit to a modest degree, and learned Zaydis dominated and were the arbiters of these matters. At the top of Yemeni society, the Zaydi leaders felt superior and found it easy to think themselves the best in the best of all known worlds. Largely confined to the highlands and cut off from the outside world, the Zaydis had little opportunity and inclination to compare their life to alternatives the outside world had to offer. They were a proud, inward-looking mountain people with a narrow, parochial perspective.

For its part, the Shafai community exhibited contradictory tendencies of submission and rebellion in the face of Zaydi power and claims to authority. More often than not, the Shafais chose or were forced to accept the imam as their secular ruler, though not as their religious leader. Denied political position and social status, some Shafais turned to trade and commerce, particularly in Taiz and al-Hudayda. Many more emigrated, to Aden and sometimes far beyond, as students, laborers, sailors, merchants, and other businessmen, and were thereby exposed to the modern world and its ideas to a far greater extent than were the more isolated Zaydis of the highlands. Many of these Shafai émigrés and their offspring returned to Yemen over the years, bringing with them some of the skills learned in the outside world. Marginal men in a Zaydi-dominated society, the more able of the Shafais were open to change and innovation. Increasingly aware of their marginality in the twentieth century, these Shafais felt more and more deprived and entitled to a fairer share, whereas their Zaydi counterparts inclined toward conservation, particularly of their privileges.

The differences between the Zaydis of the highlands and the Shafais of the uplands were less than those between either of these groups and the "Africanized" Shafais of the Tihama. Relative poverty, African social and cultural influences, and a measure of racial prejudice placed the indigenous people of the Tihama at the bottom of the social order, even a people apart and outside some common conceptions of the Yemeni society. If the Zaydis of the highlands look down on the Shafais of the uplands, both groups looked down on the Shafais of the Tihama and Yemenis born abroad, especially of non-Yemeni mothers.

North Yemen, again like Afghanistan, is distinguished by its tribal social organization. In both countries tribes and tribalism, rather than being mere vestiges of the past, are vital forces that continue to play determinant roles in the political as well as the social and cultural spheres. Despite the tendency to categorize Upper Yemen as tribal and Lower Yemen as peasant, tribes and tribalism are part of the cultural, social, and political landscape of all regions of North Yemen, even the Tihama. For centuries, what has distinguished the northern highlands from the other regions of the country is the importance, almost to the exclusion of anything else, of the tribe as a unit of identification and action and the great extent to which sub-tribes and tribes can be mobilized and organized into large tribal confederations when the interests of the tribal system or its constituent parts are at stake. Many residents of the southern uplands claim a tribal lineage, but this often seems to be less important as a basis of personal identity than place of origin—a village, wadi, or locality—or some other attribute. By contrast, many men of the highlands define themselves primarily in terms of their tribes, and many of these tribes with their present names were in existence at least a thousand years ago, often on the same land on which they currently reside. Almost all the tribes of the northern highlands and the eastern slopes are grouped into two great tribal confederations, the Hashid and the Bakil, and, as Paul Dresch estimated, the tribal population in these areas "is nowadays in excess of half a million, divided rather unevenly among some seven major Hashid tribes and perhaps fourteen from Bakil."[1]

The Yemeni social system is composed of two distinguishable but interdependent tribal and nontribal subsystems that meet primarily in the marketplace (the *souk*), be it the *souk* in a town or city or the weekly *souk* at a rural crossroads. The tribal subsystem, the domain of which is the villages and hamlets of the countryside, is made up of greater and lesser tribes, each consisting of the shaykh and his tribal following. The shaykh represents and protects the members of his tribe in their dealings with other tribes and the nontribal system; the members can hardly conceive of being and acting outside their tribe, and this sense of dependency is a key to the solidarity of the tribe. The Hashid and Bakil confederations, which have varied over time in terms of their internal cohesiveness and unity, are each headed by a paramount shaykh, a shaykh of shaykhs. The paramount shaykhs and lesser shaykhs have been preoccupied for centuries with defending both the autonomy of the tribes in relationship to nontribal authorities in Yemen and their rights to regulate affairs within their tribal domains. Although conflict between Yemeni tribes is common, the tribes do not conquer and occupy the lands of neighboring tribes, much less destroy those tribes. By contrst, there is a long history of both tribal sacking of towns in the northern highlands and tribal forays—or large-scale migrations—into richer agricultural areas of the west and south. Sanaa was pillaged by the tribes as recently as 1948, an event still fresh in the memories of people both inside and outside the tribal system.

The cities and major towns of Yemen, the foci of commerce, the state, and Islamic learning, are largely nontribal and in a fundamental way antitribal. These urban settings, even those in strongly tribal areas, consist mostly of nontribal or detribalized people, those for whom tribal ties have weakened and been replaced or at least superseded over the generations by other ties. Sanaa, though in the highlands and surrounded by tribes and tribal lands, is not tribal. The history of North Yemen is largely the history of tension if not conflict between the "land of insolence" with its tribes and their customary law, on the one hand, and the urban centers in which the Zaydi imamate or some other Islamic political institution has served to protect and propagate Islamic law, morals, and faith. Though nearly all the tribesmen of North Yemen are Zaydis, their Zaydism makes many concessions to tribal law and custom, a matter of persistent concern to the guardians of Zaydism.

The traditional social order in Sanaa and the major towns of the highlands, and with variations in the large settlements in the other regions, consisted of a stratified class system bounded on the top and bottom by castes. Still firmly in place in the sixth decade of this century, this system has changed only in part in recent decades. At the bottom were the *akhdam* (the servants), a caste consisting of black descendants of Ethiopians or other Africans who toiled as street sweepers, popular musicians, and other menials. At the top were the sayyids, descendants of the Prophet Muhammad who, in the case of the Zaydi community, traced this descent through Fatima and Ali, the Prophet's daughter and son-in-law. Zaydi law required that all candidates for the imamate be Zaydi sayyids, and most of the imams had been drawn over the centuries from several great sayyid families. The sayyid caste provided many of the small number of administrators and judges who served the imamate as well as many of the larger number of religious leaders, teachers, and scholars of Islamic law and theology. Whether comfortable or poor, and many were poor, the sayyids made up the aristocracy of North Yemen.

Just below the aristocratic sayyid caste was the qadi class, a privileged group of "commoners" who occupied positions in the imamate, often very high and sensitive positions, but were not eligible by reason of non-sayyid lineage to be imam. Indeed, the imams used members of the qadi class to protect themselves from and to make themselves less dependent upon sayyid pretenders to the imamate. In theory open to all who were schooled and became learned in Islamic law and theology, the qadi class tended over the centuries to be the preserve of an only slowly changing group of privileged families. Below the qadi class was the large group of artisans, skilled workers, merchants, and small traders, often organized into guilds. This very heterogeneous group was not closed and allowed for some upward and downward movement. Some families, through hard work, connections, and luck, even rose into the qadi class. Finally, there was the hard-to-escape muzayyan class, which consisted of those whose demeaning lot it was to be butchers, barbers, and in some areas, growers of vegetables.

The hierarchical differences that existed in traditional Yemeni society were more matters of status and role than of wealth. North Yemen was a very poor country, and the economy generated very little of the surplus required for great differences in wealth or even status. There was more than a little substance to the egalitarian ethos of the tribes, and the economically poor tribal areas imposed an austere life on shaykh and follower alike. Just as the tribesmen had easy access to their shaykhs, ordinary folk in the cities and towns had ready access to their imam or other notables. The imam lived better than most of the other prominent notables—sayyids and qadis—and the latter groups lived better than the common people, but the differences were surprisingly small by modern standards. Although there was a small number of great landowners, especially on the southern uplands and the Tihama, these landlords were often land poor, and most peasants in most parts of the country had ownership or other rights to a parcel of land and often a water source. The afternoon *qat* session, in which Yemenis gathered to chew *qat* leaves as well as to relax, converse, joke, do business, and listen to poems and the *oud*, captured the measure of egalitarianism of egalitarianism in traditional Yemen. The fact that the chewers ordered themselves roughly according to status around the rectangular diwan, the choicest section reserved to the notables present, is less striking than the fact that these notables regularly chewed *qat* with their poor relatives, tenants, petitioners, scribes, and guards.

History and the Yemeni Nation

The ideas of Yemen as a place and of the people of Yemen go back to the dawn of recorded history. Although some might wish to include the regions of Najran, Jizan, and Asir in southwestern Saudi Arabia and the province of Dhufar if not all of Oman, most Yemenis agree in the 1980s that Yemen and the Yemenis are the place and people contained within the boundaries of two territorial states, the YAR and the PDRY. (See Map 3.) Notwithstanding a quarter century of talk about unification of the "two parts" of Yemen, or the possibility that unity may indeed be realized in coming years, Yemen has been embraced by a single political system only very rarely over the past two millennia and never in recent centuries. And in these rare instances, it was a matter of the subjugation and domination of one part or faction of Yemen over the rest. For most centuries, Yemenis were divided among a few or many different political systems, much like the Germans and the Italians in the years before the creation of the German and the Italian nation-states in the nineteenth century. "The Yemens," wrote R. B. Sergeant, "closely resemble mediaeval Scotland in their tribal foraying, vendettas, murder, shifting alliances, courage and treachery, generosity and close-fistedness—the attempts by imams, kings and sultans to establish centralized law and order—that inevitably break down into dynastic strife."[2]

The emergence of two Yemens, and the homogenization within and differentiation between the two groups of Yemenis in the two Yemens, though explicable in part by the geography of the Zaydi-Shafai cleavage, is more the result of a process that began in the mid-nineteenth century with the second Ottoman occupation of North Yemen and the British seizure of the port of Aden. Just as the creation of South Yemen was the accretive result of the subsequent interactions of the British colonial rulers with the people of Aden and the indigenous political units in what came to be known as the Aden Protectorates, the creation of North Yemen resulted from the struggle until early in the twentieth century between the Ottoman occupiers and a resurgent Zaydi imamate and from the latter's subsequent efforts to extend and consolidate its rule over all of Yemen through the sixth decade of this century. The attentions of the Yemenis in the south focused on Aden and the British, whereas those of the Yemenis in the north focused on Sanaa, the Ottomans, and the Zaydi imamate. Different political cultures began to grow out of these different foci.

Memories of a glorious past, the remote past between 1000 B.C. and A.D. 750, are part of the stuff of which are made the modern ideas of Yemen as a place and a Yemeni people. Point out a pile of rubble in the interior

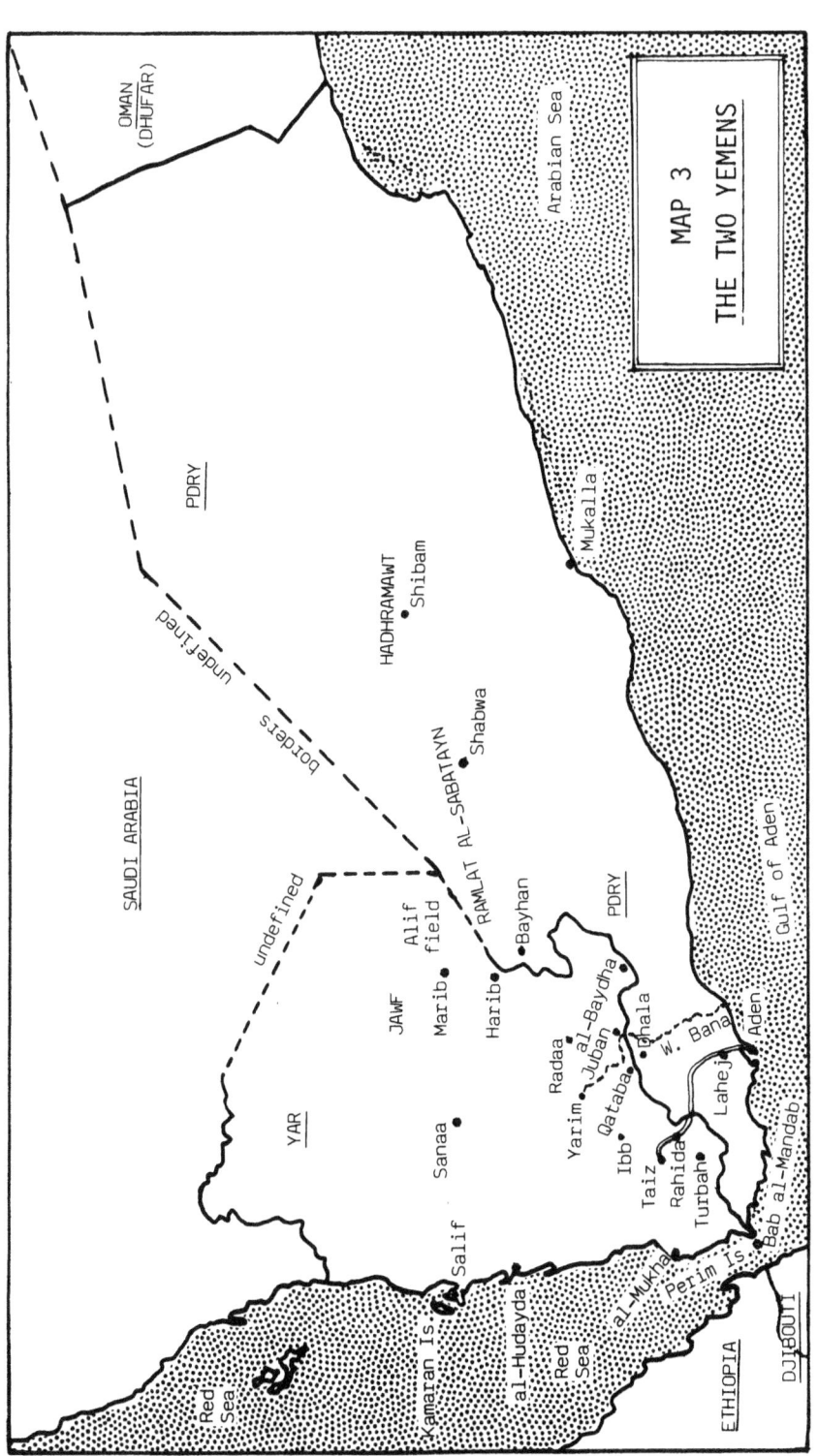

of Yemen, and an illiterate Yemeni is likely to say proudly *hadha himyari*, "that's Himyaritic," regardless of whether it is Turkish from the mid-nineteenth century or a vestige of one of the commercial kingdoms that thrived along the frankincense trail before the Himyarites established their rule early in the Christian era. The Yemenis are a proud people, proud of this historical legacy, and they are quick to compare the culture and legacy of their rich neighbors in Saudi Arabia unfavorably with their own.

Another source of the Yemenis' pride and sense of being equal to any other people is the absence of much of a colonial experience. The second Ottoman occupation in the second half of the nineteenth century was short and inconclusive, and the Yemenis take credit for having driven the Turks from their land early in the twentieth century. As a consequence, the Yemenis are not at all obsequious in their dealings with westerners, and they are not complicated and conflicted by love-hate, superiority-inferiority feelings toward the modern industrial West. Even modern, travelled Yemenis have in them a bit of the Yemeni villager who, told that you come from New York City, exclaims: "But surely it is not so grand and glorious as Sanaa."

Though conscious and proud of their Arab roots, most Yemenis probably identify themselves first as Muslims or Yemenis. This is largely the result of the location of North Yemen on the edge of the Arab world and of its long cultural and historical isolation from most of the rest of the Arab world. The modern mass media and the YAR's increased contact with the outside world have enlarged the identification of Yemenis with their fellow Arabs—among them the Palestinians—and made them far more aware than before of the friends and enemies of the Arab world.

2
From Imamate to Republic: 1904-1967

Modern state building, political construction, and socioeconomic development came late to North Yemen and were severely constrained by events and conditions after their coming. North Yemen in the late 1950s, at the dawn of the Space Age, remained one of the world's last extant examples of a relatively complex, large-scale, traditional social system. A conservative Islamic society, it was not changed in fundamental, systemic ways from the Yemen of two or even several centuries earlier. Perhaps most like the Afghanistan of about 1900, it was virtually devoid of piped water, surfaced roads, motor vehicles and engines, electricity, and telephones or radios, much less the modern ideas and institutions that go with these artifacts and amenities of modern life. North Yemen was in, but not of, the twentieth century.

The Time of Imams Yahya and Ahmad

Traditional Yemen, centered in the northern highlands and southern uplands, persisted in part because it was geographically isolated from a rapidly changing world by a forbidding coastal desert backed by high, haze-enshrouded mountains. Indeed, a diplomat with area expertise could still refer to it in the mid-1950s as "the Tibet of the Red Sea."[1] Despite close proximity to Britain's bustling Aden Colony and the modern world's major sea lane to Asia, North Yemen remained a backwater and outside the mainstream of events during the last decades of the age of imperialism and colonialism. The oil fever of the 1930s and later, which fixed attention on the other side of the arid Arabian Peninsula, served to reinforce this situation. Moreover, Yemen's traditional economic system, based upon subsistence agriculture and human and animal energy, was to a remarkable degree self-contained and self-sufficient. Although life was austere for most and severe deprivation not unknown, the Yemenis produced nearly all of what they consumed; the few luxury and essential products that they imported from abroad were paid for by the export of small amounts of coffee, cotton, and animal hides and skins. In sum, North Yemen and the modern world had little economic need for or interest in each other, and traditional Yemen remained intact partly for this reason.

To a considerable degree, however, traditional Yemen persisted by design. Noting that North Yemen had undergone some modernization during the second Ottoman occupation in the late nineteenth century, Robin Bidwell observed that "the fact that the Sanaa of the 1950s seemed a museum was not the result of centuries of neglect but of a conscious decision by . . . [two imams] to hold the twentieth century at bay."[2] In an era when the world's few remaining traditional societies were crumbling under the impact of modernity, these remarkable imams revived and reinvigorated the historic order of Yemen at the same time that they insulated it almost completely from the outside world. Imam Yahya (1869-1948), who in 1904 succeeded his father, the first member of the Hamid al-Din family to occupy the imamate, strove to contain the effects of the new ideas and practices that had come with the Ottomans. He and his son and successor, Imam Ahmad (ca. 1891-1962), were also able to limit the impact on Yemen of the rising tide of modernism and nationalism that engulfed the Arab world in the four decades after World War I brought an end to the Ottoman Empire. Between them, Yahya and Ahmad occupied the imamate and guarded Yemen's ramparts from 1904 until 1962, allowing as few Yemenis as possible to go outside and even fewer outsiders to enter Yemen with their alien ideas and artifacts.

Imam Yahya's inwardness is illustrated by the fact that he never laid eyes on the Red Sea, which delimits Yemen and is only about 30 miles from the escarpment of the highlands from which he ruled. Indeed, he never set foot outside the country. A xenophobe, he knew enough about the outside world—and of the history of the encounter of western imperialism with India, China, and the Ottoman Empire—not to want to have much to do with it. In an oft-quoted statement he once said that he would rather eat straw than risk ties that could cost Yemen its independence. On another occasion, when questioned why he had refused $2 million offered him by Americans for oil exploration rights, he replied by asking how much more would it cost to get them out later.

State and Politics in the Imamate

The imamate of Yemen was the political expression of Zaydism, the branch of Shii Islam to which most of the people of the northern highlands and the eastern slopes adhere. Founded in the tenth century A.D., the Zaydi imamate existed more or less continuously into the twentieth century, sometimes strong and sometimes weak, sometimes unoccupied or contested by rival claimants. The imamate fit comfortably into Max Weber's category of a patrimonial traditional political system in that it was sacred—that is, theocratic—and operated largely within limits set by custom and tradition. According to Zaydi political doctrine, the imam was the secular and religious leader of the community of the faithful and was elected by the ulama—the learned ones—and other Zaydi notables. He could be elected only from those males who had, among other attributes, direct descent from the Prophet Muhammad via Fatima and Ali. The imamate was theoretically nonhereditary and open to all Zaydis who possessed the required attributes. Nevertheless, the imamate tended toward dynastic rule, the Hamid al-Din family being but the latest of the handful of great Zaydi sayyid families that have occupied this position over recent centuries.

Zaydi doctrine made the welfare and protection—moral as well as physical—of the community of believers the primary responsibility of the imam. By all accounts, Imams Yahya and Ahmad were devout men who took this charge seriously. Harold Ingrams, a political officer with years of service in the Aden Protectorate, was struck by two contrasts during a rare official mission to Sanaa in 1941: the "one between the strife of the past and the order of the present and the other between the peace of the kingdom and the lack of it in the Protectorate."[3] He went on:

> It has often been said that the security in the Yemen is worse than the lack of it in the Protectorate, because of the oppression by which it is secured. The Imam's rule is stern and he keeps peace by methods which we should not like, but only a small percentage actually suffer out of a population of several millions. The taxation (and extortion) are heavy, but certainly not so heavy that it is uneconomic to labour. The cultivation—the wonderful terracing, the careful, extensive husbandry—could not be carried on if the taxation were too oppressive, nor could it be carried on without security.[4]

Imam Yahya would not have been able to insulate and reinvigorate traditional Yemen as much as he did had he not strengthened the imamate and extended its domain during the three decades after the final withdrawal of the Ottoman occupiers in 1918. As a result of his leadership in the struggle against the disliked Turks, the legitimacy of the imamate and its occupant was enhanced and a sense of national identity was reinforced, at least among the Zaydis of the northern highlands. Imam Yahya and his several princely sons established firm Zaydi rule over the southern uplands and the Tihama, areas populated by Shafais who felt no religious allegiance to the Zaydi imamate. They garrisoned these areas with troops from the highlands and even "colonized" them with Zaydis, both prominent families and minor functionaries. In consolidating and extending the imamate, the Hamdi al-Din family also tipped the millennia-old balance of power between the state and the tribes—between the center and the periphery—in favor of the former. Most of the tribes of the northern highlands and the eastern slopes, as well as rebellious elements on the Tihama, chose or were compelled to offer at least nominal allegiance to the imam. The geographic limits of North Yemen in modern times were reached in the mid-1930s when Imam Yahya acceded to a southern boundary drawn earlier by the Turks and the British, and, after losing a brief war with the then newly proclaimed Kingdom of Saudi Arabia, renounced any claim to the provinces of Najran, Jizan, and the Asir in the north. In the east, where imamate Yemen, Saudi Arabia, and the Aden Protectorate intersected in the arid waste adjacent to the

Empty Quarter, the boundary remained undemarcated and of little concern to anyone.

Under Yahya and Ahmad, the imamate was truly the imam's government, one over which he exercised direct personal control. Hugh Scott, who had audiences with Imam Yahya during a stay of some months in Yemen in the late 1930s, said it best: "He is as absolute a monarch as any left in the world. No ruler can in greater measure attend personally to every detail of his administration—as we had opportunity to see with our own eyes. ... If anyone on earth can say 'I am the State', it is the Imam of the Yemen."[5] After visiting Yemen more than a decade later, Harry Hoogstraal could say that Imam Ahmad "deals with manifold details [which include] everything from requirements of cleaning rugs and light bulbs to international affairs, road building, erection of buildings, and planting of trees along road ways."[6] Virtually no distinction was made, in theory or practice, between the imam's household and the imamate and its treasury. The imamate lacked any ministerial structure and the highest officials were usually personal confidants of the imam and often members of his household; indeed, most top positions in the 1930s and 1940s were held by the several older sons of Imam Yahya. High officials were also drawn from prominent families in the sayyid caste and in the qadi class, the latter favored in particular by Imam Yahya for presumed loyalty as well as mastery of Islamic law and theology. Below these top people, in addition to a corps of lowly clerks and scribes, there was a small, specialized, but relatively undifferentiated officialdom charged with collecting taxes, settling disputes, and carrying out other routine affairs of state.

The state that Imams Yahya and Ahmad ruled so absolutely did not amount to much by modern standards. The imamate state was neither extensive nor intensive and it was only slightly differentiated structurally from the rest of society. For example, the standing army was small, ill-equipped, and for the most part nonprofessional, forcing the imam to rely for defense on subsidized tribal irregulars. As a consequence, the capacity of the imam to penetrate his society, to regulate behavior in it, to draw resources from it, and to use those resources as he saw fit was quite limited. The constraints on the imamate are perhaps best seen in its relationship to the major tribes of the north and east. For centuries, imams and claimants to the imamate had depended for support upon the Hashid and Bakil tribal confederations, the "wings of the imamate," as they were traditionally called. The paramount shaykhs gave this support and defense in exchange for a great measure of local autonomy, the result being that the tribes were less the loyal subjects than the sometime allies of the imams.

The ragtag army and provincial administration were improved somewhat by Imam Yahya with turn-of-the-century Ottoman organization and procedures as well as some Ottoman officers and administrators who stayed on after the dissolution of the empire. However, the enhanced strength of the imamate during the four decades after World War I was primarily the result of the forceful personalities, dedication, energy, and hard work of

Imams Yahya and Ahmad. Skillful practitioners of traditional politics, they used military campaigns, the hostage system, gifts and subsidies, factional manipulation, and other arcane devices both to consolidate their power at the center where challengers to the imamate intrigued and to extend their sway slightly on the periphery at the expense of the largely autonomous tribes. They achieved these results largely within the limits of tradition and without the help of the ideas and techniques of modern statecraft. As late as the end of the 1950s, the most important modern tool of the imamate was the telegraph, a legacy of Ottoman times that the imams controlled directly and used to check regularly on tax receipts and political conditions in the major towns and cities.

Politics in the time of the imams was the preserve of a tiny minority at the top of a largely closed system; was organized into loose, shifting cliques and factions; and was conducted on a personal, face-to-face basis. The major actors were members of the ruling family, leaders of the other great sayyid clans, prominent qadis, leading ulama, and shaykhs of the major tribes. By contrast, most of the people—tribesmen and peasants as well as artisans, shopkeepers, and merchants—rarely if ever had any political relevance or role to play. The imam maintained direct contact with his subjects through daily sessions in his diwan, gatherings to which the lowliest petitioner had access. Officials and secret informers served as the eyes and ears of the imam, keeping him in touch with the society beyond the palace and his diwan. The flow of demands and supports into the political system was not handled by specialized political structures such as organized interest groups or political parties, but rather by government officials, local notables, or family heads at each level of the system. The absence of subsystems such as political parties, pressure groups, and the mass media—the absence of any real need for a differentiated political infrastructure—was a major distinction between the imamate system of traditional Yemen and the more modern political systems growing up in Aden and in much of the rest of the Arab world in the first half of the twentieth century.

The Beginning of Political Change

There were, however, breaches in the ramparts thrown up by the imams to protect traditional Yemen from the modern world and its corrupting ideas and practices. The biggest breach was Britain's fast-growing and bustling Aden Colony, one of the world's two or three busiest ports by the 1950s and the main port of entry for North Yemen's limited economic and other transactions with the outside world. Especially after World War II, an increasing number of Yemenis, mostly Shafais seeking to escape the poverty and limited opportunities in the southern uplands, went south to Aden, first for work and later for education. Indeed, most of the port workers and other laborers in Aden were migrants from North Yemen, as were many of the small shopkeepers and importers. A considerable number of North Yemenis also went abroad from Aden as sailors or to become merchants and laborers in Djibouti, Ethiopia, Sudan, and as far away as Marseilles,

Cardiff, Manchester, Brooklyn, and Detroit. More important, beginning in the 1940s, an increasing number of young Yemenis got the start of a modern education in Aden, and some of these went on for secondary and higher education in Cairo, other educational centers in the Arab world, and even Europe and the United States. Aden, called "the eye of Yemen" in classical Arabic literature, had by the 1950s become the window on and the door to the modern world for an otherwise tightly shuttered Yemen. Outside the imams' reach, this opening could not be closed by them.

Surprisingly, Aden was, like the alabaster windows for which Yemen is famous, only a translucent opening during the first half of the twentieth century. The large number of Yemenis drawn there by a desire for work or education had had little impact on their homeland to the north by midcentury. Many of the Yemenis who went to Aden stayed there or farther abroad, and apparently many of those who returned to North Yemen left most of their modernity behind them. As a consequence, a sizable number of Yemenis were by 1960 considerably more modern than were the culture and society of their homeland. Though delayed, the full impact of these more modern Yemenis was to be felt later.

A second breach in the ramparts, one that did not assume much importance until after the 1940s, was caused by the idea that tradition could be defended by the selective use of modern means. Unlike many rulers before and during his time, Imam Yahya had strongly resisted this idea. Nevertheless, he did send about a dozen young men to Iraq for training in 1936 and, more important, he allowed forty boys—later called the Famous Forty—to leave in 1947 for schooling first in Lebanon and then in Egypt and the West. The Famous Forty made up the initial wave of educational emigrants from North Yemen, and members of this group were still playing important roles in the government of their country more than a generation after they first went abroad. In the 1950s, Imam Ahmad, though no modernizing traditionalist on the order of the rulers of Iran and Afghanistan earlier in the twentieth century, succumbed to the temptations of outside ties and aid to a greater degree than had his father. Deeply concerned by Britain's new policy of increased involvement in the Aden Protectorates and later by the rising influence of Gamal Abd al-Nasir's (Nasser) brand of Arab nationalism, he looked abroad for political and military help. In 1956 he took Yemen into an anti-British pact with Egypt and Saudi Arabia, and in 1958 he joined quite improbably with Egypt and Syria in creating the shortlived United Arab States. The new link with Nasir's Egypt led in 1957 to the supply of Soviet arms and, more important, Egyptian military advisers. Economic aid agreements were also pursued, and by the early 1960s the Soviets were constructing a deepwater port at al-Hudayda and the Chinese and Americans were building North Yemen's first two modern highways. Although he did not live to see it, Imam Ahmad set in motion the roadbuilding program that in the mid-1960s would come to symbolize great power competition for influence in less developed countries: the Soviets, Americans, and Chinese each working to build a highway on a different side of the triangle formed by Sanaa, Taiz, and al-Hudayda. Imam Ahmad also allowed at least two more groups of students to go abroad, including a few members of the ruling family, and, more significantly, was unable to prevent many others in search of education from slipping over the border to Aden and on to Egypt and elsewhere. Indeed, by 1960 the trickle of educational emigrants had swelled into a torrent, the number of secondary and university students abroad doubling between 1958 and 1961, reaching well over a thousand. A few of these students became propagandists for change and a couple of them—for example, Muhammad Anaam Ghaleb in an MA thesis in 1960 and Muhammad Said al-Attar in a doctoral dissertation in 1963—wrote scholarly analyses of Yemen's backwardness.[7]

The beginnings of modern politics came to Yemen in the 1940s in the form of growing opposition to the imamate. The first major opposition organization, the Free Yemenis, was founded in Aden in 1944, although it was preceded by a few years by two small clandestine groups. The Free Yemenis played an important role in the failed effort to remove the Hamid al-Din family from the imamate on the occasion of the assassination of Imam Yahya in 1948. Although it existed as an organization for only a few years, the Free Yemenis led directly to the formation of other opposition groups in the 1950s, among them the Yemeni Unionists. The propagandizing and other activities of these groups, clandestine within North Yemen and open abroad, helped to create a climate that fostered plots and other acts against Imam Ahmad, in particular the 1955 coup attempt. Far from being radical modernists, the leaders of the Free Yemenis—Ahmad Muhammad Numan and Muhammad al-Zubayri, for example—and other dissidents such as Qadi Abd al-Rahman al-Iryani were the mid-twentieth-century equivalents of the Turkish reformers of the Ottoman Empire during the Tanzimat period in the mid-nineteenth century. They evolved only slowly from favoring a constitutional imamate to favoring a republic, and their conception of republicanism was sketchy and old-fashioned.

By the early 1950s, however, many of the still small number of young Yemenis studying abroad and a few of the far larger number working abroad had been drawn to other more modern and radical political groups. Many of these Yemenis were introduced to modern politics by way of the culturally congenial Muslim Brotherhood. Although a few stayed with the brotherhood, most of them later migrated from it to secular political movements. Based and nurtured in Aden and the major political capitals of the Arab world, Yemeni branches of the Communist party and such pan-Arab entities as the Arab Nationalist Movement and the Baath party were founded and began to attract a Yemeni following. More important, by the mid-1950s a large number of Yemenis had been profoundly influenced by the 1952 Revolution in Egypt and were coming under the spell of Nasir and his evolving brand of nationalism and socialism in Egypt. It was a heady time in the Arab world, and young Yemenis abroad sampled widely and became intoxicated by the varied forms of modern Arab politics.

"When we went out, we knew of God and the Imam—and little else." So reminisced Abdullah al-Kurshumi, one of the Famous Forty, still acutely aware of the huge place that the imams occupied in the Yemen of his childhood. As recently as 1980, the outside wall of the al-Amin Bakery in Taiz bore in English in crude but bold letters this inscription: "To see a picture before 1962, visit the museum." The museum in question was Imam Ahmad's palace, a dark, austere, not very large or comfortable pile of stone, left much as it was found at the time of the 1962 Revolution, full of modern knickknacks as well as the modest luxuries that made for the good life in traditional Yemen. Robin Bidwell, visiting the museum in the early 1970s, found it still pervaded by Imam Ahmad's immense personality and himself

> powerfully reminded of . . . King Henry VIII. Both were men of gigantic physical strength and overwhelming force of character, fierce, unscrupulous and merciless rulers when only these qualities could hold undisciplined people in check. Both were capricious rather than wantonly cruel, both were theologians and writers of distinction, both were intensely patriotic and determined to resist the slightest foreign encroachment. Neither had the least doubt of the superiority of their nation over the rest of humanity and both were determined to preserve and foster their original genius and, although deeply conservative, did not refuse to profit from all innovations. Both lived in constant danger of revolt or assassination and neither could afford to delegate substantial powers. Ahmad would have been at home in the European Renaissance, ruling a kingdom rapidly emerging from the Middle Ages.[8]

The 1962 Revolution, the YAR, and the al-Sallal Era

The Yemen Arab Republic was proclaimed after a coup by army officers under the nominal leadership of Colonel Abdullah al-Sallal (ca. 1915-   ) on 26 September 1962, a week after the death by natural causes of Imam Ahmad. Abolished forthwith were the imamate and, as important, the sayyid caste's birthright to rule North Yemen. The properties of the Hamid al-Din family and of die-hard royalist supporters were confiscated, and these persons were exiled or imprisoned. A few were executed.

Abdullah al-Sallal, of humble social origins and one of the dozen young Yemenis sent to Iraq for training in 1936, had served for nearly three decades in the imam's army. Though a political soldier and a long-time plotter against the imams, he was a high-ranking officer and had been brought into the conspiracy only on the very eve of the 1962 Revolution. The real plotters, later dubbed the Septembrists, were younger officers, especially those trained in Egypt in the early 1950s, several of the Famous Forty among them. With Egyptian backing, however, al-Sallal and his closest colleagues soon asserted control over the new republican regime, making him more than just titular head of state.

The Civil War and the Egyptian Presence

Imam Muhammad al-Badr, Ahmad's son and successor, escaped from his palace in Sanaa after the coup and rallied many of the tribes of the north and east, thereby setting the stage for a long, costly, and bitterly divisive civil war. Massive Egyptian and Saudi Arabian support for the republicans and the royalists respectively served to regionalize the conflict, and Egypt's ties to the Soviet bloc and western deference to the wishes of oil-rich Saudi Arabia then internationalized it along East-West lines. The civil war dragged on until the end of the 1960s, and in the later years spasms of fierce fighting alternated with increasingly long periods of unofficial truce and minor skirmishes.

The Egyptian intervention in the Yemeni conflict was a military and political disaster for Egypt and President Nasir as well as a mixed blessing for the fledgling YAR. Yemen's rugged terrain and scattered, self-reliant tribalists proved a match for Egyptian tanks, planes, and infantry. Unable to win militarily or, for political reasons, to withdraw with grace and honor, the Egyptian leaders came to refer to their involvement in Yemen in the mid-1960s as "our Vietnam." Although Egyptian men and material almost surely prevented the defeat of the republic by the Saudi-backed royalist tribes, the republicans increasingly had difficulty in distinguishing their Egyptian saviors from foreign occupation forces. Without question, the Egyptian presence more than any other factor shaped—some would say deformed—the YAR during its first years.

One important effect of the protracted civil war was the reassertion of tribal power and autonomy, reversing the modest trend under the Hamid al-Din rulers toward greater state power. The territory subject to the authority of the republic shrank and the "land of insolence" in which the tribes were again free of any higher authority, including that of the royalists, expanded. During the darkest days of the conflict the republic held sway loosely over little more—and sometimes much less—than the territory within the southern triangle formed by the roads connecting Sanaa, Taiz, and al-Hudayda; indeed, its rule was tenuous at best in the remoter areas of the interior of the triangle. This situation found acknowledgment in 1966 in Egypt's "strategy of the long breath," a withdrawal of vulnerable forces to secure positions on or near the roads that trace the triangle.

The leading tribal shaykhs enjoyed new power and an enhanced position in the years after the 1962 Revolution. The regime and its Egyptian patrons had renewed the old practice of granting subsidies to the tribes in their effort to compete with the royalists and the Saudis for tribal support. Shaykhs who were thought to be leaning toward the republic were granted funds as recruiters and commanders of auxiliary "popular forces" that may or may not have existed. Other shaykhs drew subsidies from the royalists and their Saudi patrons, and a few managed to collect from both sides in the conflict. As a consequence, many previously impecunious and weak shaykhs found themselves quite affluent and in command of large, well-armed forces. According to Fred Halliday, Shaykh Naji bin Ali al-Gadr received money and arms from the two sides and in the course of only a few years during the mid-1960s went from being a minor shaykh with 120 armed men at his command to being the paramount shaykh of the Bakil confederation with thousands of men under his command.[9]

The 1962 Revolution abruptly ended North Yemen's long and remarkably complete isolation from the modern world. Events during the tumultuous mid-1960s made impossible a return to isolation and a self-sufficient pattern of traditional social life. Things done or left undone during this period of civil war and deep Egyptian involvement in the internal and external affairs of the YAR brought changes and released forces that rendered irrevocable the need to further modernize Yemeni society and government. The Egyptians in Yemen, at one time numbering at least 60,000 soldiers and thousands of civil servants, teachers, and doctors, introduced many Yemenis to new ideas and ways of doing things, to a different, more modern way of life; indeed, they changed the face of—redesigned large parts of—Sanaa, Taiz, and al-Hudayda. North Yemen's enterprising Shafai merchants, particularly those from Taiz and al-Hudayda with connections in Aden, oversaw the importation of a startling array of foreign goods and a permanent change in consumption patterns. Canned foods, transistor radios, thermos bottles, pumps, and generators appeared, and cars and trucks ceased to be objects of curiosity. Paper currency was adopted for the first time in 1964, contributing further to the growth of a market economy and a system of cash exchange.

It was not only foreigners and worldly-wise Yemeni businessmen who spread new ideas and practices in the YAR. Young Yemenis with secondary and university education returned by the dozens after the 1962 Revolution, supplementing the few who had come during the last years of the imamate. A United States Embassy survey in early 1965 found nearly fifty Yemeni graduates of higher education living in the YAR, almost a third of whom were of the Famous Forty. Most of them had spent their childhood in the isolated, traditional Yemen of the imamate, but a few had been raised or even born in Aden, Djibouti, or some other Yemeni emigrant community; most were in their midtwenties when they returned, or came for the first time, to North Yemen. What they lacked in work experience they made up for in energy and in desire to end what they regarded as the poverty and ignorance—the backwardness—of their beloved homeland. For example, Muhammad Abd al-Aziz Sallam, a young native of Taiz fresh from several years in the United States with a degree in biology, was made the senior civil servant in the virtually all-new Ministry of Health in 1962. "Our offices were like classrooms," he said, speaking for his fellow graduates of higher education. "We applied and taught what we had learned as best we could, ourselves learning all the time."[10] Sallam switched to the Foreign Ministry by the mid-1960s and was named foreign minister in 1966, when he was barely thirty years of age. Another example, Muhammad Said al-Attar, a Yemeni born into a merchant family in Djibouti and French educated, was in Aden and about to go to North Yemen for the first time to do research on Yemen for his doctorate in economics when the 1962 Revolution occurred. Pressed into service by the new republican regime in Sanaa, he founded and headed the YAR's first banking institution, the Yemen Bank for Reconstruction and Development (YBRD). After taking a leave of absence from the bank to write his dissertation in Paris, he returned to the YAR in the mid-1960s to serve simultaneously as head of the YBRD and as minister of economics.

State and Politics in the al-Sallal Era

During the years of uneasy tutelage under Egypt much was done to replace Yemen's medieval Islamic state with the institutions and practices of modern government. The imamate itself was replaced by a secular head of state, the presidency. In 1963 and 1964, a host of Egyptian advisers supervised the wholesale replacement of the imam's "household" government with a council of ministers and some two dozen ministries and other government agencies. A number of mixed public-private economic enterprises were also created, among them the Yemen Foreign Trade Company, the Yemen Petroleum Company, the National Tobacco and Matches Company, the Yemen Pharmaceutical Company, and the YBRD. Some of these new enterprises played important roles during the first years of the republic, and a few of them, especially the YBRD, continue to have a prominent place in the YAR's modern sector.

This flurry of Egyptian-inspired institution building increased the capabilities of the Yemeni state and, at the very least, served to shake up and dislodge some of the ideas and practices of the imamate system. Nevertheless, this initial effort at modern state building was largely ill conceived and hastily executed, and the changes were often more formal than substantive. Egypt had tried to make the YAR over in its own image, and most of the new institutions were pale carbon copies of those in Cairo in the early 1960s; as such, they were often ill suited to conditions in Yemen and to the Yemenis for whom they were intended. Some remained inoperative paper organizations—"ghosts," as some Yemenis have called them—and others were hastily staffed by a few holdovers from the imamate who knew nothing about modern government and by young republicans who lacked prior experience with any form of governance. Most of these institutions were closely controlled by Egypt, either directly through its own advisers or indirectly through Yemenis beholden to the Egyptians. Many of the mixed public-private enterprises were partly owned by Egypt and directly linked to their Egyptian counterparts.

The distorting effect on state building of Egypt's tutelage was most apparent in terms of the armed forces of the YAR. Except for the creation of a brigade of commandos and paratroops, a modern unit with an atypically large number of Shafai officers and troops, the Egyptians did not permit the modernization and significant enlargement of the regular armed forces during their involvement in the civil war. Edgar O'Ballance claimed that in 1965 "the Yemen army was still less than 6000 men in strength, and was made up of a jumble of small infantry units scattered about the country, some of which were either incorporated into the [Egyptian] formations or in some other way under [Egyptian] command."[11] Though hard to imagine, the long civil war did not even leave the YAR with armed forces that were much larger and stronger than before.

The civil war served to mask many of the most glaring deficiencies of the republican state. To the extent that they worked at all, many of the new institutions did so largely because they were focused narrowly on the single goal of surviving the struggle with the royalists. The artificialities of the war economy and Yemen's low level of socioeconomic development made it possible for Yemenis to survive, over the short term, in spite of the near absence of the state. The fledgling private commercial sector and the system of subsistence agriculture were able to minimally meet most basic needs. Still, many Yemenis suffered severe deprivation during these difficult years, and this trying experience is stamped in the memories of most middle-aged Yemenis.

Conditions during the first years after the 1962 Revolution did not permit Yemeni republicans to take politics into their own hands much less to reorder political life in the YAR. Although political activity temporarily increased and became more open during the months after the revolution, the Egyptian intervention and the civil war soon severely distorted and arrested the development of a modern political infrastructure. Egypt became more deeply involved in the internal affairs of the YAR as the civil war dragged on, and Egyptian conduct of the war and control over much of the civil administration left little room for Yemeni politics and politicians. As Fred Halliday noted: "It was only in 1965—three years after the imam was ousted—that the first political organization, the Popular Revolutionary Organization, was set up"; an empty shell, it held its only congress in January 1967 and soon became history.[12] Indeed, Yemeni politics were run out of Cairo as much as out of Sanaa by the middle of the 1960s. At one point, President al-Sallal, by then President Nasir's puppet, was detained in Egypt for some months in order to let another group of Yemenis have a go at leading the republic. When the results proved unsatisfactory to the Egyptians, al-Sallal was returned to office in Sanaa and many members of the other group—including a number of young, educated modernists—were put under house arrest in Egypt. Many of the older generation of republicans—for example, Abd al-Rahman al-Iryani and Ahmad Muhammad Numan—withdrew from politics. Another, Muhammad al-Zubayri, joined the opposition and was assassinated.

As frustration with the civil war and the Egyptian presence deepened, the energies of many Yemeni republicans were diverted into several small, ephemeral political groupings that were in favor of some form of negotiated settlement with the royalists and were to varying degrees opposed to al-Sallal and the Egyptians. Examples include Muhammad al-Zubayri's Party of God and the various "third force" factions. At the same time, the Yemeni branches of the radical pan-Arab parties that had surfaced after the revolution found the political climate increasingly inhospitable, and they eventually joined the growing opposition and were subjected to harassment and repression. The fate of the Arab Nationalist Movement (ANM), the strongest of these groups, is illustrative. Shortly after the revolution, the ANM opened a cultural center in Taiz and assumed operation of the new republic's only radio station; it also expanded its previously clandestine trade union activities, founding in succession the General Union of Taiz Workers and the General Union of Yemeni Workers. Suspicions that President Nasir was ready to abandon the republic and to make peace with Saudi Arabia led the Yemeni branch of the ANM to break with Egypt and with ANM headquarters in Beirut in late 1964. The honeymoon over, the Egyptian-backed al-Sallal regime soon closed down all ANM activities and purged ANM members from posts in the republican administration. ANM-sponsored protest demonstrations led to further repression, and many ANM members and sympathizers fled south to Aden. Finally, the new politics of the republic took on an increasingly sectarian tone as Shafais came to the conclusion that the al-Sallal regime was perpetuating Zaydi dominance over politics and society. This seemed especially to be the case in the despised government of 1966–1967 in which al-Sallal served as both prime minister and president.

The external relations of the YAR turned sterile and unproductive as the civil war wore on, imposing upon North Yemen a new isolation, this time one not desired by its nominal rulers. The United States under President John F. Kennedy, eager to signal its receptiveness to non-Marxist reformist regimes in the Arab world, had been quick to recognize the YAR after the 1962 Revolution. Great Britain and France did not follow suit, and the former came increasingly to see protection of its interests in Aden Colony and the Aden Protectorates as dependent upon support of the royalist cause in North Yemen. Although the United States provided considerable economic and technical assistance in the mid-1960s—completing the Sanaa-Taiz-Mukha road and the Taiz city waterworks—political relations between the United States and the YAR turned cool and were finally broken off amidst acrimony in 1967. Saudi Arabia was quite successful in its efforts to portray the al-Sallal regime as Egypt's puppet on the Arabian Peninsula and to persuade the West and conservative Arab states to minimize relations with the YAR.

As a consequence, the YAR's external relations by 1967 were largely limited to Egypt and, through Egypt, to the USSR and the countries of eastern Europe. This marriage of convenience came to generate little enthusiasm on either side. This is well illustrated by a story, probably true, that involves al-Sallal, Gamal Abd al-Nasir, and Nikita Khrushchev. Allegedly, Nasir's reply to Khrushchev's angry criticism of him for having brought al-Sallal along on a Soviet cruise of the Black Sea was: "But I just wanted you to see what I have to put up with."

3

National Reconciliation and the al-Iryani Era: 1967–1971

The al-Sallal regime was ousted in November 1967 by a broad coalition of moderate republican and nationalist elements, civilian and military, under the titular leadership of Qadi Abd al-Rahman al-Iryani (ca. 1912–   ), only weeks after the withdrawal of the bulk of the Egyptian armed forces. Egypt's withdrawal was forced by its defeat by Israel in the Six-Day War in June; it was facilitated in August by the Khartoum Agreement, which ended the long confrontation between Egypt and Saudi Arabia in Yemen. Most Yemenis welcomed the exodus of the Egyptians and the ouster of President al-Sallal.

Conservative Republicanism and Its Constraints

The YAR in the late 1960s afforded a dramatic example of a country with a great need for government action and little governmental capacity to act. Part of the drama of Yemeni politics after the al-Sallal era centers on the way in which the YAR's small number of modernists perceived the task of state building and worked within severe sociopolitical constraints to increase the capacity of the state. To understand the constraints operating on this group it is necessary to recognize that, despite the unsettling effects of five years of disruptions and change, North Yemen in 1968 remained an essentially traditional society, especially outside the three cities and the major towns. Moreover, beneath the surface reality of anti-Egyptian feelings, the movement that replaced the al-Sallal regime contained a strong restorative undercurrent. In addition to seeking to return to Yemeni hands control over Yemen's destiny, it sought to restore certain traditional Yemeni values and practices that had been challenged by the rhetoric of Arab socialism and by other modern ideas during the Egyptian interlude. In sum, the mood and movement that brought Abd al-Rahman al-Iryani to the fore was conservative as well as nationalist and—with regard to the former— had many of the earmarks of a mild thermidor reaction.

The sociopolitical composition of the regime headed by President al-Iryani[1] reflected this mood and the continued vitality of tradition and traditional groups in Yemen. As Robert Stookey pointed out, the evolution of the Yemeni polity under al-Iryani involved "a progressive reassertion of the traditional loci of social and political power" and attested to "the hardiness of millennial patterns of local leadership and relationships among the various segments of Yemeni society."[2] Although the regime made room for the small group of young, educated Shafai and Zaydi modernists and for the worldly-wise Shafai merchants, it rested upon "a coalition between shaykhs of the tribes, large and small, and the community of Zaydis educated in the traditional legal and theological disciplines . . ."[3] The learned qadi families saw themselves, by training and experience, as the rightful heirs to a system ruled previously by the great sayyid families and as the proper guardians of the Islamic character of the republic. President al-Iryani, called simply "the Qadi" by most Yemenis, personified his class's confident presumption to rule. Some of the more politically astute referred to him in private as the "republican imam."

The conservative coalition was strengthened in early 1970 with the national reconciliation that ended the civil war between the royalists and the republicans. Royalist tribal leaders remained in place in their historic tribal domains, now with the blessings of the republican regime in Sanaa. Although the Hamid al-Din family was forbidden to return to Yemen, a large number of moderate royalists, including both sayyids and commoners, returned at this time. Their houses and lands were restored, and many of them reassumed positions of social prominence in the cities, towns, and countryside. Although denied access to the most politically sensitive offices, many ex-royalists were given posts in the republican state and participated actively, if discreetly, in politics. Indeed, five of them received ministerial posts and another—Ahmad al-Shami, the former royalist foreign minister—joined President al-Iryani on the multimember executive, the Republican Council. No longer able to claim governance as a birthright, many of the great sayyid families nonetheless did reemerge at this time as a force in Yemeni politics.

In 1968, nearly two years before the civil war ended in national reconciliation, political events gave the sociopolitical foundations of the al-Iryani regime greater coherence and sharper definition. With the ouster of the al-Sallal regime, the Arab Nationalist Movement (ANM) had reemerged and assumed an important role in the defense of the republic against the royalist offensive that followed the withdrawal of Egyptian forces in late 1967. The ANM was aided in this effort by the National Liberation Front (NLF), which had just wrested power from the British in Aden. The NLF, a South Yemeni offshoot of the old ANM, gave the YAR what little support it could during these turbulent months largely out of fear that a royalist victory in the north would threaten its shaky position in Aden. In Sanaa, the ANM manned and armed part of the Popular Resistance Forces (PRF), the citizens' militia created to defend the capital against the royalist siege of Sanaa in early 1968. It also took the lead in organizing units of the PRF in Taiz, al-Hudayda, and the large towns. In addition, seeking to radicalize as well as to defend the republic, the ANM organized a number of peasant leagues in the southeast near the border with South Yemen. Most of the leagues sought modest reforms, although in a couple of cases they arrested landlords and declared an end to the power of the local shaykhs.

The confrontation between the conservative core of the al-Iryani regime and the leftist partisans began after the siege of Sanaa was broken in February 1968. The burden of defending Sanaa had fallen disproportionately on young Shafai officers and troops in the Commando and Paratroop Brigade, many of whom had been influenced by the progressive ideas of the ANM and the new NLF regime in Aden. Heady with their recent victory, the more militant of the defenders began to express openly their desire to move the republic into the mainstream of revolutionary Arab nationalism. Opposed to both the royalists and the tribalists, they rejected Arab efforts to secure a compromise settlement of the civil war, called for a strengthening of the professional army and the PRF, and demanded Shafai equality with the Zaydis in the government and the army. For their part, the conservative elements in the al-Iryani regime became increasingly alarmed by these ideas and more determined than ever to eliminate the partisans from the political arena. The arrival of a shipload of Soviet arms at al-Hudayda in March 1968 was the occasion for the first test of strength, each side intent on preventing the arms from falling into the hands of the other. In the brief armed skirmish that ensued, forces loyal to the conservatives prevailed over ANM-inspired elements of the PRF. Throughout the spring and summer of 1968 the lines were more sharply drawn between the two sides, and each worked to prepare itself for the expected showdown. The left tried to regroup, and in June elements of the ANM formed a new political party, the Revolutionary Democratic party. On the other side, conservative politicians and tribal leaders met in July and adopted a plan to purge the left and leftist ideas from the YAR. Earlier, concerned by the growing influence of the NLF in the southeastern borderlands, the government had given permission to the Front for the Liberation of Occupied South Yemen (FLOSY) to conduct anti-NLF propaganda and other activities from Taiz. FLOSY had just lost out to the NLF in the fight to succeed Britain in Aden.

Efforts by moderates to defuse the situation proved of no avail. Years later, a Yemeni who was in Sanaa during these days compared the situation to that of the Paris Commune in 1871, and declared that "Sanaa was an island of revolutionary enthusiasm surrounded by a rising tide of strident traditionalism. A fight and its outcome were never in doubt."[4] The replacement of a handful of Shafai commanders provided the spark that ignited the Sanaa mutiny, a bloody three-day battle in August 1968 in which army and tribal elements loyal to the regime smashed the perceived challenge from the left. In the next several months the conservatives consolidated their position by purging the armed forces, banning the trade unions and the new Revolutionary Democratic party, and dissolving the peasant leagues and the PRF. Hundreds of militants were arrested, exiled, or forced to flee to Aden or elsewhere. This swift excision of the weak, ill-fitting left shifted the center of gravity of the al-Iryani regime in an even more conservative and traditionalist direction.

Special mention must be made of the modernists and the tribal shaykhs, poles apart in so many ways. Yemen's small group of first-generation modernists—or "graduates," as they are called by many—consisted of the first Yemenis to receive secondary and higher education in Egypt, other Arab countries, the West, and even the Soviet Union and East Europe. They returned to Yemen in two waves, after the 1962 Revolution and, in greater numbers, after the withdrawal of the Egyptians and the ouster of al-Sallal, and they came committed to working to bring the Yemeni state and nation into the modern world. These young modernists neither controlled the state nor had an independent power base of their own. Only a few of them came from prominent families or were otherwise well connected to the actual wielders of social and political power. Nevertheless, the graduates enjoyed a relatively secure place in the interstices of the al-Iryani regime. Most of them had good nationalist credentials, having proven themselves to be ardent patriots before and after the 1962 Revolution, and were able to benefit from the nationalist consensus that held together the disparate elements of the ruling coalition during the new regime's early years. However, as important as their nationalist credentials to securing them a place in the regime was the fact that the young modernists were needed by the more traditional leaders. Many of the latter knew that Yemen could not return to the isolation and self-sufficiency of the past, that the YAR had to deal continuously with the modern world, and that the graduates alone had begun to master the skills needed to operate the new state and to mediate between the YAR and the rest of the world. As one Yemeni put it, the graduates were the "modern magicians" who could transform paper into legal tender or negotiate international loans to purchase the modern goods that even the traditional leaders were coming to esteem. Though many of the traditional leaders did not particularly like the modernists or their ideas or conceits, most of the former were prepared to give the latter high office and to defer to their expertise on technical matters.

For their part, the leading tribal shaykhs continued to enjoy enhanced power and position in the years after the ouster of the al-Sallal regime. They did not give up their increased autonomy as the civil war wound down and they continued to receive subsidies from either or both sides of the conflict. Moreover, a number of "republican tribalists"[5]—among them Abdullah ibn Husayn al-Ahmar, Sinan abu Luhum, and Abdullah Tariq—had through their early and more or less continuous support of the republic established strong claims on the new political system. Their solid republican credentials legitimated future assertions of power and autonomy by their tribes.

Events immediately after the ouster of the al-Sallal regime served to further strengthen the position of the shaykhs. The withdrawal of Egyptian forces in late 1967 had made the nontribal republicans all the more dependent upon the arms of their tribal allies for defense against the royalists in the continuing civil war. No less important, tribal elements played a key military role in the successful attempt by the conservative republicans to beat back the challenge of the resurgent ANM and other progressive forces in 1968. Whatever their preferences, President al-Iryani and his colleagues were in no position in 1968 to curtail the power of the tribes.

The power of the shayks did not merely increase during and after the civil war—it assumed new forms and acquired new bases. Stookey noted that, although a pattern of shared authority between the shaykhs and the imamate's religious and civil officials was well established at the local level in Zaydi areas before the 1962 Revolution, "the basic innovation of the . . . [al-Iryani] regime consists in generalizing this collaboration to the national level, and recruiting the shaykhs, who rarely if ever held office under the Imams, into the formal ruling establishment."[6] This new practice of giving important shaykhs key consultative and executive positions in the growing central government probably contributed more than anything else to the expansion and consolidation of the shaykhs' power. No longer merely a volatile and potentially rebellious part of the environment of the Yemeni state, the tribal shaykhs were now full-fledged participants in an enlarged bargaining system that was still new and unfamiliar to all the players. In the relatively open and uncrystallized al-Iryani regime they learned quickly how to pyramid their power and influence. The shaykhs' new opportunities for enrichment and patronage at the center provided them with the resources needed to consolidate their traditional power base on the tribal periphery. In turn, the strengthening of this power base, and the credibility it gave to threats of political opposition if not armed rebellion, gave the shaykhs a further claim on benefits at the center, a claim that could be ignored by the state only at great risk.

The possibility that statist, antitribal politicians might one day attempt by force to curtail the power of the shaykhs was lessened by the "tribalization" of the armed forces. Tribal units were incorporated into the still small, unreformed regular army, and tribal leaders were placed in command of some of the key regular army units. As a consequence, the armed forces became less an instrument through which the fledgling state could extend its authority over the tribes than an instrument through which the tribes could defend their power and autonomy against the state. The question of a tribalized army versus a reformed professional army had been a major issue in the al-Hudayda incident in March 1968 and in the Sanaa mutiny in August 1968. Reorganization and reform of the army remained the most important, least publicly discussed issue in Yemeni politics during the al-Iryani era.

Finally, the position of the shaykhs was buttressed further from outside by Saudi Arabia. In choosing to take a chance and accept the republic in 1970, the Saudi leadership hedged its bet by continuing to pay subsidies to the tribes—former tribal foes as well as friends—and by presenting itself as the patron and protector of tribal interests. This arrangement both gave the Saudis a foothold in the Yemeni political system and gave the tribal leaders an external political staging area.

The loose coalition headed and held together by President al-Iryani was oligarchical in ideology and action. The regime made no serious attempt at popular political organization and, as the events surrounding the Sanaa mutiny in 1968 demonstrated, dealt sternly with major efforts of this sort by others. It early banned all political parties and its leading figures often expressed publicly the view that parties in Islamic Yemen were bad, unnecessary, or both. In an oft-quoted speech, President al-Iryani asserted that "people import ideas from outside the country" through parties and that "one begins as a partisan and ends up as an agent."[7] Given the regime's sociopolitical bases, this posture is not surprising. As Fred Halliday pointed out, the most powerful elements in the ruling coalition had reason to prevent "development of any non-tribal and non-confessional organizations; the shaykhs and religious leaders had their own traditional forms of organization and did not need parties to mobilize support."[8]

As with its predecessor, the al-Iryani regime initially operated within a vague, inchoate constitutional framework. The one institution that was given form at the outset was the Republican Council, the plural executive with, in theory at least, a rotating chairmanship. The Republic Council was clearly an expression of the leadership's desire to end one-man rule, be it that of an imam or, as in the case of al-Sallal, a soldier. This new institution quickly took root, and it did so largely because of the prestige and force of personality of one man, President al-Iryani.

The dissent and discontent surrounding the Sanaa mutiny in 1968 led to an initial effort to structure consultation among the several groups that composed the ruling coalition. Bowing to pressures, the regime announced that a consultative body would be formed, and in the spring of 1969 the appointed, forty-five member National Council held its first session. This quasi legislature quickly asserted its presence and came to play an important part in the political and decisionmaking process.

A major task of the National Council in 1970 was the drafting of the YAR's first permanent constitution. Put into effect by proclamation in December of that year, the 1970 Constitution continued the plural executive, the Republican Council. In addition, it replaced the National Council with a 179-member legislature, the Consultative Council. Twenty of the members of this new body were to be appointed by the chairman of the Republican Council and the remaining 159 were to be elected indirectly by electors chosen by the male residents of local electoral districts. National elections, another first for the YAR, were held in March 1971, and the Consultative Council was convened for its initial session in the following month.

The Consultative Council was an assembly of notables, not unlike early English parliaments. In the absence of explicit party organization and ideology, the members were grouped into shifting factions and only tenuously linked to one another and to their constituents. As a result of some fraud and a districting system skewed toward rural and tribal areas, the majority of the members were tribal shaykhs or other notables with conservative orientations or connections. Although not a sovereign lawmaking body in the western parliamentary sense, the Consultative Council nonetheless did have real powers, among them the powers to withdraw confidence from the government and to refuse to give its assent to proposed legislation and the budget. As governance under the new constitutional system settled into a more regularized pattern, the Council asserted its prerogatives and became an increasingly powerful institution.

Security Needs and Economic Constraints

The sociopolitical constraints on state building and modernization in the rather amorphous, highly decentralized system of rule that was in place by the end of 1968 either manifested themselves indirectly or remained latent during the first three years of the al-Iryani era. This was because other, more immediate imperatives constrained and took precedence over these longer-term concerns at this time. The first involved security, the need to defend the republic against the all-out royalist military offensive expected in the wake of the completion of the Egyptian withdrawal in late 1967. The first government formed in the al-Iryani era, that headed by Muhsin al-Aini, a modernist politician and member of the Famous Forty, lasted only a month. An older, more conservative republican soldier, Lt.-General Hasan al-Armi, was then appointed prime minister and commander in chief of the armed forces and charged with defending the completely encircled capital. The seventy-day seige of Sanaa, the darkest and most heroic hour of the civil war, was literally a struggle for survival; the fall of Sanaa, which many thought likely, would probably have caused the demise of the republic. Fighting as well for their very lives, the members of the al-Amri government who remained in Sanaa devoted virtually all their time and energy, as well as the meager resources of the republic, to this showdown fight.

The breaking of the siege of Sanaa in February 1968 caused the possibility of a royalist victory to recede but did not bring peace. Instead, the civil war dragged on fitfully, sometimes erupting into fierce battles, and the opponents of the republic continued to control much of the northern and eastern two-thirds of the country. The main road linking Sanaa to Taiz was wrested from the royalists only in late 1968, and the northern town of Saada changed hands several times in renewed fighting that stretched from late 1969 through early 1970. In addition, the new and tentative relations between the two Yemens waxed and waned over this period, sometimes producing tensions in the borderlands. Accordingly, Commander in Chief al-Amri, the "Sword of the Republic," was called upon to form two more successive governments in 1968 and 1969, and the needs of security continued to take precedence over most other matters at least until reconciliation with the royalists came in the spring of 1970. As one cabinet member exclaimed years later: "State building! What state building? We were struggling merely to save, not build, the state during those days."[9]

Another concern that commanded attention and severely constrained state-building and modernization efforts by the new regime was what came to be known as "the financial crisis." Several factors combined to throw the country's fragile economic and financial systems into total disarray in the late 1960s and the early 1970s: the sharp drop in the inflow of outside funds that had fuelled the artificial war economy, the prolonged drought that crippled the once self-sufficient agricultural system, and the opening of the country to an uncontrolled flood of foreign imports. The soaring rate of inflation, the collapse of the Yemeni rial, and the growing deficits in the government budget and the balance of payments were only the most dramatic of the many economic and financial problems facing the YAR as the civil war wound down. In 1969 the rial was worth less than 30 percent of what it was worth in 1964 when the silver Maria Theresa thaler was scrapped for paper money; in 1970 the value of exports amounted to 7 percent that of imports, and government revenues covered only 56 percent of current expenditures.

These pressing problems forced the YAR government to live precariously on an ad hoc, hand-to-mouth basis. The modernists in the government who might otherwise have given greater attention to increasing the capabilities of the state found themselves scrambling about and dreaming up ingenious ways to find the funds needed each month to keep the army in the field and the civil servants at their posts. The immediacy of these problems and the expedient actions they required is captured in the words of a prominent minister at the time: "About the only thing we could afford was paper, so we had money printed just as fast as we could."[10]

The financial crisis and the security imperative were not unrelated, especially in the first years of the al-Iryani era. As long as the civil war dragged on, the armed forces and the tribes loyal to the republic had preemptive claims on the limited resources of the state. More important, the financial crisis could only be eased through massive outside assistance, and it became increasingly evident that this assistance was contingent on the ending of the civil war. Most western nations and the international financial agencies they controlled were not prepared to extend aid until Saudi Arabia recognized the YAR, and the Saudi stamp of approval was contingent upon an acceptable resolution of the struggle between the republicans and the royalists.

The fiscal problems of successive governments inevitably spilled into the political arena, making the distribution of the meager budgetary pie a source of increasing instability and conflict. This more than any other factor explains why the first seven governments in the al-Iryani era lasted on the average less than six months. Between July 1969 and July 1971, three governments fell and an attempt to form a fourth failed largely because disputes over the budget had become so heated and irreconcilable. Only three months after he formed his third successive government, Prime Minister al-Amri suddenly resigned in early July 1969, at odds with both civilian modernists in the cabinet who wanted to cut the military budget and young officers who were demanding reform of the armed forces. The confused, nearly two-month-long search for a new government that followed was also confounded by disagreement over the size and distribution of the budget.

Abdullah al-Kurshumi, a member of the Famous Forty and one of North Yemen's first engineers, finally was able to put together a cabinet in early September 1969. The al-Kurshumi government was the first to make the growing financial crisis both the major topic of public discourse and the chief concern of government. From the outset, al-Kurshumi bluntly stressed in his statements the magnitude of the crisis, the severe remedies required for its solution, and the sacrifices that these remedies must necessarily impose on all claimants to the public treasury. His government addressed itself to the worsening budgetary crisis with vigor and determination. In one of its first moves, it set up four committees—one each for civil, tribal, armed forces, and security affairs—to examine expenditures. This examination resulted in new, stricter controls on spending and cuts in the budgets of most government agencies, including that of the armed forces. As a consequence, the al-Kurshumi government succeeded in bringing current revenues and expenditures into balance. In the end, however, Prime Minister al-Kurshumi's abrasive, confrontational style, particularly in his dealings with the new, assertive National Council, caught up with him. Although able to work out a budgetary compromise acceptable to the military, he failed to rally sufficient support from nontribal elements to make good his insistence that subsidies to the tribes be cut for reasons of economy. Under increasing attack, he resigned at the beginning of February 1970, after only five months in office.

The quick formation of a government by Muhsin al-Aini, his second in the al-Iryani era, ushered in a year in which the financial crisis was pushed into the background by the politics of reconciliation and an upsurge of diplomatic activity. In April 1970, on the occasion of the Islamic foreign ministers' meeting in Saudi Arabia, Prime Minister al-Aini negotiated an agreement to end the civil war, and in May the first contingent of leading royalists returned and were absorbed into the YAR government. Saudi Arabia recognized the republican regime in July, and France and Britain followed suit within a week. Peace and reconciliation were welcomed with relief by most war-weary Yemenis, and talk in government circles warmed to prospects of the increased economic aid that many were convinced would quickly flow from these new, long-sought external ties. Another factor that diverted attention from government finances was the continuation of a severe drought and the concerted international effort to secure and distribute famine relief in the second half of 1970.

Not merely overshadowed by other events, the financial crisis actually did ease temporarily in 1970, partly as a result of the stringent fiscal measures adopted earlier by the al-Kurshumi government. In addition, al-Aini bought time for his government by covering current expenses with a $6 million loan negotiated at commercial interest rates from the Netherlands Bank and guaranteed by the Saudi government. As a consequence, al-Aini was even able to increase expenditures and thereby satisfy the appetites of some of the powerful groups with claims on the budget.

Al-Aini resigned in late February 1971, after a year in office, to make way for elections to the Consultative Council, the legislative body called for in the recently proclaimed 1970 Constitution. The first government after these elections was formed in early May by Ahmad Muhammad Numan, a leading nationalist of the older generation and a founder of the Free Yemenis. Upon assuming office, the Numan government was informed that the treasury was empty and that the Netherlands Bank was demanding payment of interest on its loan. The financial crisis had returned and was immediately to preoccupy—indeed, to overwhelm—the new government.

Within ten days of taking office, Prime Minister Numan sent a message to King Faisal of Saudi Arabia in which he described the YAR's current problems and appealed for timely financial assistance. In late May, Numan painted the Consultative Council a grim picture: A large deficit in the 1971 budget was foreseen, exports would cover only an insignificant part of imports, and the government was faced with an external debt of more than $175 million, nearly two-thirds of which was owed to the Soviet Union and China. One way out of the immediate budgetary crisis was to secure more commercial loans, and al-Aini had negotiated a new Saudi-guaranteed loan just prior to the end of his tenure. Regarding it as fiscally irresponsible, Prime Minister Numan and his government refused to complete this transaction; instead, they insisted on meeting the deficit in current operations through foreign aid, more taxes, and reduced spending. Unfortunately, foreign aid was not forthcoming from Saudi Arabia or elsewhere, and the Consultative Council was unwilling to accept either higher taxes or cuts in tribal subsidies or in the size of the regular army. On July 20, Numan in a dramatic radio broadcast laid blame for the financial crisis squarely on the shoulders of the tribes and the armed forces; asserting that the YAR could not meet even a small part of its financial obligations, he called on other Arab countries to "rush to its rescue." He then tendered his resignation to President al-Iryani, only two and one-half months after taking office, declaring himself "unable to shoulder the responsibility of rule because of financial difficulties facing the nation."[11]

The Numan government remained in office in a caretaker capacity until late August 1971 when Commander in Chief al-Amri formed a new cabinet, his fourth under President al-Iryani. Within a week, however, al-Amri was sent into exile, ostensibly because of a senseless late-night argument in which he shot and killed a Yemeni photographer. There was, it seems, more to the story than this. On the morning of the day of this bizarre incident, al-Amri had sent a memo to all military commanders in which he expressed his alarm over the deterioration of Yemeni politics and declared his willingness to step aside if the armed forces chose to assume power to save the nation. Quick action by President al-Iryani and the coincidental shooting incident put an end to this extraconstitutional adventure.[12] The mercurial and perhaps unstable al-Amri, dubbed "the General Patton of Yemen" by an American, left the political scene for good.

The Numan resignation and the al-Amri affair revealed growing ill feeling between civilian and military elements based on the conviction of each that the other was corrupt, selfish, and incompetent. Numan's dramatic move triggered a rare public demonstration in Sanaa in which some seventy people were detained, including at least one high official. Protesting the effects of the financial crisis, particularly a delay in the payment of government salaries, the demonstrators directed their wrath against the armed forces, the Consultative Council, the Republican Council, and President al-Iryani. Rumors of an attempt to launch a coup in the wake of Numan's resignation provided another indication of discontent. Later, in the course of the search for a government after the al-Amri debacle, a group of senior army officers, with the assistance of a few civilian modernists, addressed to the Republican Council a memo that demanded that immediate steps be taken to eliminate the YAR's financial deficit and that the administration be subjected to wholesale reform in order to end corruption, favoritism, and inefficiency. In addition, the memo demanded that the next government stay in office for at least two years to ensure stability and that an end be put to the awarding of portfolios on a tribal basis. The financial crisis, and the political crisis it had triggered, seemed to be coming to a head in the fall of 1971.

Economic and Financial Institution Building

Given the magnitude and immediacy of the constraints within which they had to operate, the response of some of Yemen's modernists to the need for state building between 1968 and 1971 is impressive. Despite the unceasing pressure of day-to-day concerns, they were able to diagnose and to prescribe remedies for some of their country's longer-term development problems, as well as to design some of the new governmental institutions thought necessary for the proper administration of these remedies. Many of the institutions proposed by these men were in operation by the mid-1970s. Together, they rank as major building blocks in the effort to construct a modern Yemeni state.

Three modernists deeply involved in these matters at this time were Dr. Muhammad Said al-Attar, Muhammad Anaam Ghaleb, and Abd al-Aziz Abd al-Ghani. Dr. al-Attar, the founder of the Yemen Bank for Reconstruction and Development, was minister of economics in the last government under al-Sallal and in the first two governments in the al-Iryani era. The two other men were virtually interchangeable during the early years under al-Iryani. Ghaleb headed the Technical Office, the staff arm of the Higher Planning Council, during two governments in which Abd al-Ghani was minister of economics, and Abd al-Ghani headed the Technical Office while Ghaleb was minister of economics in two other governments.

State-building efforts during most of the al-Iryani era focused on economic and financial management and development planning and constitute a narrowly defined pattern of state building. By contrast, little was done during this period to create other institutions that are usually thought of as more essential to the modern state—for example, professional armed forces, a rationalized bureaucracy, and a secular legal system. This putting of the cart before the horse in state building was probably a matter of both necessity and choice. The immediate security concerns, the acute financial crisis, and the vested interests of the more powerful elements in the al-Iryani regime combined to largely determine what sort of state building could be undertaken. In addition, many of the modernists seem by training and orientation actually to have favored the path that circumstances dictated they follow. They were trained in the West, some as economists, and the institutional reforms they initially promoted were probably not unlike those upon which their western professors would have placed emphasis.

The first modest attempt at institution building in the al-Iryani era occurred in the spring of 1968, at a time when the al-Amri government was preoccupied with both the continuing royalist military threat and the growing conflict between left- and right-wing republicans. It consisted of the creation of two offices atached to the Office of the Prime Minister: the Legal Office, an agency that drafted laws and provided the state with legal advice, and the Technical Office. Ghaleb was named the first head of the Technical Office and occupied that post until early 1960 and again throughout most of 1970 and 1971. He recruited a team of young, able Yemeni graduates, as well as several foreign experts, and set them to the task of gathering the data and doing the analysis thought necessary for the YAR's development. The times, however, were not ripe for the future-oriented activities of the Technical Office. The Higher Planning Council met only once after its creation and successive governments, preoccupied with the here-and-now of political and economic survival, paid little attention to the reports and recommendations of Ghaleb and his staff. No one had to listen to the Technical Office, and few did. One person who served as a minister during this period referred to the Technical Office as "the Art Office," no doubt with Ghaleb's reputation as a poet in mind.

Nevertheless, the Technical Office was a pioneering agency. It provided a haven and a meeting place for Yemenis with ideas about the future, and it served as an incubator for many of the programs later adopted: the first development program, the national census, the creation of a central bank, and the replacement of the Treasury Ministry with the Finance Ministry. More directly, the Technical Office laid the groundwork and recruited much of the staff for the agency that was to replace it in 1972, the Central Planning Organization (CPO). On a more practical level, it began to collect the first rudimentary economic and social data on the YAR and in its last year of existence published the YAR's first statistical yearbook. Finally, the top officials of the Technical Office served as needed intermediaries between the YAR and the international aid community at the time when the former was venturing into this unfamiliar area for the first time.

Given the major contributions the World Bank and the International Monetary Fund (IMF) were to make to institution building in the YAR in the 1970s, the negotiations that resulted in membership in these organizations were crucial events in the early years of the al-Iryani era. Opinion within government circles was not unanimous on seeking membership, some ministers thinking that the requirements of membership would limit the ability of the hard-pressed government to use the printing press to finance the civil war. Nevertheless, the cabinet in July 1969 authorized completion of the application process. In the fall of that year, Minister of Economics Ghaleb presented the YAR's case for membership at the governors' meetings of both organizations, and in May 1970 it was announced in Washington that the YAR had been admitted to the two bodies and their affiliates. Earlier, in Febrary 1970, an eight-man World Bank/Kuwait Fund delegation had arrived in Sanaa to assess for the first time Yemen's needs and potential for economic development. Ghaleb led the Yemeni side of the negotiations that were subsequently to yield important agreements on development loans and technical assistance. The first of these agreements, providing for foreign technical experts, was announced in July 1971.

The major act of institution building in the first half of the al-Iryani era was the creation of the Central Bank of Yemen and the initial planning for a commercial banking system. Theretofore, the Yemen Bank for Reconstruction and Development (YBRD) had served as the YAR's only commercial bank and, with the Yemeni Currency Board, had also performed elementary central banking tasks. Although the al-Kurshumi government had taken the first steps in 1969 to create a central bank, little was done by the al-Aini government to advance this project in the next year. At the urging of the IMF, the project was revived and pushed to completion during the brief Numan government in 1971. The legislation authorizing the Central Bank was passed and Abd al-Aziz Abd al-Ghani was appointed its first governor. With the assistance of the IMF, which earlier had agreed to provide a team of experts and other technical assistance, the Central Bank opened in July 1971.

The Central Bank, the YAR's "bank of banks," was designed to perform new tasks of banking supervision as well as to take over those central banking functions previously performed by the YBRD and the Yemeni Currency Board. In addition to freeing the YBRD to operate exclusively as a commercial and investment bank, the creation of the Central Bank made possible the prudent chartering of additional domestic and foreign commercial banks, a matter long under consideration. As early as mid-1969 the cabinet had approved in principle the existence of foreign banks in the YAR, and in May 1971 the cabinet decided to allow "a number of foreign banks" to open branches in the main cities. The first of these banks, the British Bank of the Middle East, opened a branch in al-Hudayda in September 1971.

A number of other projects were conceived and nurtured during this period. Although it was not formally legislated into existence until early 1972, the decision to create the Central Planning Organization grew out of intensive study and discussions in 1971. A World Bank team concluded early that year that it was imperative for the YAR to increase its capacity to plan for economic development; it concluded further that the Technical Office was constitutionally flawed and ought to be replaced by a new and larger organization with more independent authority and greater status. In mid-1971, the YAR government both endorsed this proposal and negotiated World Bank/Kuwait Fund aid to provide the new planning organization with a team of foreign experts as well as other technical assistance.

The Treasury Ministry and most treasury ministers were not part of the institution-building effort in the early years of the al-Iryani era. One of the more unfortunate legacies of the period of Egyptian tutelage, the Treasury Ministry had surprisingly little to do even with the day-to-day financial operations of the government; indeed, it was virtually closed down for months with no apparent ill effects during a political dispute in 1969. Uncontrolled and unauthorized spending by revenue-collecting agencies of the government meant that a substantial part of all revenues never reached the Treasury. The allocation of what revenues it did receive was not determined by annual budgetary procedures. Instead, government spending was largely a month-to-month affair: ministries submitted their monthly needs to the Treasury, which as a rule did not question recurrent expenditures so long as they remained at a more or less stable level; requests for increases were negotiated as they arose but were rarely approved because of the chronic shortage of funds. In an effort to modernize this archaic fiscal system, the al-Kurshumi government in 1969 concluded an agreement with the IMF to study the YAR's procedures for collecting and distributing revenues. The study, completed in 1971, concurred in its findings with the opinion of some of the Yemeni modernists that the Treasury Ministry could not be reformed without excessive affort and should be replaced by a new financial ministry. This conclusion led the Numan government to create the YAR's first budgetary agency—the Budget Office—and to reach an agreement for an IMF-funded team of financial experts to staff that agency.

During these years the modernists also turned their attentions to the need to train Yemenis to perform new tasks in the government and in the private sector. This period saw the founding of the University of Sanaa and the adoption of a plan to create a new school of public administration. Without proper legislation and with only a provisional board of trustees, the university began in 1970 on a modest basis with a teachers' training program and a law school; the first external aid for the university, a grant from Kuwait, was secured in the same year. The attempt to meet the need to train personnel for the YAR's public institutions centered on a proposal of a United Nations' expert that the small clerical and secretarial institute created in 1963 be revitalized and expanded. In 1971 the government accepted this proposal, thereby opening the way for the creation of the National Institute of Public Administration (NIPA) in 1974.

Finally, preliminary work toward both a national census and the preparation of a development plan was done during this period. From the outset, the Technical Office had viewed these two tasks as central to its mission. In 1969, Ghaleb hired a Soviet expert to advise the Technical Office on censustaking and to conduct pilot census projects. Although the Technical Office in 1969 was able to secure commitment of the government to prepare a general plan for the YAR, it was not until late in the Numan government in 1971 that the project received its first big push forward. The agreement by the World Bank and the Kuwait Fund in that year to assist the proposed Central Planning Organization was tied to the goal of preparing the YAR's first plan in the near future.

4

Contradictions in the al-Iryani Regime: 1971–1974

The months after the one-week government and exile of Hasan al-Amri in the summer of 1971 did not appear so different from those that preceded these dramatic events. There occurred neither the bankruptcy of the Yemeni state directly predicted by Prime Minister Numan nor the military coup anticipated by others. Instead, the financial crisis eased and the civilian politicians gave signs of providing the stability demanded by the officers' corps. In retrospect, however, the period from late 1971 to 1975 constitutes a separate phase in the short history of the YAR. The new phase was one of transition and had a confusing, ambiguous, almost incoherent quality, the result of cross-cutting inchoate forces. The dynamic underlying the transition was a growing and only gradually apparent contradiction between the sociopolitical composition of the al-Iryani regime and the possibilities for—and the requirements of—a major breakthrough in state building and modernization. Unresolved old problems and new events were by 1974 to place Yemeni politics and state building on a new course, the trajectory of which was not to become apparent until after 1975.

The first half of the period was marked by unprecedented governmental stability. The two governments that followed that of al-Amri each remained in office for more than a year: the cabinet formed by Muhsin al-Aini in September 1971 lasted until December 1972 and that headed by the conservative Qadi Abdullah al-Hajri remained until February 1974. At the same time, it was a period of external and domestic strife and turmoil. Relations between the YAR and its southeastern neighbor, renamed the People's Democratic Republic of Yemen (PDRY), had become increasingly strained after 1969 as the former drifted right and the latter lurched left. Fanned by the revolutionary fervor of the NLF regime in Aden and especially by Saudi-backed efforts to raise a rebellion and overthrow that regime, the smoldering conflict between the two Yemens rose to a serious level early in 1972, erupted in a brief border war in September of that year, and flared up again in the spring of 1973. The banned Revolutionary Democratic Party reemerged in the YAR and engaged in a program of underground political organizing and agitation in rural areas close to the border with the PDRY. The Organization of Yemeni Resisters, a group formed of members of the banned Popular Resistance Forces and soldiers purged from the YAR army in 1968, made its first appearance at this time. The political activities of these PDRY-supported groups were accompanied by numerous acts of sabotage and violence by guerrillas in the border area. In response, the al-Hajri government in 1973 unleashed the harshest campaign of repression to occur during the al-Iryani era, including arrests, imprisonments, and public executions. These inter-Yemeni and intra-YAR conflicts were important catalysts in the transition to a new pattern of politics and state building. Strains associated with the approaching end of this transition were manifest in the major political events in 1974: the short-lived government of Dr. Hasan Makki, the coup led by Colonel Ibrahim al-Hamdi, and the post-coup struggle for power.

Improved Prospects

One side of the growing contradiction was a set of conditions that by 1974 held out the prospect for a rapid increase in the pace of state building and modernization in the immediate future. Things came together and pieces fell into place in such a way as to relax some of the constraints that previously had tied the hands of the YAR's economic and financial managers and development planners. These conditions fall into three categories: (1) the middle-term solution of the financial crisis, (2) the increased availability of external development aid, and (3) the modest increase in the capacity of the state to plan and to manage.

The budget and balance-of-payment deficits that had loomed so large in the financial crisis began to evaporate after 1971. The major cause for the decline in the payments deficit was the massive increase in the flow of remittances from Yemenis working abroad, especially in Saudi Arabia. With the normalization of relations in 1970, Saudi Arabia stopped interfering with the transfer of workers' remittances to the YAR and the number of Yeminis leaving for work there increased dramatically. As a result, remittances for 1972 were nearly twice those for the years 1969–1971, and for 1974 they were nearly twice those for 1972. These remittances were the YAR's single most important source of foreign exchange, and they made it possible for the YAR to offset the huge balance-of-trade deficits caused by soaring imports and even to record modest surpluses in its balance of payments. Indicative of the improved situation, the value of the Yemeni rial, which had plummeted after 1966, stabilized in the 1970s despite the removal of exchange controls in 1971.

The solution to the government's chronic budget deficit involved increased customs duties and, as important, the beginning on a regular basis of budget subsidies from Saudi Arabia. Although prime ministers Numan and al-Aini had sought budgetary aid from the Saudis in 1971 and 1972 respectively, the breakthrough in the search for a solution to the government's inability to raise revenues to match its growing expenditures did not come until

1973. Prime Minister al-Hajri travelled to Saudi Arabia in March of that year and during this visit finally secured Saudi agreement to make state-to-state cash payments to cover most of the deficit for as long as this aid was needed. It was agreed that the amount of the subsidies would be negotiated annually and that the payments would be made in regular quarterly installments. Saudi Arabia deposited the first quarterly payment with the Central Bank of Yemen in mid-1973, and during the next twelve months provided the YAR with nearly $25 million in direct budgetary aid. Subsidies of at least 50 percent more than this figure were negotiated in the early summer of 1974 to cover the projected deficit in the 1974-1975 budget.

The remittances helped to solve the YAR's balance-of-payment problem and the subsidies both erased the budget deficit and moderated the intensity of the politics of the budgetary process. Together, they provided at least a middle-term solution to the financial crisis. In so doing, they also released the modernists in the government from many of the seemingly insoluble financial, economic, and political problems that had preoccupied them on a day-to-day basis from 1968 through 1971. The modernists were afforded new freedom to apply their time and energies to the development of institutions and substantive programs for the longer term.

Two further causes of the improvement in the YAR's prospects by 1974 were the marked increase in the flow of development funds and technical assistance and the likelihood that this external aid would increase still further in the second half of the 1970s. The YAR's major aid donors in the 1960s had been Egypt and the socialist countries, especially the USSR, China, East Germany, and North Korea; the United States, a major donor in the early 1960s, had suspended aid before relations with the YAR were broken at the time of the Six-Day War in 1967. The opening to the wealthier western aid community came in July 1969 when West Germany agreed to provide considerable aid in exchange for the YAR's decision to reestablish diplomatic relations with Bonn, a decision strongly opposed by the Arab League and the socialist countries. Although aid from West Germany began to arrive in the YAR in 1970, substantial aid from other western sources was not immediately forthcoming. Contrary to Yemeni hopes and expectations, the establishment of diplomatic relations with Saudi Arabia and the major industrial states of Western Europe in 1970 was actually followed by a hiatus in the flow of new aid to the YAR. The socialist countries became less generous because of the YAR's apparent political shift, and the western aid community moved slowly through the process of studying and evaluating the YAR's needs and aid requests.

By 1974, however, this situation changed dramatically. The disappointing trickle of new aid in the early 1970s swelled into a torrent of loans, grants, and technical assistance from a variety of donors: the United Nations' Development Program and the UN's specialized agencies, the World Bank/International Development Agency, West Germany and other Western European countries, the United States, Saudi Arabia, and the Gulf Arab states and their development funds. Capital expenditures for 1973-1974, wholly financed by foreign loans and grants, were two and one-half times those of 1972-1973; those for 1974-1975 were nearly double those for 1973-1974. By 1974, these funds were being applied to a growing number of development projects, particularly in the areas of transportation and communications: the Sanaa international airport was constructed, telephone links among the major cities were established, work continued on the Sanaa-Saada highway, the Sanaa-Taiz highway was paved, and a number of other major road projects were planned. Construction of many schools, mosques, medical facilities, and government buildings was begun in the cities and major towns, and the electrical and water systems of the three major cities were extended and improved. The Tihama Development Authority was established and the first of its projects to expand irrigated agriculture, the Wadi Zabid Project, was brought to the implementation stage. Preliminary planning also began on a number of other large agricultural schemes. Furthermore, negotiations conducted in 1973 and 1974 indicated that even larger amounts of aid were available for the next generation of projects.

Finally, and no less important, the period embracing the al-Aini and al-Hajri governments was marked by a significant increment in the capacity of the Yemeni state to manage its economic and financial affairs and to plan its future development. Although these governments did not take major new initiatives in state building, their tenure was a time of implementation, a time during which institutions conceived between 1968 and 1971 were put into place and began to function. The presence of these institutions, and the growing number of young graduates available to staff them, increased the likelihood that the YAR would be better able to take advantage of both the available external aid and the easing of the financial crisis.

The Central Bank of Yemen, headed by Abd al-Aziz Abd al-Ghani and supported by technical aid from the IMF, made progress in building up an effective management between 1972 and 1974. The important Banking Control Department commenced work and began to regulate banking operations with a view to establishing sound commercial banking practices. Minimum interest rates for private deposits were established in April 1972, and a statutory reserve requirement was imposed in December of that year. Under the supervision of the Central Bank, the commercial banking system expanded rapidly and without major mishap in the early 1970s. Between 1971 and 1973, the number of commercial banks rose from one to five—the Yemeni-owned Yemen Bank for Reconstruction and Development and four foreign-owned banks. The commercial banks recorded a strong rise in banking operations over this period, and between 1970 and 1973 savings and time deposits rose fivefold. The Central Bank established the Banking Committee, composed of the managers of the commercial banks and chaired by the deputy governor of the Central Bank, and its periodic meetings after 1971 provided for an informal exchange of views on bank and exchange-related matters.

The gradual replacement of the Treasury Ministry with the new Finance Ministry increased the likelihood that the state would in the future be able to exercise more effective control over government expenditures. In early 1972, based on the IMF recommendations of the previous year, the Budget Office was created and staffed with a number of young Yemeni graduates and an IMF-funded team of foreign experts. As conceived by the modernists, the mission of the new office was to introduce modern budgetary procedures as well as to serve as the nucleus of a modern financial ministry that would be created in the near future. Though under the jurisdiction of the treasury minister, the Budget Office was housed outside the Treasury Ministry and not involved in its day-to-day operations.

Ignored and isolated by an unsympathetic treasury minister and a suspicious Treasury establishment, the Budget Office had little to do and negligible impact during the first year of its existence. This situation changed in 1973 with the appointment of Muhammad Ahmad al-Junayd as treasury minister in the al-Hajri government. Al-Junayd, British trained and agriculture minister in six successive governments before becoming minister of state for development affairs in the previous government, brought a modernist outlook and much energy to the top post in the Treasury Ministry. Determined to proceed with the reform of government finances, al-Junayd directed the Budget Office to go through the motions of preparing a trial budget for fiscal 1973-1974. He had the Budget Office develop an elementary budget format and a set of budgetary procedures, created budget departments headed by members of the Budget Office in each ministry and brought the more able officials in the Treasury Ministry together with experts from the Budget Office to simulate the preparation of the budget. Despite the initial fear and hostility of some Treasury officials, the experiment caught on and was brought to what was judged to be a successful conclusion. Encouraged by the results, al-Junayd declared 1974 the "Year of the Budget" and directed the team of Budget Office and Treasury officials to prepare a budget for actual application in fiscal 1974-1975. In addition, the government at al-Junayd's urging informed the IMF that it wished to proceed to the creation of a single institution that would end the bifurcation between the Budget Office and the Treasury Ministry. After convincing a skeptical IMF that the new staff was sufficient in size and experience, the decision was made to go ahead and merge the Budget Office and salvageable elements from the Treasury Ministry into the new Finance Ministry.

The most important act of state building between 1972 and 1974 was the establishment of the Central Planning Organization (CPO). With the active support of Prime Minister al-Aini, the legislation creating the CPO was issued by decree in January 1972. The legislation followed many of the recommendations contained in the 1971 World Bank study and was designed to overcome the constitutional defects that had limited the effectiveness of the Technical Office. Responsibility for the formulation of national development policies and a national development plan was vested in a central planning committee under the chairmanship of the prime minister. The CPO was designated the Secretariat of the Central Planning Committee and made responsible for the day-to-day management of its affairs. In this capacity, the CPO was charged with the formulation of development policies, priorities, and strategies; the preparation of the national development plan; the collection and processing of socioeconomic information; the preparation of an annual development budget; and the coordination and supervision of plan implementation by the various ministries. In addition, the CPO was to assess proposals for external assistance, make recommendations to the government on the utilization of foreign aid sources, and act on behalf of the government in the conclusion and signing of foreign aid agreements.

Dr. Abd al-Karim al-Iryani, a Yale University Ph.D. and head of the Wadi Zabid agricultural project since 1968, was appointed the first chairman of the CPO, and Muhammad Anaam Ghaleb was named its official adviser. Dr. al-Iryani was both exceptionally well qualified for the position and a nephew of President al-Iryani, attributes that gave the CPO more than just a constitutional basis to insinuate itself into the existing machinery of government. The nucleus of the CPO consisted of a team of foreign advisers provided by the World Bank, as well as several able Yemeni holdovers from the staff of the Technical Office. Additional Yemeni university and secondary graduates of superior quality were recruited, a process that was aided by a provision in the enabling legislation that gave the CPO the exceptional privilege to offer salaries up to 50 percent higher than the regular government scale.

The CPO was fashioned into a functioning institution in a remarkably short time. This was the result of a number of factors, among them the strong support of the government, the experience of the Technical Office, the leadership of Dr. al-Iryani, and the caliber, esprit, and cooperativeness of the foreign and Yemeni staff. In 1973 the foreign experts relinquished most operational activities in the CPO to their Yemeni counterparts and assumed a more purely advisory role. In Yemeni hands, the CPO by 1974 had in fact as well as in law become the focal point for the formulation of development policy and programs, the principal point of contact with aid donors, and the main generator of data and analyses on Yemen's economy and society. Regarded by many modernists as the model for future institution building, the CPO had in less than three years established itself as the most dynamic and influential—as well as the most glamorous and prestigious—component in the modern sector of the Yemeni govenrment.

The major ongoing task of the CPO in 1973 and early 1974 was the preparation of the Three Years' Development Program for 1973/1974-1975/1976. A first draft of the program was presented to the cabinet in August 1973. This draft was subjected to a review process within the government and then was revised by the CPO on the basis of this review and other new data; a second draft, submitted to the cabinet in April 1974, was adopted by that body in the following month. The Three Years' Development Program was a first attempt by the YAR at general prospective thinking. It was not a plan in the strict sense; instead, it was an attempt to determine and to assess where Yemen was in the early 1970s, and to specify a set of objectives, priorities, and projects for the mid-1970s. Nevertheless, along with the first national census and the statistical yearbooks, it was a milestone in the new effort to subject the future development of the YAR to a greater degree of rational thought and choice.

In retrospect, the main catalysts in the coming together of state-building and development activities in 1973 and 1974 were the establishment of the CPO and the preparation of the Three Years' Development Program. The former provided a single place where Yemeni modernists involved in these activities could meet among themselves and with foreign experts and donor representatives; the latter provided a temporal frame and sequence in terms of which Yemeni modernists and foreign experts could locate and evaluate their ideas and proposals. Al-Junayd's decision in 1973 to have the Budget Office begin the process of budgetmaking was motivated in part by a desire to link this process with the YAR's first comprehensive attempt at development programming. The aid package of the United Nations' Development Program for Yemen for 1972-1976, which was prepared in 1973 and adopted in 1974, was also designed to mesh with the development program being prepared in 1973 at the CPO. Finally, the very nature of the Three Years' Development Program, which lists and describes projects through 1976, served to compel negotiators for Yemen and external donors to get down to specifics and to make and act upon a large number of decisions.

Manifest Political Constraints

On the other side of the contradiction evident in the YAR by 1974 was a sociopolitical configuration that placed veto power over state action in the hands of individuals or groups that were increasingly indifferent if not hostile to further state building and to many aspects of socioeconomic development. The tribal leaders, from the outset the physically strongest component in the al-Iryani regime, had become more deeply entrenched and assertive as the decentralized system of political bargaining and brokerage crystallized into a regular and accepted pattern of governance. Their determined use of their growing power to defend their prerogatives and autonomy meant that the bargaining system increasingly produced an antimodern, antistatist bargain. The tribalists had the support of urban conservatives who, though proponents of a strong traditional state on the order of the imamate, did not support many of the goals toward which the modernists sought to apply the republican state.

As noted earlier, the Consultative Council created in 1971 was dominated by tribal shaykhs and conservative notables. Many of the 179 members of this increasingly powerful body quickly learned to use the leverage their votes afforded them to enrich themselves and to protect their interests. As a result, the Consultative Council had by 1973 become the key instrument and symbol of tribal and conservative power on the national level. The growing influence of the council and its members was not unrelated to the fact that since its inception its speaker was Abdullah ibn Husayn al-Ahmar, paramount shaykh of the Hashid confederation, the most powerful tribal grouping in Yemen. A tribal aristocrat and sure of his prerogatives, Shaykh al-Ahmar moved easily between his tribal and government positions and derived symbolic and tangible benefits from each. The acknowledged national spokesman for the tribalists, he shared in most of the inner deliberations of the al-Iryani regime. An additional source of his influence in government circles was his increasingly close patron-client relationship with Saudi Arabia, a relationship both he and the Saudis valued highly and took care to nurture.

The degree to which tribal and other conservative elements had insinuated themselves into the national political system is readily apparent in the number of key executive and administrative positions they occupied during the government of Prime Minister al-Hajri in 1973. Qadi al-Hajri, a former royalist, was himself a deeply conservative and traditional man, the only person of this persuasion to head a government after the 1962 Revolution. Members of tribal families held three ministerial portfolios in the al-Hajri government—those of information, communications, and health—as well as six of the ten provincial governorships. Given the weakness of the central government outside the major cities and towns, the governorships were particularly important sources of tribal power.

Two prominent governors with strong tribal connections were Shaykh Mujahid abu Shuwarib and Shaykh Ahmad Abd al-Rabbou al-Awadi, the governors of Hajja and Taiz provinces respectively. However, the most important by far was Sinan abu Luhum, long-time governor of al-Hudayda province and a leader of the Nahm tribe in the Bakil tribal confederation. In an obvious reference to Sinan abu Luhum, a United Nations' report describes with surprising candor the multi-based power of the tribal governors: "Several governors remain powerful because of their tribal leadership, maintain almost complete independence from the central administration and report directly to the Republican Council. Their power and influence not only dominates the life of the people of their tribe, which administratively belongs to a different province, but also of those in the province over which they have administrative authority."[1] Relatives of Sinan held key army commands and his brother-in-law, Muhsin al-Aini, was the leading modernist politician during the al-Iryani era. Sinan was perhaps Yemen's shrewdest and most successful tribal politician during this period, and he seemed to move with even greater skill and ease than Shaykh al-Ahmar between modern and traditional politics, between the center and the periphery. He was reputed by many to have become the chief broker of Yemeni politics, able to make and unmake governments almost at will.

The shaykhs and other conservatives also became well entrenched in the police and civil bureaucracies. Their penetration of the central government and provincial administrative systems had increased with the expansion of government, and by 1974 their influence was pervasive. In Sanaa, this was especially true of the large, unreformed ministries that went back to the early days of the 1962 Revolution. In addition to acquiring top positions for themselves, these leaders adapted well to the burgeoning system of political patronage. They used their influence to place their client-followers in official positions and those so placed in turn increased the influence of their patrons.

The armed forces of the YAR remained small, ill equipped, and unreformed throughout the al-Iryani era. The only major upgrading of those forces after the 1962 Revolution occurred at about the time of the Egyptian withdrawal in late 1967, and it involved the transfer of obsolete Soviet arms and the supply of a number of Soviet military advisers. Thereafter, attempts to reequip and to reorganize the armed forces were blocked or delayed for various political reasons, most often because of objections of the tribal leaders to the strengthening of the professional army. The pattern for the rest of the al-Iryani era was set in the al-Hudayda incident in March 1968 when conservative and progressive republicans fought over whether a new shipment of Soviet arms should go to tribal irregulars or to the more professional units in the regular army—it was the tribalists who won the dispute and got the arms. When agreement was finally reached in the early 1970s on a new supply of Soviet arms, the Soviet Union reneged on delivery at the last moment when it found itself caught between a radical PDRY and a YAR that seemed to be moving toward the West.

Tribal influence over the armed forces remained extensive and may have increased during the early 1970s. Powerful tribal leaders had gained command of some of the most important military units. For example, Shaykh Mujahid abu Shuwarib, the governor of Hajja province and brother-in-law of Shaykh al-Ahmar, commanded the Glory Brigade; and Ali abu Luhum, a brother of Sinan, commanded the Reserves. Indeed, four of Sinan's relatives—two brothers, a cousin, and a son—held command positions. As a result of the institutionalization of tribal and other parochial influences, the army remained extremely fragmented and virtually at war with itself, less a unified and hierarchical instrument of the state than a collection of nearly autonomous and mutually suspicious units each with primary loyalty to some tribal grouping, locality, or powerful personality.

In the final analysis, the tribalized armed forces were the linch-pin of the system of tribal power. It was their considerable control over the instruments of coercion that gave the tribal leaders the freedom required to develop and apply their various noncoercive techniques of political influence. By blocking reform of the army—and thereby keeping it weak, divided, and partially under their control—they were able to minimize the likelihood of the army becoming an autonomous center of power or an effective instrument of state power. Furthermore, the tribal irregulars outside the army, subsidized by the government and by Saudi Arabia, were formidable only because of the weakness of the regular forces of the state. The credibility of these irregulars both kept alive the historic fears of rebellion and urban pillage by the tribes and made it possible for the shaykhs to deny the state access to, much less control over, large areas of the north and east.

The Coalition Strained

The domestic sociopolitical constraints upon state building and socioeconomic development only became salient and apparent with the relaxation after 1972 of the more immediate economic and financial constraints. Planners and managers in the government became increasingly aware that the application of their modest but growing planning capabilities and material resources to the further development of the YAR was inhibited by other shortcomings in the Yemeni state—for example, its very low coercive and adminstrative capabilities. In turn, they increasingly traced the failure to correct these defects to the political constraints inherent in the highly decentralized, tribalized system of power and political brokerage that had evolved during the al-Iryani era.

The modernists and the conservative leadership had not been at odds often during the early years under President al-Iryani. Many differences were initially submerged in the mood of reconciliation and restorative nationalism that al-Iryani personified. Most of the tribalists and other conservatives had realized early their need for the skills of the modernists but had not regarded this small and relatively powerless group as a threat to their interests; indeed, few had appreciated the intentions of the modernists or the implications of modernity. For their part, most of the modernists had accepted the tribal system as a part of present reality but had taken comfort in the belief that it would soon give way before the advance of modernization. Some had regarded the tribal leaders as anachronisms who had to be tolerated because of their power, and a few had thought of them as resources that could be won over and enlisted in the cause of modernity. Even when tinged with mutual disrespect and suspicion, the relationship between the modernists and the conservatives had usually been conceived as one of live-and-let-live in a world large enough to accommodate both. Few had regarded the existence of the one as antithetical to the continued existence of the other, at least over the short run.

By 1973, the expansion of development activities had caused the world containing the modernists and the conservative leaders to shrink, with the result that their interests and activities intersected and clashed with greater frequency. The tribalists and other conservatives became increasingly aware that the plans and projects passing through the Central Planning Organization had the potential either to enhance or to threaten their wealth, power, and position. At the center—in Sanaa, Taiz, and al-Hudayda—they insisted on being informed, consulted, and even courted on matters pertaining to development. On rare occasions, they acted to block the adoption of reforms or projects; more often, they intervened in the implementation stage to bend the results to their purposes or to those of their clients. In particular, their stake in the patronage system led them to interfere in adminstrative reforms and personnel changes. On the periphery, particularly in the least accessible areas, the local tribal shaykh exercised an effective veto over projects that did not suit his interests. Both at the center and on the periphery, the tribalists were in a position to exact a heavy price for their support of the schemes advanced by the modernists.

For their part, the modernists in the government entered the mid-1970s with conflicting thoughts and feelings. On the one hand, they shared a sense of momentum and a growing belief that the YAR was near the threshold of rapid modernization and development. The modest but real achievements of the recent past gave them a new feeling of self-confidence—touched, perhaps, with self-importance and arrogance—and convinced them that they at least had acquired much of the knowledge, skills, and organizational capabilities needed to take hold of Yemen's destiny. On the other hand, the modernists increasingly came to regard the tribalists and other conservative notables as threats if not impassable barriers to future state building and socioeconomic development. Many of them bridled at the need to cater to the parochial and selfish interests of the tribalists on matters that they somewhat unrealistically and self-righteously regarded as technical, above politics, and in the interests of all Yemenis. Many believed their efforts to develop the YAR were being obstructed and put into jeopardy by the corruption, favoritism, cynical bargaining, and petty bickering that they regarded as endemic to the politics that revolved around the Consultative Council. The influence of the tribalists in the bureaucracy and in the provinces was a cause of additional despair, especially for those modernists who believed that further development required administrative reform at the center and the increased presence of the government on the periphery.

The resolution of the contradiction between the tribalized political system and the requirements of further modernization might have been deferred or achieved less dramatically had it not been for an event that was only obliquely related to state building and socioeconomic development: the complex and protracted conflict between the two Yemens in 1972 and 1973. This was the catalyst in the transformation of the muted differences between the modernists and the tribalists into an open confrontation. Although the conflict between the two Yemens diverted attention from development and placed new strains on the YAR's financial resources, these considerations were secondary in importance to the way in which that conflict exposed as by x-ray the underlying defects of the Yemeni state and political system. What stood out most clearly was the utter powerlessness of the state to prevent the tribal periphery, with Saudi Arabia's encouragement and assistance, from dragging the YAR into a war with the PDRY. Unable to secure the borders and to control events within those borders, the central government and the armed forces were for the most part helpless bystanders in a conflict in which the YAR was used by Saudi Arabia as a surrogate in regional politics and became a battleground on which Saudi-backed tribal irregulars and Adeni refugees fought with PDRY-backed guerrillas and the regular forces of the PDRY. On a more general level, the conflict revealed that the interests of the tribalists could clash fundamentally with those of the state and the rest of the nation, and that the state as then constituted was unable to prevent the tribes from acting on their interests.

Though discredited by the PDRY's rout of their irregular forces in the fall of 1972, the tribal leaders reached the apogee of their power in 1973 and 1974. In part this was because the state and the armed forces had by their impotence discredited themselves to an even greater degree. Most important was the sharp decline in the prestige and influence of President al-Iryani, a crucial development in light of the vital role he had played as the bridge between various groups—republicans and royalists, modernists and traditionalists, civilians and soldiers. People of all political persuasions in the YAR, as well as members of his own family, began to question both the efficacy of his remaining in office and the viability of the political formula and system that he had come to personify. The tribalists came to think that they could better protect their interests without him, and many modernists came to think that modernity could not be advanced with him. This was a very new situation in that President al-Iryani theretofore had been able to influence the political process by trading on his widely assumed indispensability and threatening to resign. Another cause of President al-Iryani's growing powerlessness was Saudi Arabia's loss of confidence in him and its decision to place greater reliance on its tribal clients in Yemen, especially Shaykh al-Ahmar. The withdrawal of Saudi and domestic support for the Yemeni head of state ushered in a period of political stalemate and drift. Uncertainties about the future, the unbridled pursuit of self-interest, and a growing normlessness and cynicism in public life gave the period an end-of-an-era flavor.

The al-Iryani regime did make one last effort at political construction with the creation of an official political organization, the ban on parties notwithstanding. Established in early 1973, the National Yemeni Union was proclaimed the political body for all Yemenis; its political bureau, topped by President al-Iryani, read as a "who's who" of YAR politics. Nevertheless, although accorded ample funds and high priority, the National Yemeni Union failed to develop to the point of having any lasting political impact. It never launched an organizing and indoctrination campaign among the people; indeed, it was not opened for membership until the spring of 1974, fifteen months after its creation. In retrospect, it is apparent that the Union was less an expression of a new commitment to political organization than a hastily designed attempt by the regime to preempt the political arena during the period of uncertainty following the agreement in late 1972 by the two Yemens to end their border war through political unification. As the prospect for unification with the PDRY receded, the leaders of the regime seemed quickly to lose interest in the National Yemeni Union, and no one appeared to mourn its passing when it was abolished in 1974.

The modernists, with the support of President al-Iryani, engineered the resignation of conservative Prime Minister al-Hajri in early 1974. The government formed by Dr. Hasan Makki at the beginning of March represented an attempt to change the political formula that increasingly had constrained and immobilized its predecessors. President al-Iryani himself had come to feel the despair shared by most modernists and was keenly aware of his own declining ability to exert direction or control over political events. In an effort to break out of this situation, he selected Dr. Makki, a modernist with some radical political views, as prime minister, and instructed him to choose a government on the basis of technical qualifications and without the customary consultations with the tribal leaders. The result was a government that was regarded at the time by most modernists as the best qualified in the YAR's history, the first in which graduates outnumbered nongraduates.

The Makki government is significant less for its concrete accomplishments during its short tenure than for its attitude and approach to the further development of the YAR. Its main achievement was the redefinition of the YAR's major domestic problem and the adoption of a strategy to deal with that problem. As seen by Makki and his colleagues, the problem was the weakness and short reach of the state. The remedy was conceived of as an increase in the capacity of the state to deliver services, especially to areas on the periphery, combined with exchange of these services for allegiance to the state. This redefinition of the problem was accompanied by a realization of the need for a more generalized pattern of state building, one which went beyond those institutions responsible for economic and financial management and development planning.

The Makki government was too short-lived to translate these ideas into an established pattern of action. Driven by a sense of urgency—and, perhaps, an awareness that its days were numbered—the government nevertheless was able both to complete a number of pending reforms and to advance or initiate a number of others. Teams of experts and political leaders were sent to Marib and other areas on the periphery in order to study local problems and needs for government services. In an effort to upgrade agencies charged with the delivery of services, decrees were issued in early April that created the Ministry of Supply and the Ministry of Social Affairs, Labor, and Youth. More important, a decree issued in late May replaced the Treasury Ministry with the new Finance Ministry and named the treasury minister, Muhammad Ahmad al-Junayd, as the first minister of finance. On this occasion, those Treasury employees who were deemed retrainable were brought into the new ministry, whereas the rest were either pensioned off or absorbed into other ministries or agencies.

In another action, the Three Years' Development Program for 1973/1974-1975/1976 was all but formally adopted during the Makki government. CPO Chairman al-Iryani submitted the second draft of the program to the cabinet in April, and the cabinet adopted and sent it to the Consultative Council in May, along with the budget for 1974-1975.

The Makki government also advanced a far-reaching reform of the legal system and the judiciary with the aim of lessening inefficiency and corruption. Work had been done in the previous government to prepare legislation that would reorganize the hierarchy of courts and establish new procedures for the selection and disciplining of judges. The project was revived by the Makki government and the task of drafting the legislation in its final form was completed by the Ministry of Justice with the aid of the Legal Office. The new judicial reform law was adopted by the Makki government and sent to the Consultative Council in the early summer.

A modest plan to modernize the armed forces was also initiated during the Makki government. With the government's approval, the Armed Forces High Command prepared a reform plan in early 1974, building on some preparatory work done during the al-Hajri government. The program was to be financed by Abu Dhabi and was to involve the use of Jordanian military advisers and instructors to increase the administrative efficiency of existing units in the army. Although a number of Jordanian officers arrived in Yemen during the Makki government, serious implementation of the program was delayed until after the resolution of differences between its proponents and those tribal leaders who feared that the reform could undermine their influence over key units in the armed forces.

5

Political Adjustment and Socioeconomic Development Under al-Hamdi: 1974-1976

President al-Iryani was sent gracefully into exile following a bloodless coup on 13 June 1974. The Command Council, composed of army officers and under the chairmanship of Colonel Ibrahim Muhammad al-Hamdi (ca. 1943-1977) was created and assumed all legislative and executive powers. This council immediately suspended the 1970 Constitution and the Consultative Council and dissolved outright the moribund political organization, the National Yemeni Union. A new government was appointed several days later with Muhsin al-Aini, the head of three governments during the al-Iryani era, as prime minister and foreign minister. It included a number of other modernists and several members of the previous government, including its prime minister, Dr. Hasan Makki.

As the composition of the new government suggests, the change in regime did not mean a fundamental change in general orientation or specific policies. Nor did the change mean a radical shift from civilian to military rule, as military politicians had played prominent roles under President al-Iryani and the armed forces were only beginning to develop into a well-differentiated corporate body with interests of its own. Ibrahim al-Hamdi, barely in his midthirties at the time of the coup in 1974, epitomized the blurred lines between the civilian and military politicians. The son of a respected Zaydi qadi, he had studied for and begun a traditional legal-administrative career only to switch to one in the military shortly after the 1962 Revolution. A young man known to be able and ambitious, al-Hamdi rose quickly to public prominence in the latter half of the al-Iryani era. He commanded the Reserves, an elite army unit, in the early 1970s, was deputy prime minister during the year-long al-Aini government in 1972, and held the post of deputy commander in chief of the armed forces from 1973 until the time of the coup. He was also a leader in the growing movement for local-level economic and social development, and as such became the first president of the Confederation of Yemeni Development

Associations in 1973, a position that he continued to hold after becoming head of state of the YAR.

The 13 June Correction Movement, as the new regime was called, had most of the familiar earmarks of a protest against civilian misrule by young reform-minded officers. On the day of the coup, President al-Hamdi[1] explained that the armed forces had assumed power both to end the "exhaustive feuds" between President al-Iryani and the Consultative Council and to deal with the "collapse in the internal political situation, administrative slackness and corruption in the bureaucracy."[2] Similarly, upon appointment of the al-Aini government, the Command Council declared that the former regime had "resigned" because of "administrative and financial chaos and indiscipline prevailing . . . to the extent of making many despair of reform or of restoring a normal atmosphere suitable for progress and development."[3]

These statements accurately reflect some of the motives and concerns of President al-Hamdi and the officers who conspired with him. However, the nature and dynamics of the coup were far more complex. It had been promoted if not engineered by tribal and other conservative leaders who viewed the overthrow of the faltering al-Iryani regime as an opportunity to shore up the decentralized political system from which they had derived so many benefits during the previous several years. At the center of this cluster of conspirators were Sinan abu Luhum and the major tribal shaykhs of the north, including Abdullah ibn Husayn al-Ahmar and Ali Ahmad al-Matari. The promoters of the coup also had the blessings of the regime in Saudi Arabia. Having bided their time for more than a year, the opponents of President al-Iryani took as their excuse his mild response to an alleged Iraqi-backed plot against the YAR, a response that caused Shaykh al-Ahmar to threaten to march on Sanaa.

Political Adjustment Under al-Hamdi

The first eighteen months of the al-Hamdi era were dominated by a protracted and convoluted struggle for power. The upbeat rhetoric and the professions of unity with which this period began were belied almost at once by important policy differences among President al-Hamdi and other political leaders over relations with Saudi Arabia, alternative sources of military aid, and, above all, restoration of civilian rule and the 1970 Constitution; and behind these differences lurked the fundamental, unresolved issue of the relationship between al-Hamdi and the politicians who initially had backed his assumption of high office. The struggle intensified as al-Hamdi became more assertive and made clear his intention to be more than an interim ruler or puppet, a development that did not fit the agendas of Muhsin al-Aini, Sinan abu Luhum, or Shaykh al-Ahmar.

President al-Hamdi's hold on his office during the early months was extremely tenuous and depended primarily upon key figures in the fragmented armed forces, most notably his brother, Abdullah al-Hamdi, commander of the elite Giants Brigade; Ahmad Husayn al-Ghashmi, the chief of staff of the armed forces; and Abdullah Abd al-Alim, commander of the paratroops and commandos and the highest ranking Shafai in the armed forces. President al-Hamdi's personal popularity with the people grew quickly, but institutions were absent to convert this popular support into a political resource. For their part, the civilian modernists had little power to bring to bear on the struggle and, in any case, were divided in their assessment of the new regime. Some were suspicious of either or both the military and the involvement of the tribalists and the Saudis in the coup. Many of those who knew al-Hamdi well, and realized that he was a strong nationalist with modernist views, thought either that he would not have the courage to act against his promoters or, if he did, that he would be swept from power.

The sequence of dramatic political events in 1975, beginning with the dismissal of Prime Minister al-Aini in January and ending with the permanent adjournment of the suspended Consultative Council in October, ranks with the 1962 Revolution and the overthrow of the al-Sallal regime as a major turning point in the modern history of North Yemen. In a series of swift, deft moves, President al-Hamdi sharply curtailed the national political power of the most prominent tribal leaders; in so doing, he changed the configuration of forces in Yemeni politics and altered the sociopolitical bases of the YAR. At the time, many Yemenis who understood and approved of what the young president was doing followed his actions with awe and disbelief. "We did not—could not—believe our eyes and ears," one such person said in 1976.[4]

President al-Hamdi followed a divide-and-conquer strategy in his attempt to consolidate his power in 1975. The several months of political maneuvering between him and Prime Minister al-Aini ended with the abrupt replacement of the latter by Abd al-Aziz Abd al-Ghani in January. The move was widely interpreted at the time as a victory for Saudi Arabia and conservative elements in the YAR, and it is true that Saudi leaders were wary of al-Aini's Baath party ties and that Shaykh al-Ahmar backed his ouster. Nevertheless, President al-Hamdi acted primarily on his own initiative and for the purpose of eliminating from the scene a powerful competitor who many Yemenis thought had a better-than-even chance of outmaneuvering him after the coup in 1974. Al-Aini was regarded as a consummate politician and, with Sinan abu Luhum as his patron and brother-in-law, was one of the few civilian modernists with a political base. For his part, al-Hamdi had developed a healthy respect for al-Aini's political skills and ambition when he served as deputy prime minister in the al-Aini government in 1972.

Early in the spring of 1975, and again with Shaykh al-Ahmar looking on benignly, President al-Hamdi acted to curtail the influence of Sinan abu Luhum and the rest of the powerful Luhumi clan. In this instance, he probably played on traditional enmity between the Hashid and Bakil confederations and convinced al-Ahmar that Sinan and the Bakil confederation of which Sinan's tribe is a part had become so powerful as to pose a threat to his position as Yemen's leading tribalist. Using loyal army units,

President al-Hamdi forced the resignation of four Luhumis who commanded units of the armed forces, including Lt.-Col. Ali abu Luhum, his successor as commander of the Reserves and a member of the Command Council. He then acted against some of ex-Governor Sinan's allies in al-Hudayda province, thereby denying him his political base on the Tihama.

By this time, Shaykh Ali Ahmad al-Matari, the powerful leader whose tribal domain straddles the vital highway between Sanaa and al-Hudayda, was engaged in an effort to alert al-Ahmar and the other shaykhs to the necessity of closing ranks against the assertive al-Hamdi. Aware of these political activities, al-Hamdi moved quickly later in the spring and seized the weapons caches of tribal forces loyal to Shaykh al-Matari. At about the same time, and despite the vigorous opposition of a now alarmed Shaykh al-Ahmar, he also removed Lt.-Col. Mujahid abu Shuwarib from a broad array of key military and political posts, including those of deputy commander in chief of the armed forces, member of the Command Council, and governor of Hajja province. Mujahid, a Hashid tribalist and a brother-in-law of Shaykh al-Ahmar, made his way secretly to Hajja where he attempted to use the threat of a tribal uprising to regain his offices. Al-Hamdi stood his ground, and Mujahid had to back down after a month when the army garrison and other elements in Hajja refused him support. In turn, Lt.-Col. Yahya al-Mutawakkal, who had opposed the dismissal of Mujahid, was forced in July to resign from the Command Council and as minister of the interior and then persuaded to accept appointment as ambassador to the United States.

The ouster of Mujahid abu Shuwarib in the spring of 1975 brought relations between President al-Hamdi and Shaykh al-Ahmar close to the breaking point and ushered in several months of intense but muted conflict. While Shaykh al-Ahmar tried to rally the support of the tribes and other conservative elements, President al-Hamdi sought both to strengthen his position in the armed forces and to convince the lesser shaykhs that his dispute was with the big shaykhs and not with the tribal system as such. Both antagonists sought support from Saudi Arabia in their struggle. Publicly, their differences centered on the question of a return to constitutional government and elections for a new Consultative Council, Shaykh al-Ahmar's power base in the central government during the al-Iryani era. Reversing a decision taken by the Command Council a month earlier, President al-Hamdi announced in May 1975 that constitutional government and elections would not be restored on the first anniversary of the 13 June coup; Shaykh al-Ahmar responded by pressing still harder for the early holding of the promised elections and a return to civilian rule. The controversy was brought to a head in October 1975 with a bit of political theatre on both sides. President al-Hamdi staged demonstrations against the old Consultative Council and its tribal members; and then, bowing to these expressions of the popular will, he permanently adjourned that body and deferred elections to an unspecified time in the future. At this point, Shaykh al-Ahmar held a tribal convocation at which he broke publicly with al-

Hamdi, denounced the regime as illegitimate, and called upon the tribes to unite behind him in open rebellion.

Shaykh al-Ahmar failed to gain the initiative in late 1975 because many tribal leaders questioned his motives and were unwilling to support his call for overt action against the al-Hamdi regime. The result was the onset of a long "no war, no peace" standoff between the state and those tribes that controlled large areas of the north and east of the YAR. Saudi Arabia worked hard to stabilize the stalemate by providing each side with aid on condition that it not act to eliminate the other by force of arms.

Time seemed to be on President al-Hamdi's side after 1975. He refused to allow the armed forces to get drawn into a military campaign that would be hard to win and that could serve to unite uncommitted tribes against him. His strategy was to isolate and to ignore the quasi rebellion, and to devote the resources of the state to the development of those areas of the country that were under his control and that recognized his authority. He anticipated that with time tribesmen in the "land of insolence" would come to see the positive relationship between their future well-being and allegiance to the state, and would either oust their present shaykhs or force them to end the rebellion and come to terms with the state. On occasion, al-Hamdi used small incidents as carrot-and-stick object lessons. When tribal elements in the Arhab area challenged the state in the spring of 1976, the regime unleashed a strong military assault against the offending parties. President al-Hamdi insisted that the responsible local shaykhs come before him in Sanaa both to pledge allegiance to the state and to present the grievances of their followers; he then accepted their pledge and ordered the government to act quickly to meet most of the grievances. Some Yemenis began to refer to the "Arhab model" in discussing al-Hamdi's strategy toward the rebellious tribes.

At the other end of the political spectrum, relations of the al-Hamdi regime with the partisans and the progressive parties following the 1974 coup were more ambiguous and less dramatic than those with the tribalists. The official ban on political parties remained in effect, and the regime often warned the partisans against open activity and occasionally—for example, in the summer of 1976—subjected them to harassment and arrest. Moreover, the commando and paratroop forces under Lt.-Col. Abd al-Alim carried out a successful program of pacification and local development in order to lessen the influence of the partisans in the countryside near the southeastern border with the PDRY. In balance, however, the al-Hamdi regime did not deal as harshly with the progressive parties as had the previous regime in 1968 and 1973. Al-Hamdi himself turned a blind eye to most of the partisans' barely clandestine activities. As a young army officer, he had been associated with the Yemeni wing of the Arab Nationalist Movement before it was forced underground after its confrontation with the conservative republicans in 1968. He had kept up his personal ties with many of the partisan leaders after he went his separate political way in the late 1960s and he continued to maintain contact with them after he assumed power in 1974.

On their side, the partisans warmly applauded President al-Hamdi's actions against the tribalists and most of them came to respect him for his nationalism and his goals of national strength and development. Many of the younger partisans, among them the so-called Nasirites who were less social radicals than strong Yemeni nationalists, were won over to the regime by al-Hamdi and his offer of positions of responsibility in the national effort. The leaders of the progressive parties hoped and campaigned for an open and formal partnership with President al-Hamdi as a way back into the political system from which they were expelled in 1968. In part with this in mind, six of the parties announced the formation of the National Democratic Front (NDF) in mid-1976. The six parties—the Revolutionary Democratic party, the Organization of Yemeni Resisters, the Labor party, the Popular Democratic Union, and the two wings of the Yemeni Baath party—proclaimed both their desire to collaborate with al-Hamdi and a moderate program calling for more planning, a stronger state, and greater independence for the YAR.

State Building and Modernization Under al-Hamdi

The surgical operations performed by President al-Hamdi on the political system in 1975 were narrowly political in motivation and were designed primarily to strengthen his initially shaky position. A secondary effect, perhaps unintended, was the relaxation of some of the domestic political constraints that had worked to thwart or distort efforts at state building and modernization during the last years of the al-Iryani era. This new situation was reflected in the greater freedom of action enjoyed by the Abd al-Ghani government in 1975 and thereafter. The technocrats in the government, including the prime minister, who was a former minister of economics and the founding chairman of the Central Bank, were released from much of the petty politicking, obstructionism, and corruption that they associated with the Consultative Council and the system of political bargaining and brokerage it had come to symbolize. Less constrained than before by what they regarded as ignorant and selfish forces, they felt able to get on with what they perceived to be the major tasks facing the Yemeni state and nation. As one minister said with satisfaction in early 1976: "A small group of us—ten to fifteen in number—are free for the first time to make and to act on decisions affecting development. We are having an impact."[5]

As was the case in governments under the previous regime, Prime Minister Abd al-Ghani and his fellow technocrats did not have an independent political base, individually or collectively. Instead, they depended for their positions and decisionmaking freedom upon President al-Hamdi and his military colleagues. Their dependence was not without its drawbacks, as was evident in al-Hamdi's unexpected switching of Dr. Abd al-Karim al-Iryani from minister of development to minister of education in the summer of 1976. Dr. al-Iryani and most other modernists, including the prime minister, were unhappy with the move but were powerless to do anything about it. Nevertheless, President al-Hamdi's overriding political concerns and his commitment to national strength and development dovetailed nicely with the specialized skills and technical concerns of the modernists, and he chose to give them considerable leeway in the formulation and implementation of domestic policy that was not politically sensitive. The parallel but not identical interests of the military politicians and the civilian modernists made for a good working relationship and division of labor. Despite the predictable irritations between the two groups, each respected and realized its need for the other. Moreover, the partnership between President al-Hamdi and the Abd al-Ghani government was bound together in part by a strongly held if uncodified ideology of state building. Both parties regarded state building as the primary task of the current phase of Yemen's development, and both recognized the need to strengthen the state at the center and to increase its capabilities to reach and have an impact on the periphery. Their strategy was to increase the capacity of the state to deliver services and then to exchange those services for allegiance to the state, a quid pro quo designed both to advance socioeconomic development and to strengthen the state. In most regards, the perspective shared by President al-Hamdi and the Abd al-Ghani government resembled that advanced by the Makki government, the last to serve under the al-Iryani regime.

Generalized State Building

The elimination of the leading tribalists from the central government and the statist orientation of the al-Hamdi regime paved the way for a more generalized pattern of state building than that pursued during the al-Iryani era. The process was extended from agencies of economic and financial management and development planning to other institutions characteristic of the moden state. Although it did not abandon the earlier concerns—and, indeed, made good use of the Central Planning Organization, the expanding banking system, and the other new economic and financial agencies—the al-Hamdi regime increasingly turned its attention to the tasks of reforming and strengthening such institutions as the armed and security forces, the legal system, and the state bureaucracy.

President al-Hamdi and his military colleagues paid early attention to the security services, which were modernized, enlarged, and reorganized into the Central Organization for National Security under the direction of Lt.-Col. Muhammad Khamis. The potentially most far-reaching act of state building by the al-Hamdi regime involved the complex and delicate task of strengthening the armed forces. The leaders of the regime realized that the capacity to coerce—or, putting it more benignly, to maintain internal order and security—is perhaps the most elementary attribute of the modern state and that its absence makes it easy for opponents of the state to prevent efforts to advance other aspects of state building and modernization. In addition, they were aware that al-Hamdi depended for his position largely upon the more professional elements in the armed forces and that the continued support of these elements depended upon his satisfying their desires for a stronger, more modern military establishment. As a consequence, strengthened armed forces were widely regarded as the sine qua non both for al-Hamdi's long tenure in office and for the state building and modernization to which his regime seemed committed.

Little was done to strengthen the armed forces in 1974 because the political maneuvering among President al-Hamdi, Prime Minister al-Aini, and the tribal leaders turned in part on differences over sources of military assistance, with al-Aini favoring a triangular arms deal with Iraq and the USSR and Shaykh al-Ahmar favoring one with Saudi Arabia and the United States. Even the modest army modernization plan prepared before the end of the al-Iryani era had to wait for full implementation until after al-Hamdi ousted al-Aini and purged the tribal officers in early 1975. This done, the Abu Dhabi–financed program to use Jordanian military advisers to introduce modern methods of management, administration, and communications was implemented in 1975 and 1976.

This modest but important effort to make the army more efficient and businsesslike did not attack its main organizational defect: the fact that it consisted, even after the purge of the tribalists, of a large number of relatively self-contained fighting units, little armies within the army. Despite shakeups in command, some of these units continued to have parochial loyalties and to serve as power centers for contending factions within and without the officers' corps. In short, the army was still something other than a unified instrument of state power. To correct this situation, President al-Hamdi and the Command Council adopted a major plan in 1976 that envisaged the reorganization of the army into a smaller number of more interdependent units. Implementation of this reorganization plan was delayed over the next year because of its great sensitivity: it had real power implications, both inside and outside the army, and it promised at the very least to affect the careers of many senior officers. Moreover, President al-Hamdi's efforts to end the fragmentation and competition within the army through this reoganization were complicated by the fact that he had gained and consolidated his position through the support of some of the units whose power the new plan would curtail, including his brother Abdullah's brigade, the Giants.

The military assistance agreement between the United States and the YAR, approved in the summer of 1976, provided President al-Hamdi with some of the leverage he needed to proceed with the reorganization of the armed forces. It gave him new arms and equipment to use as inducements in the politicking that was bound to accompany efforts to secure compliance with the reform plan. Most observers in 1977 felt that the reorganization and reequipping of the armed forces, if carried through as expected, would both strengthen President al-Hamdi's links with those forces and tilt the balance of military power between the state and the tribes decidedly in favor of the former.

The armed and security forces were not the al-Hamdi regime's only objects of reform. The Abd al-Ghani government made a major effort to modernize the courts and the legal system. The plan to reorganize the court hierarchy and to revise the procedures for selecting and disciplining judges, prepared before the 1974 coup, was subjected to final review in late 1975 and put into effect by decree in the spring of 1976. In a more important effort at legal reform, the government drafted and adopted the YAR's first commercial law code in mid-1975. A team of Sudanese judges arrived in Sanaa in the summer of 1976 in order to set up and initially operate the new commercial law courts. The commercial code and courts were regarded by many as the opening wedge in the creation of a system of civil law, at least in those areas beyond the traditional competence of the *shariah*—that is, the traditional Islamic law. In a related effort, the government began a thorough revision of court procedures that was to be applied first to the commercial courts and then, after modification, to the rest of the court system. It was thought that, taken together, these several reforms would rationalize and modernize the Yemeni legal system to a considerable degree and, in turn, help to provide the legal framework required to facilitate the further modernization of the YAR.

The Abd al-Ghani government was working at the same time on a number of fronts to increase the capabilities of the state bureaucracy that had grown from almost nothing since the 1962 Revolution. Leading modernists had concluded as early as 1973 that further advances in public finance and planning would come to naught so long as the ministries and other government agencies in Sanaa and the provinces lacked the skills required to implement programs and make effective use of public revenues. In an effort to begin to remedy this situation, the Central Planning Organization and the United Nations' Development Program (UNDP) put together a package of institutional support projects designed to introduce teams of foreign experts into selected government agencies. By 1974, UNDP had a team of experts on a long-term basis at the National Institute of Public Administration and a large team of experts at the Ministry of Education, and by late 1975 small teams were also operating in the Ministries of Economics and Agriculture. With financing provided by the Kuwait Fund, a more general approach to administrative reform was started in 1976. A team of Sudanese experts was attached to the Office of the Prime Minister and charged with the study, evaluation, and revision of rules, procedures, and personnel policy, starting with that office and then moving on to each of the ministries and possibly the Office of the President. The team began its work in 1976 with a survey of the entire civil service of the YAR.

In late 1975 the Abd al-Ghani government launched an effort to increase the ability of the state to extract taxes and other revenues. To start to correct a situation in which taxes amounted to less than 10 percent of Gross Domestic Product, the government reorganized the Tax Office and the Customs Office and replaced many of the old functionaries in these two offices with new graduates. In another move, a team of tax experts from the IMF was attached to the new Ministry of Finance that only two years earlier had begun for the first time to subject government expenditures to formal budgetary procedures. The mission of this IMF team was to increase the capacity of the ministry to tap new sources of taxes and to make the existing system of taxation more efficient and less prone to corruption—all matters of special concern to Finance Minister al-Junayd.

The Yemeni technocrats and their foreign advisers knew full well that underdeveloped human resources imposed the most severe constraints on the capacity of the YAR to absorb external aid and to implement development projects in coming years. The education system in the mid-1970s was a hodgepodge of ill-fitting foreign gifts tacked on to archaic and jerry-built Yemeni foundations. The Ministry of Education was one of the largest and best-fortified bastions of traditionalists and antimodern thinking in the government, refusing in the mid-1970s to be affected much by the largest of the UNDP's institutional support programs in the YAR. The appointment of Dr. Abd al-Karim al-Iryani as minister of education in 1976 offered some hope that this situation might change. Dr. al-Iryani proceeded slowly with al-Hamdi's backing to modernize gradually the traditionalist curriculum of the schools—for example, to increase time devoted to mathematics and the sciences—and to reduce the maze of departments in the ministry from thirteen to five. Already by early 1977 he was being attacked in the mosques by religious leaders and in private by their Saudi allies, and it remained to be seen whether he would be able to stay in office long enough to impress his educational reforms upon the ministry.

Modernization and Development Planning

Favorable economic conditions joined with the political changes to make possible modest gains in modernization during the years after al-Hamdi came to power. The financial constraints on development activities eased considerably as a result of further increases in the Saudi budget subsidy and the dramatic rise in both external development aid and remittances from Yemenis working in Saudi Arabia and elsewhere. Aid donors were favorably impressed by the al-Hamdi regime, leading them to step up the already considerable flow of funds and projects. Workers' remittances more than doubled from $225 million in 1974-1975 to $525 million in 1975-1976, and they grew at as fast a rate in 1976-1977. This growing flood of funds made it possible for the YAR to build up a sizable balance-of-payments surplus over this period, despite negligible exports and a four-fold increase of imports. By mid-1977, the increasing supply of imported consumer goods and the boom in commercial and residential construction were everywhere evident in the cities and even in villages in the countryside. Yemenis were enjoying an unprecedented prosperity. Public and private development activities were gaining momentum and becoming noticeable; even the man on the street was talking about "the development."

New Yemeni graduates as well as foreign experts and other technical assistance contributed to a marked improvement in the functioning of the Central Bank, Finance Ministry, Central Planning Organization, and other modern institutions, and this improvement in turn increased the capacity of the YAR to absorb the new funds available for development activities in the mid-1970s. The commercial banking system continued to expand under the supervision of the Central Bank, which Prime Minister Abd al-Ghani still chaired. Under its first chairman, Dr. al-Iryani, the CPO became both the vital center of the YAR's development activities and its model modern institution in the mid-1970s. The Three Years' Development Program had been formally adopted just after al-Hamdi assumed power, and it had been implemented with considerable success by the end of 1976. Preparation of the more ambitious and elaborate First Five-Year Development Plan (1977/1978–1981/1982), begun by the CPO in 1975, was completed in early 1977 after much work. Arrangements were being made in mid-1977 for an international development conference in the fall of that year, at which time an effort would be made to match up the growing list of the YAR's external donors with the many projects included in the plan.

As in the last years of the al-Iryani era, government-sponsored development activities under the al-Hamdi regime focused on basic infrastructure—roads, port facilities, communications, and electricity—and on the heavy construction involved in these activities and in the building of schools, hospitals, and offices. The blasting, bulldozing, grading, and surfacing of roads was the most ubiquitous of these activities. A lesser but still considerable emphasis was placed on providing health, education, and other basic services. By mid-1977, the Wadi Zabid Project, designed to increase irrigated farming in a major wadi in the Tihama, was nearing completion, and plans for similar projects in other wadis had been prepared by the four-year-old Tihama Development Authority. Work was begun on the ambitious Southern Uplands Rural Development Project, and other integrated rural development projects were in the planning stage. Sanaa University and the National Institute of Public Administration underwent rapid expansion during these years.

Light industry and most commercial activity, largely left to the private sector, thrived and grew rapidly after 1974. The generous provisions of a new foreign investment law, Law No. 18 of 1975, and the planned opening of industrial parks in Sanaa, Taiz, and al-Hudayda offered hope for much more light industry in the near future. The regime praised and encouraged the small number of "national capitalists," men like Taiz's very wealthy Hayl Said, who were prepared to invest long-term in Yemen's future. At the same time, the countryside was alive with the construction of feeder roads, cisterns, small clinics, and one- or two-room schoolhouses, and most of this activity was financed with remittances from workers outside the country and carried out by the local development associations that were being set up in many localities.

The al-Hamdi Regime and Political Construction

President al-Hamdi's behavior after 1974 provides an unclear index of his concern for political construction—that is, the development of ideas and organizations that support the political process. Certain of his actions seemed to indicate an awareness of the need for a stronger political infrastructure and a desire to act on this need, whereas other actions seemed to suggest that his approach to this matter was one of extreme caution if not a more basic ambivalence. To the extent that he was uncertain about the virtues and the feasibility of political construction, he was reflecting the various sides of a growing debate within the Yemeni political community on this basic question.

Al-Hamdi's Record on Political Construction

The al-Hamdi regime did not launch a major and sustained effort to strengthen the political infrastructure of the YAR during the three years following the abolition of the National Yemeni Union and the suspension of the Consultative Council and the 1970 Constitution. Elections to a new legislature were not held, and the 1970 Constitution was not reinstated, amended, or replaced. The Command Council, declared at the time of the coup to be an interim body during a transitional phase, remained the sole repository of legislative and executive authority; and even the Command Council existed only in a formal sense by 1976, its membership reduced by political attrition to just President al-Hamdi and three others. More and more, the regime revolved around the person of President al-Hamdi, in fact as well as in the popular imagination.

President al-Hamdi promised elections to a new legislature or a constituent assembly with increasing frequency after early 1975. Except for the creation and subsequent meetings of the Higher Electoral Commission, chaired by ex-Prime Minister al-Hajri, little action was taken to fulfill these promises during the next two years. It is, however, difficult to infer President al-Hamdi's true intentions from his promises and inaction regarding elections. Until late 1975, the issue of elections to a new Consultative Council was the chief public expression of his political struggle with Shaykh al-Ahmar and the other leading tribalists; thereafter, the holding of elections was made difficult if not impossible by the quasi rebellion of the tribes in the north and east. Nevertheless, the fact that al-Hamdi repeatedly revived the promise of elections after 1975 would seem to suggest that he felt a need for electoral legitimation even if he was unwilling or unable to act on this felt need at the time.

The al-Hamdi regime did not replace the previous regime's still-born National Yemeni Union with a new political party or movement. President al-Hamdi put himself on record as opposed to parties, and in early 1975 said that government in Yemen is "based on principles of the Islamic faith ... far removed from all affiliations and loyalties which take the form of ... parties."[6] As previously noted, the ban on parties was maintained, and the regime subjected the partisans to frequent warnings and occasional acts of repression.

President al-Hamdi's wariness or ambivalence regarding the expansion of politics is evident in his involvement in the Confederation of Yemeni

Development Associations (CYDA) and in the Correction Movement. The local development association (LDA) movement began with the founding of a cooperative in al-Hudayda just before the 1962 Revolution and a second one in Taiz in the mid-1960s. The movement, rooted in a Yemeni tradition of local self-help and supported primarily by local funds and some foreign gifts, spread rapidly by example throughout the southern provinces of the YAR in the early 1970s. The growing number of LDAs soon became a major factor at the local level in the construction of feeder roads, schools, clinics, cisterns, and other water systems. Ibrahim al-Hamdi was an early convert to the LDA movement—reputedly sensing its political as well as its economic potential—and during the al-Iryani era established the first LDA in the rural north of the country. When the spread of the movement led to talk of a national organization, it was Colonel al-Hamdi who seized the initiative from others in the movement and orchestrated the creation of the Confederation of Yemeni Development Associations in 1973; he was elected its first president late in that year and retained that post after the 1974 coup. CYDA organized and conducted the elections of the development boards of all of its approximately one-hundred member LDAs in August 1975. The elections were held with much fanfare and required a great amount of effort on the part of the regime, suggesting that al-Hamdi regarded them as of considerable importance. Circumstances suggest that the attention he paid to those elections was related less to the role that the LDAs might play in development than to political considerations: he reputedly planned to follow these elections quickly with elections for a new national legislature, believing that the expected pro-regime results of the former would produce a strong pro-regime majority in the latter. This scenario was not followed, and the apparent reason, discussed below, is suggestive of al-Hamdi's hesitancy regarding political construction.

The Correction Movement, a subsequent initiative, was viewed by some Yemenis primarily as a device to generate a new political structure and to identify and develop young political cadre loyal to the al-Hamdi regime. The movement was launched in June 1975, on the first anniversary of the al-Hamdi coup, and marked a return to the regime's initial theme of combatting administrative corruption and inefficiency. On this occasion, the Higher Correction Committee was set up under the chairmanship of Ahmad Damash, a friend and political confidant of al-Hamdi. The Higher Correction Committee was charged with the task of forcing the public bureaucracies and the mixed public-private bureaucracies to end their isolation from the people and to meet popular needs and desires. Correction committees were established for this purpose in each of the provinces; in turn, each provincial committee in early 1976 appointed many small committees to study, evaluate, and recommend reform in the organization, staffing, and operations of every administrative unit in its province. For example, the Taiz Province Correction Committee set up and supervised the work of between sixty and eighty of these small workplace committees. Bringing together the members of all of these committees, the Correction Movement held its first national conference in Sanaa in June 1976, during the celebrations of the second anniversary of the al-Hamdi regime. The announced purpose of the conference was to decide the direction and methods of the new movement, and to instruct and generate enthusiasm among the committee members. On this occasion, the Correction Movement received much publicity and the renewed endorsement of President al-Hamdi.

The histories of CYDA and the Correction Movement raise as many questions as they answer with regard to President al-Hamdi's involvement in political construction. Yemeni observers noted a waxing and waning of his commitment and attention to each of these major organizational efforts. It has been suggested that the results of the local development board elections in 1975 dampened his enthusiasm for the LDA movement and caused him to rethink the prudence and efficacy of using it as the basis of a grass-roots political organization. Although conservative local notables and shaykhs lost control of many of the development boards, a result desired by al-Hamdi, the victors in some instances were leftist partisans who were not identified with the al-Hamdi regime; indeed, in a few cases, candidates who were explicitly pro-regime were defeated by members of constituent groups of the yet-to-be-formed National Democratic Front. Whether or not these election results did cause him to have second thoughts, President al-Hamdi was less publicly involved in the LDA movement after 1975 than previously; moreover, he felt compelled in the summer of 1976 to lecture CYDA and the local development boards on the need to focus on development and to stay out of politics.

The fact that the Correction Movement was promoted heavily by the regime for the first time in the fall of 1975, only several weeks after the mixed results of the LDA elections were tabulated, has been interpreted by some Yemenis as evidence of a decision by President al-Hamdi to build his political base on that movement instead of on the LDAs. Even here, however, his initial enthusiasm was not followed by sustained attention and promotion during the several months before and after the first national Correction Movement conference in June 1976. Even allowing for the many other demands on his time, al-Hamdi's sporadic if not half-hearted involvement in CYDA and the Correction Movement after mid-1976 suggests either that he did not place high priority on political construction at this time or that he questioned the appropriateness of these organizations as means to this end.

The Yemeni Debate Over Political Construction

President al-Hamdi's ambiguous political moves after 1975 took place against the backdrop of a growing debate among Yemenis over whether the current phase of development in the YAR would be helped or hindered by additional political construction. Conducted largely in private, the debate revealed at least four different orientations toward political construction. Two of these orientations opposed the expansion of politics, and two supported it; the two that opposed it did so for antithetical reasons, and the two that supported it differed over the form and locus of new political innovation. Each of the four orientations toward politics was usually paired with a particular orientation toward state building and modernization.

The traditional establishment—urban conservatives, local notables, and tribal leaders—generally continued to oppose political construction as well as extensive modernization and social change toward greater equality; they also generally opposed further state building that might advance these social goals. The members of the traditional establishment had been to varying degrees the chief beneficiaries of the prerepublican status quo ante, and continued in most cases to benefit greatly from the republican status quo. As long as politics remained amorphous and unstructured, they did not feel a need for new political organizations and procedures; they were able to exert influence and to protect their interests through a network of traditional relationships and personal ties. They tended to identify parties and other popular organizations with secularly educated youth, unwanted modernity, and radical if not "communist" thinking; indeed, some saw parties as inherently un-Yemeni and un-Islamic. Some members of the establishment—Shaykh al-Ahmar and his colleagues, for example—favored the creation of a new legislature but only so long as it was a council of notables and nonpartisan. Others were somehow able to square their general antipathy for parties with support for the Muslim Brotherhood and other militant guardians of tradition that use modern organizational forms.

The most thoughtful and articulate opponents of political construction in the mid-1970s were modernists, especially first-generation modernists educated in the West. The leading technocrats in the Abd al-Ghani government shared with many other modernists a preference for what could be called "administered development." They believed that the overriding priority for the YAR in the late 1970s was state building and the implementation of projects designed to create the beginnings of a modern socioeconomic infrastructure and that politicization and political construction at this time would be destructive of these new and still-fragile processes. "Let us first build the state and a framework for modernization," they said. "Once these elements are in place, then we can end the moratorium on popular politics. Just now, this form of politics is a luxury the YAR can ill afford." For them, present reality was drawn along lines of "State vs. Party." Although committed to greater social equality and to future democratization, the technocrats were opposed to what they regarded as the premature introduction of parties, popular organizations, and representative bodies. They were convinced that innovations such as these would be taken over by traditionalist opponents of state building and modernization or by well-meaning radical modernizers who were ignorant of the requirements of these processes. The technocrats were at the time more fearful of the traditionalists than of the radicals. They were confident, however, that they could trick the powerful traditionalists into modernization and reform by moving incrementally and by concealing their modernist motives and goals. Self-confident elitists, the technocrats regarded modernization as a technical and an administrative problem; they believed that they had or could acquire the requisite skills for development and wanted to be free to get on with this task unencumbered by politics.

In arguing their case, the technocrats reminded others of the political turmoil and immobilism of the last years of the al-Iryani era, and they pointed in particular at the obstructionist role of the tribally dominated Consultative Council. The frustration and disgust felt by many of them during that earlier period were stamped in their memories, strongly affecting their attitudes toward politics and political development. The technocrats also cited what they perceived to be the negative effects of overpoliticization on development in the PDRY, claiming that fear and suspicion had caused decision-makers in Aden to procrastinate and to evade responsibility to a greater degree than in the YAR. Finally, many of the technocrats viewed with skepticism if not hostility the LDA movement and the Correction Movement. They regarded the former as an attempt to create local power bases and political pressure groups rather than "true" local self-help agencies and the latter as an invitation to second-rate careerists and amateurs who knew nothing about "scientific" management and administrative reform to insinuate themselves into the development process.

The tribalists and the technocrats, at opposite ends of the spectrum on virtually all other issues of modernization, combined without design to make predominant an antipolitical climate of opinion during the 1970s. The tribalists, until weakened by President al-Hamdi in 1975, had been in a position to insist on only a minimum of political construction; the technocrats, enjoying their new freedom of operation after 1975, argued the same point from a modernist perspective. Acknowledged to be largely responsible for the new prosperity and development in the YAR, the latter were accorded a respectful hearing.

There were, however, modernist voices that spoke on behalf of the need for more politicization and political construction, and these voices became more numerous and vocal in the second half of the 1970s. Increasingly, the "State *vs.* Party" thesis of the technocrats was challenged by the "State *and* Party" thesis of other modernists. Most of these advocates of political construction were younger, second-generation modernists educated in the Arab world or Eastern Europe between the early 1960s and the early 1970s. Most of them were subsequently employed by the government, some attaining important middle-level postions in the mid-1970s. Finally, most regarded themselves as socialists of one sort or another, although this was by no means true of an overwhelming majority. Even those with strong egalitarian commitments tended to base their arguments for parties, popular organizations, and representative bodies on nationalist grounds and on the need for a stronger state and more rapid modernization. Like the technocrats, they began their argument with the present fragility of the state and the development process; unlike the technocrats, however, they reasoned from this to the conclusion that politicization and political construction were needed to protect the vulnerable and embattled nation-state from its enemies. They argued that only with the support of a stronger political infrastructure would President al-Hamdi be able both to defeat the tribalists and other conservative foes of modernization and to limit the influence of Saudi Arabia and other foreign powers over the domestic and external policies of the YAR. Indeed, the power of the conservatives and the influence of Saudi Arabia—and the dependence of the former on the latter—was an almost constant topic of conversation and source of resentment among most of the proponents of increased political construction.[7]

The advocates of political construction differed among themselves over whether the process should be generated from above or allowed to spring from below. Although exceptions abound, those advocates who were somewhat older, less radical, and closer to the al-Hamdi regime tended to think in terms of political construction from above. These people, the Nasirite group among them, would have had President al-Hamdi use his popularity to create and legitimate a political organization to support his regime and its goals; the model they often suggested he follow was that of the Arab Socialist Union at the height of the Nasir era in Egypt. Some of them viewed this official political construction as much as a means of taming foreign-influenced and pro-PDRY leftists as of limiting the influence of the traditionalists and Saudi Arabia; they saw it as a means both to "Yemenize" the leftist partisans and to strengthen politically the YAR in anticipation of closer ties and even unification with the PDRY in the future. Short of the launching of a new movement of this sort, many of the advocates of top-down political construction looked with some approval on President al-Hamdi's involvement in either or both the LDA movement and the Correction Movement.

By contrast, many of the advocates of political construction who were younger, more radical, and more remote from the al-Hamdi regime—and often members or ex-members of one of the groups in the newly formed National Democratic Front—tended to favor a more autonomous and spontaneous process of political construction from below. Although usually quite pragmatic and instrumental, the more radical politicizers were somewhat more revolutionary and populistic; they spoke of the need to harness the support and to increase the influence of the people, especially the young and the more secular. Although they regarded President al-Hamdi as a true nationalist leader, they were concerned as much with keeping the al-Hamdi regime on what they perceived as the correct path as with eliminating the influence of the tribalists, traditionalists, Saudi Arabia, and the imperialist powers. Most of the radical politicizers had been influenced by the form— and many by the goals—of political construction in the PDRY since the National Liberation Front came to power in 1967. They argued that people in the YAR had had considerable experience with parties in the 1960s and the early 1970s, and that the required new effort at political construction should build upon this experience and upon the remnants of the old political parties and their cadres. Some maintained that an attempt from above that ignored the existing parties would result in both a lifeless formalism and the alienation of the only elements with experience in building popular political organizations. Unlike many of the advocates of top-down development, these people viewed Egypt's Arab Socialist Union in negative terms. They also cited as support of their position the ephemeral nature of the National Yemeni Union during the last years of the al-Iryani era. What they proposed was an alliance between President al-Hamdi and a national front created out of old and new political elements. This was, of course, precisely what the National Democratic Front, formed in 1976, proposed and pursued.

6

Domestic Stalemate and Fast-evolving External Politics: 1975-1977

The domestic politics of the YAR, which had undergone such dramatic change during the first eighteen months of the al-Hamdi era, settled into the political equivalent of stationary trench warfare by 1976. By contrast, the external politics of the YAR evolved rapidly, changed character, and became more salient and important, particularly after 1975.

The Domestic Stalemate

President al-Hamdi's popularity as a nationalist leader grew dramatically in 1976 and 1977. Not at all physically imposing, he nonetheless proved to be a charismatic figure with great appeal and an object of growing respect and affection for an ever-widening share of the populace. He became no less than North Yemen's first great populist. Although he used his personal magnetism to political advantage in large gatherings as well as initimate settings, al-Hamdi did not do so in a manner or to a degree that interfered with practical affairs of state; politics in the YAR in 1977 was not subverted by a cult of personality and excessive political showmanship.

In the minds of many Yemenis, particularly the educated young, al-Hamdi came to personify a modern version of the historic Yemeni identity, one that cast this identity in terms of the nation-state and denied the relevance if not the existence of distinctions between sayyid and non-sayyid, tribalist and nontribalist, and above all, Zaydi and Shafai. Indeed, some young Yemenis in 1976 were crediting him with saving the YAR from the sectarianism of what they called the "Lebanese model." Al-Hamdi tapped the strong sense of pride and dignity for which the Yemeni people are known, in part because he seemed to be standing up to their rich and demanding neighbor, Saudi Arabia. Moreover, and without assuming a militantly antitraditionalist posture, al-Hamdi committed his regime to—and identified himself with—the goal of modernization. This captured the popular imagination and helped to nurture and spread widely a development ethos that focused the attention and efforts of Yemenis on this new goal. Young, educated recruits to the government came to feel a part of something important, developed a sense of being somebody. An annual occasion as modest as National Tree Day, an afforestation effort begun under al-Hamdi, came to be personified by him and equated with the growth of a new and better, more prosperous Yemen.

Nevertheless, the growth of President al-Hamdi's popularity as a national leader took place against the backdrop of only modest attempts to organize political support and the unresolved standoff between the state and the tribes—between al-Hamdi and Shaykh al-Ahmar. Al-Hamdi's wariness regarding political construction was especially evident in his dealings with the National Democratic Front, created in 1976 by six of the illegal progressive parties. When apprised by partisan friends of their intention to launch the NDF, he reportedly had not discouraged them; indeed, some say he had encouraged them to proceed. In the year after the formation of the NDF, however, he did not acknowledge its existence, much less endorse it in public. Issued in early October 1977, the NDF's program calling for a centralized state and independence from Saudi Arabia was met with complete silence on the part of the al-Hamdi regime. Although many of the partisans arrested in mid-1976 were released in 1977, the oft-predicted dialogue between the regime and the partisans never came about. In his wooing and warning of the partisans, President al-Hamdi seems to have been trying to keep them both powerless and unalienated until such time as he could decide what role, if any, they might safely be allowed to play in the political system. Perhaps he hoped with time to win over the partisans individually, rather than having to deal with them as a group with its own political organization and agenda. In any case, there is no evidence to suggest that he seriously considered the reincorporation of the progressive parties as such into the political system of the YAR.

At the same time, moreover, President al-Hamdi favored with high positions and other benefits members of the one major progressive group that was not a constituent of the NDF, the Nasirites. Mostly Shafais who as students in Egypt in the 1960s had been swept up by the Arab nationalist and socialist ideas of Gamal Abd al-Nasir, ideas championed later by Libya's Colonel Muammar al-Qaddafi, the Nasirites had been denied inclusion in the NDF in 1976 on the grounds that they were opportunists already in al-Hamdi's pocket. For his part, al-Hamdi apparently regarded them as a more reliable, safer bet than the NDF or its constituent parts.

Early 1977 was witness to a third political initiative in as many years by the al-Hamdi regime, one that seemed to acknowledge that both the LDA movement and the Correction Movement were not meeting certain perceived needs. In this instance, President al-Hamdi announced plans to convene a general people's congress in al-Hudayda in the summer of that year. According to official statements, the General People's Congress (GPC) would bring together several thousand delegates selected by the LDAs, the Correction Movement, and other popular organizations. The declared purpose of the congress would be to review the experience of the YAR since the 1962 Revolution and to chart the future course of the republic. Some Yemenis interpreted this to mean that the congress would propose the drafting of a new constitution; it was also suggested that the results of the congress would be used as the basis of a nationwide political education campaign, and that this would be followed in turn by a national plebiscite and national elections. Most political observers, including the tribalists who opposed and denounced it, regarded the congress as an attempt by the al-Hamdi regime to constitutionalize itself, to wrap itself in the mantle of political legitimacy. By mid-1977, however, observers were wondering whether the General People's Congress, for whatever purpose and in whatever form, would come to pass. Skeptics found significance in the fact that the congress was postponed from the summer until sometime later in the year.

After a year of relative calm, the cold war between the tribes and the state heated up during the first half of 1977, only in part as a response to the proposed General People's Congress. Allegedly at the instigation of Sinan abu Luhum, a group of tribal leaders met in the north in early January in order to mount a renewed effort to organize tribal opposition to the al-Hamdi regime. The assembled shaykhs denounced the regime as "communist and atheist," threatened it with "holy war," drew up a list of grievances and demands, and established an "information and mobilization council" to advance their cause.[1] In February, an attempt by Saudi Arabia to reconcile the differences between President al-Hamdi and Shaykh al-Ahmar failed when the former balked at some of the latter's demands for changes in public policy and the restoration of the tribal leaders to high offices of state. The cause of reconciliation was set back further in April by the assassination in London of ex-Prime Minister Abdullah al-Hajri, the older confidant of al-Hamdi whose good conservative credentials had made him an apt mediator among his Saudi friends, al-Hamdi, and the shaykhs. Throughout the spring of 1977, acts of harassment and defiance by tribesmen against the armed forces and other agencies of the state increased in number and severity. By late spring, Sanaa was full of ominous rumors about the growing threat of a tribal rebellion and about the likelihood that an impatient al-Hamdi would soon take vigorous action against the tribalists. These predictions seemed to be coming to pass in July when President al-Hamdi responded to provocations in the northern towns of Saada and Khamr—Shaykh al-Ahmar's town—by mobilizing armored units and sending planes against targets in the north.

Political tensions eased suddenly after July, largely because of another initiative by the Saudis, and the stalemate between the tribes and the state appeared reestablished. Later in the summer, persistent rumors suggested that the Saudis were reducing their support for the tribes, negotiations between the parties were again underway, and a reconciliation agreement was imminent. Giving some credence to these rumors, Ahmad Damash, al-Hamdi's long-time confidant, suddenly resigned from the government and fled Sanaa in the early fall, leaving behind a statement in which he bitterly condemned the president for having carried the sacred struggle against the tribes only halfway, thereby partitioning rather than uniting the Yemeni nation.

Foreign Policy and External Relations

External politics were overshadowed and largely determined by domestic politics during the months after the al-Hamdi regime assumed power. At the outset, the regime continued and elaborated further the policy shift begun during the al-Iryani era: rapprochement with Saudi Arabia and opening to the industrial West. This came quite easily to al-Hamdi as he had been one of several army officers who had joined together at a crucial moment in the late 1960s to pressure some of the more senior veterans of the 1962 Revolution—some of the Septembrists—to overcome their reluctance to pursue this new policy. By 1977, however, President al-Hamdi was cautiously projecting himself onto the regional stage, taking initiatives that, although not sharply at variance with the policy of the mid-1970s, suggested that national self-interest called for a greater degree of independence and a redefinition of the ever-stronger Saudi connection.

Tilting West and Opening to All, 1974–1975

President al-Hamdi had had little prior exposure to the outside world and virtually no experience in international politics when he became head of state in mid-1974, a condition that put him at a disadvantage in his struggle with his internationally known and experienced prime minister and foreign minister, Muhsin al-Aini. The ouster of Al-Aini in January 1975 allowed the appointment of an equally skilled practitioner of international politics, Abdullah al-Asnaj. Al-Asnaj's role as architect and builder of the YAR's foreign policy during the second half of the 1970s is quite remarkable. Aden's most prominent politician, a Shafai with no sociopolitical roots or base in the YAR, al-Asnaj forged a career of prominence and influence in Sanaa after the political group he led, the Front for the Liberation of Occupied South Yemen, lost out to the NLF in the struggle to succeed the British in South Yemen in 1967, and he did so in the field of diplomacy, long a preserve of the Zaydi community in North Yemen. The need for his diplomatic skills, his opposition to the PDRY regime, and the fact that he was an outsider and posed no threat to YAR politicians help account for his success. By 1976, it was apparent to many that the stamp of al-Asnaj's thinking was on most of the YAR's policy moves, and some were saying that al-Hamdi was proving to be the very able student of a very able teacher.

Foreign Minister al-Asnaj fashioned a pattern of external relations based on three overriding needs. First, the need to prove to Saudi Arabia that the al-Hamdi regime was sufficiently trustworthy a friend to justify both shifting support from the tribes to the state and providing the generous budget subsidies and funds for development and security upon which the

YAR was increasingly dependent. Second, the need to normalize relations with the PDRY so as to lessen the likelihood of PDRY-supported leftist agitation and armed rebellion against the YAR. And third, the need to establish and maintain good relations with all possible aid donors, especially the oil-rich Arab states and the developed industrial countries of the West.

The YAR met these needs quite successfully during the first two years of the al-Hamdi era. In addition to al-Asnaj's skillfulness, other reasons for this success were worldwide and, more important, regional detente. During this unusual period, close ties to Egypt did not have to come at the expense of good relations with other Arab nations, and friendship with the Baath regime in Iraq did not preclude friendship with Saudi Arabia or even the Baath regime in Syria. Most important, good relations with Saudi Arabia and the PDRY were not mutually exclusive at this time. The winding down in 1975 of the PDRY-backed rebellion in Dhufar against Oman raised the prospect of normal relations between the PDRY and the conservative Arab states, especially Saudi Arabia, relations that might be based on an exchange of political moderation on PDRY's part for financial aid from the Arab oil states. Increasingly civil if not friendly relations between the PDRY and Saudi Arabia in 1976 freed the YAR from the need to choose between its two most proximate and important neighbors.

Even if secondary to domestic politics during the first eighteen months of the al-Hamdi regime, external politics could not be ignored because of the extensive interpenetration of the two political domains. Relations with Saudi Arabia were closely tied to al-Hamdi's attempt to put the tribalists in their place, and—to an equal degree—relations with the PDRY bore directly upon the regime's efforts to control the southeastern borderlands and to win the support of progressive elements, particularly the educated youth. Finally, the attempt by the new regime to gain widespared acceptance turned on continuation and expansion of the new prosperity, and this depended in turn on an increasing flow of development aid from abroad, especially from Saudi Arabia.

Nevertheless, immediately pressing domestic political concerns meant that the al-Hamdi regime only slowly began to formulate, enunciate, and act on a foreign policy. Early statements were predictable and unexceptional, including expressions of friendship and appreciation for Saudi Arabia, calls for unity with the PDRY, and reaffirmations of a desire for friendly relations with all countries willing to assist the YAR in its development—that is, the YAR's "open door policy."

Not surprisingly, President al-Hamdi's first trip abroad was to Saudi Arabia, in July 1974, little more than three weeks after he assumed power. The primacy of relations with the Saudis was further underlined when Shaykh al-Ahmar led a delegation on an official visit to the kingdom in August. President al-Hamdi visited Saudi Arabia three times in 1975, in part no doubt to reassure the Saudi leaders that his actions against their tribal clients were not prelude to a radical restructuring of Yemeni politics and in part to urge them to end their subsidies and other support to the tribalists and to fund the purchase of arms from the United States for the YAR armed forces. Although Saudi development assistance and budget subsidies had increased significantly since mid-1973, it was Prime Minister Abd al-Ghani's visit in August 1975 that regularized the flow of those funds at a massive level. This meeting ended with an announcement of a Saudi pledge of $273 million in budget subsidies and development loans and grants as well as the creation of the Saudi-Yemeni Joint Coordinating Council, a body that would meet each year to assess and act on the YAR's development needs.[2]

The Saudi connection crystallized further when serious negotiations began in 1975 on the subject of a Saudi-financed transfer of U.S. arms to the YAR. The al-Hamdi regime early made known its interest in U.S. arms, following up on an approach made to the United States by the al-Iryani regime in 1973. President al-Hamdi asserted as early as January 1975 the willingness of the YAR to accept arms without strings from any source. Throughout the year rumors as well as public statements alluded to al-Hamdi's eagerness to make a deal for U.S. arms and to the possibility that military relations with the Soviet Union would be "frozen" and Soviet military advisers expelled in the bargain. There were also rumors of Saudi ambivalence and reluctance at the prospects of financing the reequipping of the armed forces of a former enemy, one with which it had fought a territorial war in the 1930s and had battled by proxy for years during the civil war in the 1960s. These rumors were often coupled with other rumors of al-Hamdi's growing impatience with the Saudis over the arms-purchase delays. Probably to spur the Saudis to action, al-Hamdi sent a military mission headed by his Command Council colleague, Major Abdullah Abd al-Alim, to the Soviet Union in November 1975. In any case, the Saudis were acting in 1976 as if they had gotten this message.

Unlike YAR-Saudi relations, relations between the two Yemens got off to a slow start after the al-Hamdi regime replaced that of President al-Iryani. High-level contacts that began in late 1974 led to the resumption in early 1975 of meetings of the joint unification committees that had been set up after the border fight and unification agreement in 1972. Relations quickly worsened, however, and by March 1975 the YAR was publicly accusing the PDRY of permitting saboteurs to operate over the border in YAR territory, a situation reminiscent of the early 1970s. Although these accusations continued through April, relations then improved as fast as they earlier had deteriorated. High-level diplomatic contacts resumed in May and by August the joint unification committees were again holding meetings. The improvement in relations between the two Yemens was facilitated by the cautious approaches that the al-Hamdi regime and the NDF dissidents were making toward one another and by the efforts of each Yemeni regime to limit on its side of the border the political-military activities of dissidents and refugees from the other Yemen. Clearly, both Yemens saw benefits in a normalization of relations in 1975.

The United States quickly concluded that the al-Hamdi regime was a worthy recipient of friendship and development aid, both because of evolving strategic considerations on the Arabian Peninsula and because the regime seemed to be a good example of the noncommunist reformism favored by policymakers in Washington. Nevertheless, the U.S. government's desire for close, friendly ties with the YAR did not fit so well with its concern for its interests in Saudi Arabia. As its special relationship with Saudi Arabia overshadowed all other United States concerns on the Arabian Peninsula—especially after the OPEC-led price increases and Secretary of State Henry Kissinger's assignment to Saudia Arabia of a key role in the Middle East peace process—Washington deferred almost totally to the Saudis on the subject of the YAR and took at face value their private assessments and pronouncements on the two Yemens. YAR leaders, President al-Hamdi included, resented this and made known their resentment to Washington. For their part, the Americans and the Saudis tended to ignore these Yemeni sensitivities in pursuit of their shared desires to get the Soviet military advisers out of the YAR and to contain the Marxist regime in Aden.

Most other countries responded positively to the YAR's efforts to promote its "open door policy." Western industrial countries more removed from strategic considerations than the United States merely saw the new regime in the YAR as attractive and deserving of development assistance, as did United Nations agencies and such other international aid bodies as the World Bank and the International Monetary Fund. The West Germans, British, Dutch, and Scandinavians initiated or increased existing aid programs after al-Hamdi assumed power. For their part, the small, oil-rich Arab Gulf states—for example, Kuwait and the United Arab Emirates—saw a strong and stable YAR as a desirable counter to Saudi hegemonic ambitions on the Arabian Peninsula, and the al-Hamdi regime indicated privately a willingness to play this role in exchange for generous development aid. Generous amounts of aid were forthcoming from nearly all quarters.

Some Lines Are Drawn, 1976–1977

Diplomatic activity involving the YAR increasingly accelerated from early 1976 through the fall of 1977, and this period was marked by the emergence of President al-Hamdi and the YAR on the regional and world stages. The modest rise in the YAR's status in the world arena was indicated in spring 1976 by the announcement of the long-sought and long-discussed military assistance agreement between the United States and the YAR. The arms agreement, financed by Saudi Arabia and valued at $139 million, provided for the rearming and general reequipping of a number of infantry batallions. Though modest in scope, the agreement was billed in private by United States officials as only the first in a number of such agreements between the two countries; indeed, negotiations were already underway in 1977 on a second triangular YAR-Saudi-U.S. deal that would involve F-5E fighter planes and other heavy weapons. Though unresponsive to Yemeni pleas that it persuade or pressure the Saudis to be more understanding of the YAR's situation and to speed up the transfer of arms, the United States acknowledged in public and private the strong interest that it and its Saudi ally had in a stable, prosperous, and friendly YAR. Washington also became obsessed with the prospects of getting the Soviet military advisers expelled from the YAR, prospects heightened by a YAR refusal to accept new Soviet arms.

In the summer of 1976 President al-Hamdi got his first taste of international diplomacy when he headed a YAR delegation to Sri Lanka for the Conference of Non-Aligned Nations, an experience that proved very satisfying and whetted his appetite for a bigger role in world affairs.[3] A year later he travelled to Europe for the first time and made a much-publicized state visit to France, a visit that was seen as an attempt to break out of a diplomatic pattern largely dominated by Saudi Arabia and the United States. Although the weapons sought by the YAR were not forthcoming, the trip did result in a significant increase in France's role as a commercial partner and as a source of development aid for the YAR.

The role of President al-Hamdi and the YAR on the regional scene increased substantially and for the most part involved or was driven by changes in the triangular relationship among the YAR, Saudi Arabia, and the PDRY as well as by a major realignment of forces on the Red Sea and the Horn of Africa. Moreover, the sides of this core triangle became firm and sharply focused, revealing potential conflicts and differences, at the same time as the regional and international environment was becoming less benign and more demanding. The climate of detente, which had allowed the YAR the luxury of not having to choose between Saudi Arabia and the PDRY, began to change by early 1977. The PDRY, which a year earlier had muted its support for revolution in the Gulf and Oman's Dhufar province in return for financial aid from Saudi Arabia and the lesser Gulf oil states, edged or was nudged by some of the socialist states toward alliance with revolutionary Ethiopia and against Somalia and most of the rest of the Arab world in what appeared to be a growing struggle over the Red Sea and the Horn of Africa.

The YAR's relationship with Saudi Arabia, by far its most important concern, was complicated after 1975 by the fact that President al-Hamdi, for reasons of domestic politics and personal pride, felt compelled to assert a measure of political independence for the YAR at precisely the moment when its dependence on the Saudis for financial aid was becoming total and when the Saudis were again becoming concerned about their southern flank, on the Horn of Africa as well as on the Yemeni corner of the Arabian Peninsula. Al-Hamdi's efforts to secure for the YAR some breathing space in its patron-client relationship with Saudi Arabia focused on improved relations with the PDRY and claims to a leadership role in Red Sea security. The noticeable improvement in ties with the PDRY, a marked contrast to the adversary relationship of the early 1970s, involved a mutually beneficial quid pro quo: al-Hamdi put the anti-PDRY refugee groups from South Yemen on a short leash and the PDRY did the same with the constituent groups in the NDF that had fled or been expelled from the YAR in 1968 and thereafter. The ability of the Yemeni regimes to deliver on this arrangement was partly a result of modest increases in their strength and popular acceptance in the mid-1970s. The improvement in relations had been aided by the reactivation of the joint unification committees, providing a format and forum for regular contact if not serious steps toward formal unification of the two Yemens. In addition, improved ties between the YAR and the PDRY were facilitated by good personal relations between al-Hamdi and his counterpart in the PDRY, Salim Rubaya Ali. The heads of state of the two Yemens held meetings twice in 1977, the first time in Qataba on the YAR side of the border in the spring and then in Sanaa as Salim Rubaya Ali was returning to Aden after his historic visit to Saudi Arabia in early August. Al-Hamdi strongly supported his PDRY counterpart in his desire, often over the objections of some of his NLF colleagues in Aden, to improve relations with and to secure financial aid from Saudi Arabia and the Gulf states. Al-Hamdi quietly planned to go to Aden on the occasion of Revolution Day in October 1977 and thereby to become the first YAR head of state to visit the PDRY.

Throughout 1976 and 1977, President al-Hamdi used the thinly veiled threat of closer ties if not unification with the PDRY to get the Saudis to do certain things and to refrain from doing others—for example, to maintain generous levels of aid to the government in Sanaa and to cut back support for the tribes. Similarly, he used his Red Sea initiative during the same period to give the YAR some leverage in its unequal relationship with Saudi Arabia. The Red Sea, a vital international waterway, albeit less so than prior to the closing of the Suez Canal in 1967, became the focus of renewed attention because of political changes triggered by the revolution in Ethiopia in 1974. The beginning of the process by which the Soviet Union and the United States "swapped" Ethiopia for Somalia, bringing the latter back into the main Arab camp at the same time that it put pressure on an otherwise moderating PDRY to choose between the Arabs and a socialist camp that included Ethiopia, was already being felt in 1976. There were also conflicts that centered on Ethiopia's territorial integrity—the long-standing Arab-backed Eritrean rebellion and the just-beginning Somali-inspired Ogadan rebellion—as well as the potential for conflict in the imminent independence from France of the colony of Djibouti, scheduled for mid-1977. Finally, there were charges of Israeli probes at the southern narrowing of the Red Sea. Things were suddenly in flux on the Horn of Africa and the margins of the Red Sea, and this both created opportunities that the YAR might possibly turn to its advantage and undermined the regional detente that had helped make the YAR's external environment so benign in the mid-1970s.

According to the thesis that President al-Hamdi and Foreign Minister al-Asnaj were expressing frequently by 1977, the problem of Red Sea security was one about which all of the Arab and African states bordering on that vital waterway should be concerned. They maintained that the issue of securing the Red Sea as "a zone of peace" should be solved only by these bordering states and that the YAR acting singly or jointly with the PDRY was best positioned to act on their behalf to maintain security—provided Saudi Arabia made available the economic and military wherewithal for it to do the job. The YAR's litany called for a strong, well-armed YAR with normalized relations if not close ties with the PDRY, conditions that caused the Saudis to wonder if the secure Red Sea they desired was worth the political price and the risks entailed.

President al-Hamdi's attempt to capitalize on the issue of Red Sea security came to something of a climax on 22–23 March 1977 when he hosted in Taiz a summit meeting on the subject that brought together the heads of state of the two Yemens, Sudan, and Somalia. Although the summit served to focus the regional spotlight on al-Hamdi and the YAR for a short period, it almost failed to take place and was doomed by events to lead to naught. The continuing retreat from detente made futile the summit's concluding call for "efforts to convene an expanded meeting that will include all the countries overlooking the Red Sea." Growing conflict among some of these countries—and a very violent conflict between Somalia and Ethiopia—was to make impossible such a meeting in the coming years.

The drama of higher diplomacy and international politics after 1975 served as a backdrop against which the YAR and Saudi Arabia dealt more routinely with matters that recurrently concerned and sometimes divided them. High level visits continued, with President al-Hamdi visiting Saudi Arabia once in 1976 and twice in 1977 and Prime Minister Abd al-Ghani going there in each of these years. Al-Hamdi continued to urge the Saudis to end their direct subsidies to the tribes and to channel aid for the tribes through the central government. In 1977, the Saudi leaders were privately expressing alarm over al-Hamdi's stubbornness and impetuosity, concerns probably heightened by al-Hamdi's requests that they get Shaykh al-Ahmar out of the YAR so that his regime might deal more freely with some of the more troublesome tribalists. Good feelings generated by the conclusion of the triangular arms deal notwithstanding, the YAR was complaining to the United States by early 1977 that Saudi Arabia was delaying the delivery of arms under the agreement and was refusing to consider promptly requests for additional arms. Nevertheless, the Saudi-supervised delivery of U.S. arms did begin and by the fall of 1977 was moving along in a manner more or less to the satisfaction of the three parties. The Yemenis continued to complain in private over Saudi foot-dragging on their request for more impressive additions to their arsenal. A joke circulating in Sanaa at the time had the Saudis agreeing to the sale of tanks to the YAR only upon invention of a tank that could drive and shoot south but not north.

Despite unofficial threats that President al-Hamdi was going to restrict emigration and organize workers abroad in response to reports that Yemeni workers were being mistreated in Saudi Arabia, additional workers continued to leave the YAR and the remittances continued to flood in. The Saudi-Yemeni Joint Coordinating Council met early in both 1976 and 1977—on the former occasion in Sanaa, to which Prince Sultan led a big ministerial delegation—and on each occasion Saudi Arabia committed itself to a high level of budget subsidies and development aid. However annoyed or dissatisfied the Saudi leaders may have been with al-Hamdi, they apparently concluded that it was not in their interest to cut their aid and to lessen whatever leverage they had over him and his regime. On their part, al-Hamdi and his colleagues acted with some restraint, not yet prepared to bite the hand that fed them.

7

The al-Ghashmi Interlude: 1977-1978

Sanaa was infused with optimism around the time of the 26 September Revolution Day celebrations in 1977. Independence Square was its most festive in memory and the Yemeni on the street and in high government office seemed confident and even self-congratulatory. Most knowledgeable persons agreed that the YAR's current economic situation and longer-term development prospects were bright: Workers' remittances and external aid were rushing in like a torrent and the YAR's public and private sectors seemed increasingly able to take advantage of this new bounty. Many were keenly anticipating the international development conference and the formal presentation of the First Five-Year Plan. Political prospects were also judged to be relatively bright. President al-Hamdi had spoken on Revolution Day and on other recent occasions of the imminence and great significance of the reorganization and reequipment of the armed forces. It was widely rumored that the elusive on-again, off-again reconciliation between the state and the tribes—between al-Hamdi and Shaykh al-Ahmar—was also imminent and that it would be effected on terms favorable to President al-Hamdi and with the blessings of the Saudi rulers who had finally soured on the tribalists. The YAR's relations with its Yemeni brothers in the PDRY were regarded as cordial and improving, and those with its more important neighbor and patron, Saudi Arabia, seemed to be more firmly grounded than before on mutual interst and national dignity. In short, the mood in Sanaa was decidedly upbeat.

The Death and Legacy of al-Hamdi

The mood in the country changed swiftly to one of profound shock and great uncertainty when on the evening of 11 October 1977 President al-Hamdi and his soldier brother, Abdullah, were shot dead and left in a private house on the outskirts of Sanaa. The initial wildly conflicting and often bizarre or scandalous accounts of the event gave way over the following weeks to a widely held belief that the killings were the work of a small group of senior army officers acting with the prior knowledge and probable encouragement of persons high in the Saudi regime. Some said that Prince Sultan and other members of the Saudi royal family had become alarmed by al-Hamdi's growing populism, assertiveness, and near threats of much closer ties if not unity with the PDRY, seeing him as "a little Nasir," one who should be cut down before he got too big to control.

Although there probably was official Saudi complicity at some level and to some degree, it is most likely that the Yemeni army officers who assassinated the al-Hamdi brothers acted less on behalf of Saudi patrons than out of the belief that they had better get President al-Hamdi before he got them. More specifically, these officers probably became convinced that the reform and reorganization of the armed forces that al-Hamdi was pushing to implement would prove to be the occasion or excuse for their elimination. They had the purge of 1975 as a precedent, and al-Hamdi apparently did little to allay the fears of some of this fellow officers as 1977 wore on; indeed, communications between him and these officers seem to have virtually broken down. In the end, the politics of leadership at the top around al-Hamdi degenerated or collapsed into a kill or be killed struggle for survival. And the al-Hamdis were killed.

In retrospect, there appears to have been something amiss with al-Hamdi's personality and resultant political style as they affected his relationship with persons of actual or potential power or influence. Some confirmation of this is found in a comment by no less an authority than al-Hamdi himself. At an informal gathering in 1974, shortly after coming to power, al-Hamdi leaned over to one of his ministers and confided: "Brother, my biggest weakness is that I am *too* suspicious. I don't trust *anyone.*"[1] Other Yemenis have said things that support this bit of self-analysis. One young admirer of al-Hamdi, who served him in the Office of the President, has noted that he was "very intelligent but too suspicious—he isolated himself."[2] It seems that al-Hamdi was an uncommonly distrustful person and that he viewed the world as a threatening place. Suspicious by nature, he perceived persons whom he and others regarded as his equals or near equals in knowledge and talent as threats to his power if not his very being and was unable psychologically to share power with such people. The result was that the strength of the al-Hamdi regime was progressively corroded after 1976 by a crisis of trust and confidence at the top.

It became fashionable after al-Hamdi's death to say that he had an "autocratic urge" or a "hunger for power." If he did, it is perhaps best viewed as a response to the more basic fear of exposure or sense of vulnerability that overcomes many who have reached the pinnacles of power. The need to gain control and the fear of losing control once gained often go hand in hand.

The legacy of the young and dynamic al-Hamdi is modest because the shortness of his tenure, like that of John F. Kennedy, made it more a matter of promise than fulfillment and because his regime depended so much upon his physical presence. During his brief time, he fostered a political environment that advanced the prosperity and development activity begun during the al-Iryani era, tilted the political balance in favor of the modern sector and came to personify national strength and development in the minds of many Yemenis. However, much as did his two republican predecessors, President al-Hamdi left to the future the task of lasting and significant political construction in the YAR. His personalist regime was not institutionalized at the top and had very shallow and amorphous political underpinnings. Running what was increasingly a one-man show, he failed to foster a strong leadership structure and to generate a political organization capable or reaching down into the society. Al-Hamdi's greatest achievement in state building came early in his tenure and was his effort to expel from the state and hold at bay the leading tribalists. But this considerable political accomplishment was of an essentially negative sort, a change in the political equation that was more an act of destruction than of construction: although he eliminated powerful enemies, al-Hamdi did not aggregate and organize supporters into powerful groupings. As a result, he created and left a political vacuum. A Briton who knew Yemen well from his days as a royalist mercenary said that al-Hamdi had "hollowed out" the political system but that after quite wisely ousting al-Aini and the Luhumis had been so overtaken by fear and suspicion that "his hollowing out left only an empty shell."[3]

The Accession and Rule of al-Ghashmi

Deputy Commander in Chief and Chief of Staff Ahmad Husayn al-Ghashmi (ca. 1940–1978) was promptly chosen chairman of the Command Council. Al-Ghashmi possessed none of al-Hamdi's personal magnetism, and he was thought by many—erroneously, it seems—to be devoid of both intelligence and ambition. He was a man of limited formal education and was of tribal origins, the brother of a shaykh in an area close to Sanaa.

In his first message to the nation, Al-Ghashmi called for calm and pledged both to punish the assassins of al-Hamdi and to maintain the domestic and external course of the 13 June Correction Movement. Some were unconvinced. An al-Hamdi supporter in the army tried to shoot him almost immediately and the mourners who pressed against his car in al-Hamdi's funeral procession were heard to chant repeatedly: "Al-Ghashmi, al-Ghashmi, where is our al-Hamdi? Al-Ghashmi, give us back al-Hamdi!" The fear spread and stayed that the country was in store for turmoil and instability, and that these could shatter the fragile prosperity and development of the previous few years. Nevertheless, despite other minor protests and mutinies by al-Hamdi supporters in the cities and big towns, and the subsequent purge or flight of those persons, the political system of the YAR was marked by relative calm during the fall and winter of 1977.

The story of the al-Ghasmi interlude is less a matter of what happened than of what was expected to happen—and did not. On the one hand, the people did not rise in revolt against the presumed reactionary killers of their beloved al-Hamdi. On the other hand, the tribalists and other conservatives in league with the Saudis did not undo what al-Hamdi and his colleagues had done to strengthen the state and to provide the YAR with a modicum of independence. Indeed, the year that followed al-Hamdi's assassination left the YAR quite unchanged, and what did not occur says much about the nature or condition of the YAR in 1978. The people had neither the organization nor the inclination to act in protest in the name of the slain al-Hamdi, however much beloved. Regarding the former, they lacked the labor unions, student organizations, and business associations through which to resist, demonstrate, or riot. Regarding the latter, the popular response suggested that many of the Yemenis who revered al-Hamdi or were keenly interested in politics were political spectators— subjects, not participants, of politics—much as they had been in the days of the imam. That is to say, the popular reaction, or lack thereof, was a reminder of Yemen's low level of socioeconomic development in general and political development in particular. However, if not modern enough to support a popular uprising, the YAR of 1978 was too modern, too changed, for the past to reassert its grip. Some things had changed during the previous decade—between the late 1960s and the late 1970s—making it unlikely that al-Hamdi's successors could hand Yemen over to the tribalists and the Saudis, even if they had wanted to. Finally, the prosperity of recent years also militated against political change in the wake of the assassination of al-Hamdi. As Dr. Abd al-Karim al-Iryani put it in 1978: "Now, here in my own country, I finally see how you can have the political apathy and indifference that so baffled me during my ten years in the United States. A whole nation can be too busy pursuing money and profit to be concerned at all with politics."[4]

The al-Ghashmi regime proceeded to do what it could to establish itself and to increase its chances of survival in the domestic political environment of the YAR and in the larger regional and international systems. In external relations, the task was to convince the rest of the world that nothing had changed—that the well-received domestic and external lines taken by the al-Hamdi regime would be continued—at the same time that Saudi Arabia was assured that the regime would make certain alterations in policy when circumstances were more favorable. The al-Ghashmi regime knew that its survival depended on continued prosperity, that this new prosperity depended on increased development aid, and that the flow of aid depended on its being able to convince a large number of donors that it was no less committed to development and no less able to absorb development assistance than had been the widely respected al-Hamdi regime. For this reason, al-Ghashmi and his colleagues went ahead with plans to hold the international development conference in order to promote the First Five-Year Plan. The conference was carried off smoothly in a climate of political calm on 17-20 November 1977, only several weeks after the assassination of al-Hamdi. The participants were favorably impressed and funds and technical assistance were pledged at about the hoped for levels. The enemies as well as the friends of the al-Ghashmi regime in Yemen worked to make a success of the bid for support for the plan as no one wanted to kill or be accused of killing the goose that laid the golden egg.

As al-Ghashmi had been reputed to be the Saudis' man in the al-Hamdi regime, relations between the client YAR and its Saudi patron were not regarded at the outset as problematic. In fact, however, the al-Ghashmi regime was caught by nationalist sentiments and other political considerations squarely between the PDRY and Saudi Arabia. The new and very suspect regime in Sanaa had to convince the radicals in Aden and their North Yemeni comrades that it was not about to hand the YAR over to the tribalists and Saudi Arabia at the same time that it had to convince the Saudis that it intended to accommodate the tribalists and to be more responsive than al-Hamdi had been to Saudi security and strategic concerns. Although more patient with al-Ghashmi than with al-Hamdi, the Saudis quickly came to question the new head of state's loyalty and competence. Indeed, they were beginning to have second thoughts by the spring of 1978 as to whether the cure of al-Ghashmi was better than the disease of al-Hamdi.

With no prospects for an alternative to Saudi-funded transfers of U.S. arms, the al-Ghashmi regime had an added reason to secure the support and approval of the government in Washington. In this regard, the regime had to allay the concerns of a U.S. government that began with grave doubts about al-Ghashmi's abilities and became increasingly convinced that he had been intimately involved in the assassination of the popular al-Hamdi. American concerns lessened, however, after only several months as it became apparent both that al-Ghashmi's presumed involvement in the assassination might not be politically fatal and that he was more able than previously guessed.

Neither feared nor respected by many, the al-Ghashmi regime faced tasks in the domestic political domain that were more formidable than those related to external politics. The two major tasks were to secure the loyalty of the fragmented armed forces—the strongest and immediately most important political actor—at the same time that beginnings were made in the longer-term effort to build support and legitimacy for the regime outside the armed forces. Regarding the armed forces, the initial purge of most units loyal to al-Hamdi, especially his brother's brigade, the Giants, took place in the immediate wake of the assassinations. Officers loyal to al-Ghashmi and his coterie were placed in key positions. After the first weeks, however, the process by which commanders and units of suspect loyalty were purged became more protracted and subterranean. The first major conflict broke the surface in early 1978 when Major Mujahid al-Kuhhali, a strong al-Hamdi loyalist with good tribal ties, raised his troops in mutiny when the regime ordered him to step down as commander of the garrison in Amran, a large town on the main road north from Sanaa. The standoff of some weeks ended in March when al-Kuhhali was persuaded to end his challenge to the central government, turn over his garrison, and accept safe conduct and a diplomatic post abroad.

The departure of al-Kuhhali left more exposed the position of Major Abdullah Abd al-Alim, the commander of the commandos and paratroops, and, except for al-Ghashmi, the only remaining member of the Command Council formed at the outset of the al-Hamdi era. Abd al-Alim had been a friend and loyal supporter of al-Hamdi as well as the self-appointed guardian of Shafai interests in the Zaydi-dominated armed forces. He and al-Ghashmi were known to have a long and intense personal dislike for each other. Most observers thought that Abd al-Alim's break with al-Ghashmi and his colleagues was inevitable, and many thought that he would make his break on the occasion of the al-Kuhhali mutiny; when he did not, some called him prudent and a realist, and others accused him of indecision if not cowardice. In late April, several weeks after the al-Kuhhali mutiny was ended, Abd al-Alim, apparently fearful for his own safety, fled from Sanaa with loyal forces and went to his homeland south of Taiz and near the border with the PDRY. Forces loyal to al-Ghashmi and under the command of the military governor of Taiz, Major Ali Abdullah Salih, moved into the area and, after three weeks of negotiations failed to result in a peaceful resolution of the new mutiny, launched an assault against positions held by Abd al-Alim's supporters. A discredited Abd al-Alim fled without a fight across the border into the PDRY as the forces under Major Salih were closing in on him; he was further discredited when his followers took as hostages and then murdered a group of local notables who had tried to mediate between him and the al-Ghashmi regime. With the flight of Abd al-Alim, the last major pocket of known al-Hamdi loyalists was purged from the armed forces of the YAR.

Ahmad al-Ghashmi's effort to build support and legitimacy for his regime outside the armed forces was made formidable by virtue of his being doubly condemned. Whereas he and his colleagues were judged illegitimate by the supporters of al-Hamdi, the institutional framework that he inherited from al-Hamdi was still regarded as illegitimate by the tribalists and other elements who had thrived under the 1970 Constitution and its institutions. In late 1977, al-Ghashmi seemed to be trying to appeal to both groups at the same time. On the one hand, he declared that the 1970 Constitution remained "the legal framework governing our work," and, in a rare public criticism of his predecessor, said that al-Hamdi's biggest mistake had been the dissolution of the Consultative Council, "thus disrupting constitutional life." On the other hand, he announced the formation of a preparatory committee for a general people's congress, reviving al-Hamdi's last institutional initiative and at least raising the possibility of an alternative to the 1970 Constitution and its institutions, including the Consultative Council.

In an effort to fill the institutional vacuum and provide for broader participation, the Command Council issued a constitutional decree in early February 1978 that created the People's Constituent Assembly (PCA). This ninety-nine-member appointed body was given mostly advisory powers and described as being part of the transition to a new, elected legislative body. In turn, the People's Constituent Assembly in late April abolished the Command Council, created a Presidential Council consisting of a president and two vice presidents, and appointed Ahmad al-Ghashmi as president.

The abolition of the Command Council denied Abd al-Alim his base of authority in the state, and it was this that occasioned him to flee for his safety from Sanaa. The Abd al-Ghani government submitted its resignation on the day after al-Ghasmi became president, and Abd al-Ghani, who had been prime minister for more than three years, was then asked to form a new government. In part because of the political turmoil surrounding the Abd al-Alim rebellion, the process of forming a new government with Abd al-Ghani as prime minister was not completed until the end of May, several weeks later. The new government assembled, a transitional institutional framework consisting of the PCA and the new presidency seemed to be in place. President al-Ghashmi seemed finally to be taking command, much to the surprise of many, Yemenis and non-Yemenis alike.

Al-Ghashmi's Demise

The al-Ghashmi interlude ended only eight months after it began with the bang of a bomb that killed President al-Ghashmi in his office on 24 June 1978. Killed with him was a man who only moments before had arrived with a briefcase, a man assumed at the time to be the personal emissary of the PDRY head of state, Salim Rubaya Ali. Apparently unbeknownst to the emissary, the briefcase he carried was booby-trapped. Within twenty-four hours, Chairman Salim Rubaya Ali himself was dead in Aden, the loser in the final episode of his long-simmering feud with his co-leader in the PDRY regime, NLF Secretary General Abd al-Fattah Ismail. The assassination of al-Ghashmi probably was the work of Ismail's militant wing of the NLF and probably involved an ingenious switch in both emissary and briefcase. It surely had less to do with the domestic politics of the YAR or the relations between the two Yemens than with the power struggle within the NLF in the PDRY. Nevertheless, the bizarre occurrence did not bode well for politics within the YAR or between the two Yemens. Outraged, the friends and foes of President al-Ghashmi in the YAR condemned the regime in Aden and persuaded Arab League members in emergency session to freeze relations with the PDRY.

The regime in Sanaa responded quickly to the assassination of President al-Ghashmi with the formation of a four-man Presidential Council chaired by Vice President Abd al-Karim al-Arishi and also consisting of Prime Minister Abd al-Ghani, Chief-of-Staff Ali al-Shayba, and Major Ali Abdullah Salih, the military governor of Taiz province. Although the surface of Yemeni politics appeared placid, intense politicking took place behind the scenes during the weeks following al-Ghashmi's demise. Qadi al-Arishi, a traditionally trained functionary of modest abilities and reputation, aspired to accede to the presidency. The power to decide, however, was in the hands of the military, not the civilian politicians, and it quickly became clear that Ali Abdullah Salih, promoted to lieutenant colonel a week after al-Ghashmi's assassination, would either assume the presidency himself or govern indirectly through al-Arishi. In mid-July, less than a month after the assassination, Lt.-Col. Salih was elected president and commander in chief by the People's Constituent Assembly. Qadi al-Arishi resumed the posts of vice president and chairman of the PCA, and Prime Minister Abd al-Ghani stayed on to serve in that capacity under his third president in considerably less than a year. The consensus prognosis after the violent end of the second YAR president in eight months is caught in a joke that circulated widely in the country in the fall of 1978. Al-Ghashmi, just arrived in Heaven, waved off al-Hamdi's angry tirade for having forgotten to bring *qat* from Sanaa. "Don't worry," said al-Ghashmi, "President Salih has promised to take care of the *qat*—and he should be joining us any time now."

8

The Salih Regime: Bleak Prospects and Faint Hopes, 1978-1981

The period 1978-1981 was one of widespread political pessimism as well as one during which President Ali Abdullah Salih (ca. 1945-   ) labored to improve his political prospects. The rough fabric of Yemeni politics during this time included a number of interrelated threads. One important thread, largely hidden from view, involved the fraying and attempted mending of the YAR's vital patron-client relationship with its rich and demanding neighbor, Saudi Arabia. Two other threads, closely tied to the Saudi one, involved the Salih regime's troubled dealings with the major tribes of Yemen and its changing relations with countries with which it had important ties, including the two superpowers. A fourth thread had to do with the YAR's attempt to reverse both the faltering of its development effort and the international development community's growing disenchantment with the YAR as a recipient of aid. A fifth thread, by its nature quite visible, pertained to the specific efforts by the Salih regime to renovate and legitimate the political system and—in the process—to increase its own legitimacy and public support. Although each was important, none of these threads was more central to the politics of this period than the efforts of the Salih regime to end an armed rebellion by the National Democratic Front and to normalize relations with the other Yemen, the militantly Marxist PDRY. This double thread was at times tied to or intertwined with one or more of the other threads. Indeed, on occasion it formed with most or all of them a great knot, one difficult to untie or cut.

The Salih Regime Hits Bottom: Spring 1979

In early 1979, the fortunes of the Salih regime reached their lowest point and many observers were confidently predicting its imminent demise. Indeed, the CIA station chief in Sanaa was taking bets—and giving good odds, too—that President Salih would not survive the spring. Many informed Yemenis agreed that a change would come soon and that it would probably reach to the top. The question was how it might best be effected to avoid turmoil and long struggle.

Two recent events had highlighted the troubled state of Yemeni politics. The first was the October 1978 coup attempt against President Salih, coming only three months after he had succeeded al-Ghashmi to the presidency. The coup was the work of followers of the slain President al-Hamdi—especially members of the Nasirites—and was led by the young and highly respected minister of social affairs, labor, and youth; the head of the Office of the President; and the commanders of four military units in the Sanaa area. It also had the backing of al-Hamdi people in exile, among them Mujahid al-Kuhhali and Abdullah Abd al-Alim, and received moral and material support from the Qaddafi regime in Libya. A major undertaking, the coup attempt was crushed by armed might only after it was well in motion in the early morning darkness on 15 October. Many suspected of involvement or mere sympathy were arrested, and the leaders, both civilian and military, were tried and executed in a matter of days. Although put down efficiently, the coup attempt belied the sense of stability that had been fostered by the new Salih regime and confirmed the fears of some—and the hopes of others—that forces for fundamental change coursed just beneath the placid surface of Yemeni politics.

The second event was the February–March 1979 border fight between the forces of the YAR and those of the PDRY and the National Democratic Front. Although treated abroad and in Sanaa almost solely as an interstate conflict between the two Yemens, the fight also embraced a rebellion against the Salih regime by North Yemeni dissidents grouped under the banner of the NDF. In the months after the October coup attempt, the supporters of al-Hamdi, now calling themselves the 13 June Movement, had merged with the two-year-old NDF and together they had pledged to struggle for the Salih regime's destruction. They had the support of the PDRY leaders in this effort. During the same period, moreover, the Salih regime and other elements in the YAR were giving aid and comfort to anti-PDRY refugee groups that had been revived and augmented by the unrest and fighting in the PDRY after the execution of Chairman Salim Rubaya Ali in June 1978. Although the immediate origins of the actual fighting are complex and even unclear, responsibility for its escalation probably should be borne about equally by both sides. What started as a war of words at the end of 1978 gave way to armed skirmishes in the border areas of the two Yemens in early 1979. In turn, these soon escalated into pitched battles and successful thrusts deep into YAR territory by PDRY and NDF forces, the latter consisting largely of ex-YAR soldiers. The tribal and regular forces of the YAR performed dismally, and a new wave of officers and men defected to the NDF side. For a time, the advance from the south threatened to sever Ibb and Taiz provinces, the populous southern third of the YAR, from the rest of the country.

The heavy fighting ended abruptly in early March, largely as the result of the mediation and pressure of the Arab League and certain of its members, particularly Kuwait, Iraq, and Syria. Their concern was with ending a conflict that threatened to divide the Arab world at a time when unity was required to meet the challenge of events after Camp David and in Afghanistan and Iran. A ceasefire was arranged and took hold with surprising ease in mid-March. On 28 March, the heads of state of the YAR and the PDRY held a summit meeting under Kuwaiti auspices in Kuwait, and, for the second time in seven years, the two Yemens agreed to end a border fight by agreeing to unify. Under this latest accord, a reaffirmation of the unification agreement of 1972, major steps toward complete political unification were to begin after four months.

The border fight and the unification agreement, coming hard on the heels of the October coup attempt, served to strip President Salih of much of what little support and credibility he had managed to garner since he assumed power only months before in mid-1978. At best, the post-Hamdi regime, headed in succession by presidents al-Ghashmi and Salih, had elicited a negative kind of support among politically aware Yemenis. These Yemenis had vivid memories of the long civil war and the privation that had accompanied it in the 1960s, and many chose not to oppose the regime only out of a deep fear that any attempt to seek an alternative to it could easily lead to a political struggle that would threaten the unprecedented prosperity that Yemen had enjoyed over the previous few years; they were prepared to tolerate the regime, however repugnant, if that were what was required to insure the flow of worker remittances, Yemeni investment capital, and external development aid. The events of early 1979, however, challenged this rationale for acquiescence and led many Yemenis to conclude that political change was required precisely for the sake of continued prosperity. They were appalled by the way in which the regime had provoked or allowed itself to be drawn into what became a runaway fight with the PDRY and the NDF; they believed that President Salih had been outwitted by Abd al-Fattah Ismail at the Reconciliation Summit in Kuwait and that the unification agreement, when it inevitably broke down, would be used to justify new acts of aggression against the YAR. By April 1979, as a result of declining civilian support, the base of the Salih regime had shrunk to little more than the military, a military that was divided, depleted, and discredited by both the corrosive effects of the al-Hamdi assassination and the dismal showing in the border fight. Many civilian leaders who earlier had said that they were helpless because matters were in the hands of the military were now asking, "What military?" Talk was openly of political change, for the first time in nearly eighteen months.

The coup attempt and the border fight were indications of a more fundamental problem that worked to weaken the Salih regime. From the outset, it was plagued by questions of legitimacy, and these questions focused on the worthiness of the man, Ali Abdullah Salih, and on the constitutional status of the regime itself. Many Yemenis believed that President Salih had had a hand—quite literally, some maintained—in the overthrow of the popular al-Hamdi. Moreover, because many assumed that al-Hamdi had been eliminated on behalf of the tribal shaykhs and Saudi Arabia, President Salih also stood accused of being an ally if not a stooge of the tribalists and the Saudis. Young Yemenis, particularly those educated abroad, found him unacceptable on most counts, and he was dismissed with contempt by many of the older civilian and military politicians as a "mere soldier," and a tribal one at that. Many of them derided him as a half-literate, raw, and inexperienced young man, a cause for national worry and embarrassment. Jokes were made about his ragged reading of speeches, and rumors circulated about the bad first impressions he had made on the monarchs of Saudi Arabia and Jordan. Some were shocked by the ineptitude by which he had allowed the YAR to become isolated from the Arab mainstream during the Baghdad Summit called to respond to Egypt's peace talks with Israel, and— as mentioned—some thought that he had committed a serious blunder in fighting and then agreeing to unification with the PDRY.

The inclination to think the worst was easy because most civilian politicians knew so little about this thirty-five-year-old junior officer. A member of the minor Sanhan tribe in the Hashid confederation, Ali Abdullah Salih had been a tribal irregular in the imam's army who then joined the republicans and the regular army during the civil war. The young Salih came under the patronage of Chief of Staff al-Ghashmi in the mid-1970s, and the latter persuaded al-Hamdi to appoint him military governor of Taiz province, the post he held until succeeding al-Ghashmi as president in 1978.

The widespread belief that the institutions and practices of the regime headed by al-Ghashmi and Salih were not morally right and proper is a burden it has shared with the al-Hamdi regime. There is rather broad agreement among Yemeni leaders—among some tribalists as well as modernists and urban conservatives—that legitimacy in republican Yemen inheres in the constitutional system put in place by President Abd al-Rahman al-Iryani at the beginning of the 1970s. It is this system, and not the traditional Zaydi imamate or the "revolutionary" Arab socialist al-Sallal regime, that is the standard against which subsequent regimes have been judged wanting by many. For their part, the tribalists valued the 1970 Constitution because it had incorporated them into the state for the first time; their domination of its quasi legislature, the Consultative Council, had allowed them to enrich themselves and to protect tribal interests. Although most modernists had been critical of the 1970 Constitution when it was in force, many of them had second thoughts during the years after President al-Hamdi suspended the constitution and replaced its executive and legislative organs with the Command Council. The subsequent atrophy of that body resulted in an institutional vacuum that al-Hamdi failed to fill before his demise. Al-Ghashmi, although he promised elections and talked at times as if the constitution were in effect, did not formally reinstate the 1970 Constitution or its major institutions. Instead, he created a new presidency and the People's Constituent Assembly, all the time emphasizing their transitional status. President Salih inherited this rickety extraconstitutional framework. Given his background and alleged path to power, the regime he headed was particularly vulnerable to being labeled a mere military dictatorship.

Attempts to Stem and Turn the Political Tide: 1979–1981

Political events appeared out of control during President Salih's first year. Enjoying little support and beset by mortal challenges, the Salih regime seemed to be relying on improvisation and failed to project to outsiders a sense of political will and direction. Nevertheless, despite drift and confusion, real as well as apparent, the regime made and began to act in terms of a major choice on broad strategy for domestic and external politics in the second half of 1979. The choice made was not one thought likely by most observers during the months surrounding the border fight. It was widely assumed at this time that the changing political equation would inexorably push the vulnerable President Salih into a relationship of even greater dependence on Saudi Arabia and the major tribes of Yemen. To many, this seemed the surest path to survival at a time when mere survival was an issue—indeed, perhaps *the* issue. Instead, and at the risk of straining relations with the Saudis and the leading tribalists, President Salih chose to seek a political solution to the NDF rebellion and a normalization of relations with the PDRY. If the effort failed—a real possibility—then chances were good that the result would be the worst-case situation of renewed conflict with the NDF and the PDRY, on the one hand, and strained relations with the Saudis and the tribalists, on the other. What made this grim prospect more likely was the unwillingness of the Salih regime to offer concessionary terms in its effort to resolve the substantial differences it had with the NDF and the PDRY. To do so would have cost the regime much of what little support it still received from the political middle in the YAR and would have produced an outright break—not just a strain—in relations with Saudi Arabia and the tribes. In short, political prudence required that the regime drive a hard bargain with those to its left.

President Salih was prepared to take the risks involved in pursuit of an understanding with the NDF and the PDRY in part because of mounting pressure in the Arab world in 1979 for solidarity in the wake of the recent Egyptian-Israeli peace treaty. The Arab states that had provided good offices to end the border fight, especially Kuwait and Iraq, expected and urged the YAR to make a sincere effort to resolve its differences with its Yemeni brothers. As these states provided the YAR with considerable development aid, their wishes could not be ignored with impunity.

Pressure from other Arab states, however, was not the main reason. Though a tribalist, President Salih came from a minor tribe and did not identify with the most powerful tribal shaykhs. Moreover, he and his closest advisers were statists and nationalists of various sorts. For them, survival at the price of moving deeper into the embrace of the major tribalists and the Saudis was an anathema because it would have turned the clock back to the early 1970s when these same tribalists severely constrained the state and Saudi Arabia treated the YAR as a virtual dependency. Revulsion at the prospect of Yemen's future held hostage in this manner was strong within the regime, particularly within the officers' corps upon which President

Salih depended most immediately for support and among the other republican nationalists—businessmen, modernists, and youths as well as some urban conservatives—who were its potential supporters.

Moreover, a small number of modernists viewed an effort to resolve differences with the NDF more positively as a means to correct a serious imbalance in republican Yemen. The NDF traced its roots back to the Yemeni left of the 1960s, to the parties expelled from the body politic in the intrarepublican fight after the siege of Sanaa in 1968. This expulsion had produced a Yemeni republic in the 1970s that was weighted strongly toward the interests of the leading tribalists and many of the urban traditionalists. In 1975, President al-Hamdi had attempted to redress the balance by purging these tribalists. As it did not involve the reincorporation of the left, however, this change had shifted the regime's center of gravity toward the modern sector at the cost of greatly narrowing its base of support. In 1979, farsighted Yemenis realized that the tribalists had to be accommodated, but felt that this could be done safely only if some of the elements represented by the NDF were also readmitted to the body politic, an addition that would both broaden the regime's base and strengthen its statist orientation.

The NDF Rebellion and the YAR's External Relations

The decision of the Salih regime to seek survival through a resolution of the PDRY-backed NDF rebellion thrust external relations to the forefront. Indeed, these relations provided much of the environment within which domestic politics were played out during the early 1980s.

The PDRY and the NDF Rebellion. Official statements, especially those emanating from Sanaa, shed little light on the long minuet danced by the two Yemeni regimes and the NDF during the three years after the border fight in early 1979. As the YAR never officially acknowledged its existence, much less negotiating with it, the NDF did not appear in the cast of characters in YAR statements except under the guise of vague references to "dissidents" and "subversives." Statements on relations with the PDRY took their cue from the March 1979 Reconciliation Summit and masqueraded under the theme of the unification of the "two parts" of Yemen. In fact, however, unification was not regarded by either side as an immediate issue. What was of concern to both of them was the normalization of relations and the avoidance of another round of serious conflict. What made these more modest goals difficult to attain was PDRY support for the NDF's opposition to the Salih regime. Put simply, the YAR wanted the PDRY to end unconditionally its political and military support of the NDF, and the PDRY wanted the regime in Sanaa to reincorporate the NDF into a more progressive—that is, antitribal, anti-Saudi, anti-imperialist—YAR. Caught uneasily between the two regimes, the NDF wanted to be reincorporated into the YAR on generous terms and, to this end, wanted continued PDRY support and protection. Complicating matters further were differences in ideology and interest that made the NDF very heterogeneous and not inclusive of all the North Yemeni dissident groups. In the spring of 1979, five of the six parties that had originally founded the NDF united to form the Yemeni People's Unity Party. The new party, avowedly Marxist, remained in the NDF, along with part of the non-Marxist 13 June Movement; a number of independents; and the Septembrist Grouping, a faction of army officers with roots in the 1962 Revolution. The Yemeni branch of the Iraqi Baath, the sixth NDF founder, pulled out of the NDF, as did part of the 13 June Movement.

The policies and actions of the YAR and the PDRY toward each other and toward the NDF shifted suddenly on several occasions during these three years, leading many to judge either or both parties as capricious if not mendacious or malevolent. In fact, however, these shifts were largely the result of the strong and direct impact of domestic politics on these policies and actions in each of the two Yemens. Indeed, dealings among the two Yemens and the NDF were very salient and sensitive issues in the domestic politics of both Yemens. In the PDRY, stands taken on the NDF and the YAR served as a litmus test by which revolutionaries were grouped and graded; in the YAR, political alignments and assessments of the Salih regime were based largely on the issue of the NDF and the PDRY. Furthermore, in each of the Yemens, the domestic opponents of a negotiated settlement of differences had formidable external support. The Saudis strongly backed the tribalists and other conservatives in their insistence that President Salih deal sternly with the NDF and the PDRY, and support for the pro-NDF faction in the PDRY regime came from Libya, Syria, and probably the Soviet Union and some of its allies. As a consequence, every understanding or agreement between the two Yemens designed to resolve the NDF rebellion on the basis of compromise immediately generated strong pressures on both regimes to repudiate it or to violate its letter or spirit. This made it extremely difficult for the leaders of both regimes to keep their promises and to follow through on a policy of moderation, whatever their inclinations or intentions.

The tight linkage between domestic and external politics was evident within months of the March 1979 Reconciliation Summit. The several joint YAR-PDRY committees, created under the first Yemeni unification agreement in 1972 and allowed to fall into disuse after al-Hamdi's assassination, were quickly resurrected and held meetings between the late spring and early summer. The special envoys of the two heads of state met or exchanged messages several times during these months. Although the heads of state did not meet in May as stipulated in the summit agreement, the YAR foreign minister did go to Aden for talks in early August. On a related front, President Salih quietly initiated talks with NDF representatives in Sanaa in June, and rumors ciruclating in July suggested that certain politicians on the fringes of the NDF—for example, Yahya Muslih, a colleague of al-Hamdi—had already made peace with the regime and that a settlement was imminent under which key elements of the NDF would be reincorporated into the YAR.

Instead, August and September were marked by a pause in contacts between the YAR and both the NDF and the PDRY, a pause parallelled in each Yemen by domestic political problems that largely turned on inter-Yemeni affairs. On August 9, a major cabinet reshuffle occurred in Aden, precipitated by policy differences between the head of state, Chairman Abd al-Fattah Ismail, and Prime Minister Ali Nasir Muhammad. Four ministers, including the foreign minister, were dismissed. At issue in the dispute was, euphemistically, "the path to unity" with the YAR, with Chairman Ismail favoring all means, including armed struggle, and Prime Minister Muhammad favoring a peaceful path. For its part, the regime in Sanaa had to deal with equally acute political problems. A plot against President Salih was uncovered in late June, and the several high-ranking army officers involved in the plot allegedly had Saudi connections and were motivated by their opposition to rapprochement with the PDRY and the NDF. Late in the summer, the major tribalists and other conservatives who since the March 1979 Reconciliation Summit had been sounding alarms over unification proceeded with their announced plans to form an "Islamic Front" to oppose the NDF and its "communist" allies in the PDRY. It was presumed at the time that they had the moral and material support of Saudi Arabia, a presumption that later provied to be true.

Contacts between the two Yemens picked up with the visit of Prime Minister Ali Nasir Muhammad to Sanaa in early October. The increased tempo of meetings, joint statements, and minor agreements peaked in January 1980 and then, except for a brief period in March, dropped off sharply from late January until late April. The hiatus in contacts in the spring of 1980 was directly related to an intensification of the political struggle in Aden, a struggle that resulted in the bloodless overthrow of Chairman Abd al-Fattah Ismail by Prime Minister Ali Nasir Muhammad on 21 April. The hiatus in inter-Yemeni contacts was also related to the stalemate of discussions between the Salih regime and the NDF. Talks between the two parties had resumed in late 1979 and the leader of the NDF, Sultan Ahmad Umar, had come to Sanaa for meetings in January 1980. By the end of that month, rumors were again circulating that an accord and a change in the YAR government were imminent, and Sultan Ahmad Umar announced in February from Aden that he and President Salih had signed an agreement resolving major differences on 31 January. This claim was belied by the complete silence of the YAR government on this matter over the subsequent months.

The leadership change in Aden in April 1980 ushered in several months of intensive inter-Yemeni diplomacy, much of it focused on the problem of the NDF. Most observers thought that the reputed moderation and pragmatism of the PDRY's new head of state, Chairman Ali Nasir Muhammad, and the widespread desire for peace in Aden that his takeover seemed to reflect probably meant a decline in PDRY support for the NDF. Although cloaked in the usual euphemisms, statements by President Salih and his unity adviser suggested that the regime in Sanaa anticipated or at least hoped for such a development. On 3 May, the YAR prime minister, Abd al-Aziz Abd al-Ghani, was warmly received when he arrived for talks in Aden, the city where he had lived as a schoolboy and later as a teacher.

An economics accord was signed, and the joint statement that followed this visit stressed economic cooperation rather than the more unlikely goal of political unification. The PDRY's minister of defense was in the YAR in May, and Chairman Muhammad arrived in Sanaa on 9 June for several days of discussions. Agreements were concluded to create three joint Yemeni companies for overland transport, sea transport, and tourism. More important, the two heads of state reached a secret agreement under which each regime pledged not to support military, political, or propaganda activity directed against the other regime, an agreement which, if implemented, had obvious implications for the future of the NDF.[1] The PDRY's chief of staff visited Sanaa in July and the minister of defense was there in August. Chairman Muhammad was in the YAR twice in September, first for talks and then for the celebration of Revolution Day. In late November, the YAR's vice president, Abd al-Karim al-Arishi, paid an official visit to Aden on the occasion of Independence Day.

Confusion over what, if any, agreement had been reached in January 1980 did not prevent talks between the Salih regime and the NDF from continuing intermittently through the summer of that year. Sultan Ahmad Umar and his NDF colleague, Yahya al-Shami, were in Sanaa in March and May, as were other NDF representatives in August, and the NDF was referring months later to a "May agreement" and an "August agreement." On balance, however, the improved relations between the two Yemens in the months after the accession of Chairman Muhammad were parallelled by increasing conflict between the YAR and the NDF. At the end of April, only days after the leadership change in Aden, the NDF accused the Salih regime of retreating from "the principles of national unity" on which it claimed both sides had agreed in January. The accusations continued, and in late summer it blamed the regime for "terminating the dialogue." The government in Sanaa acknowledged neither these charges nor the alleged agreements of May and August.

More serious than the NDF's verbal attacks on the Salih regime was the sporadic fighting that started in May and continued through the summer of 1980. The clashes involved NDF insurgents and both YAR uniformed forces and tribal irregulars fighting under the banner of the year-old Islamic Front. Most of the engagements occurred where NDF elements had long had a presence, in Yemen's rugged "middle region," especially the southeastern border area east of the town of Ibb. Many observers attributed the increased fighting in large part to the improved relations between the PDRY and the YAR. Fearful that Chairman Muhammad would limit its freedom of action, a fear heightened by the June 1980 agreement between the two heads of state, the NDF had moved most of its fighters over the border into the YAR, thereby increasing the chance of clashes with YAR forces. For its part, the YAR was more inclined to engage NDF units near the border because of a growing belief that PDRY forces would not intervene to protect those units.

The fighting increased in frequency and severity in the last quarter of 1980, largely because the Salih regime had come to the conclusion that fruitful discussions could not take place until the military balance was tilted more clearly in its favor. The clashes took place in the fall in a tribal region northeast of Sanaa as well as in the usual NDF strongholds in the southeast. Using well-equipped regular forces and the tribal irregulars of the Islamic Front, the regime escalated the conflict by launching a major offensive against NDF positions in the border area over a three-week period in December. Under heavy pressure, most of the rebel fighters retreated across the border into the PDRY. In January 1981, NDF leader Yahya al-Shami declared that all negotiations with the YAR had been suspended. He asserted that the regime in Sanaa had turned from dialogue to all-out fighting, and that given the scale of the fighting, President Salih must be responsible for this turn of events.[2]

Although subsiding after the December offensive, the fighting continued fitfully through the early spring of 1981. Better equipped than in the past, the guerrillas proved increasingly able to stand their ground against the YAR's regular and irregular forces. Moreover, during the last months of 1980, they had established a presence in the remote and heavily populated highlands deep inside the Sanaa-Taiz-Hudayda triangle, far to the northwest of the southeastern border. The NDF increased its presence in this new area in early 1981 and reports had it starting to set up rudimentary services and administration. Despite claims that the strength of the rebels was being exaggerated, the government admitted in private that the rebellion was straining its resources and that the situation had deteriorated in the spring. Observers were beginning to take the rebellion more seriously and to refer to it as a war of attrition.

The Salih regime adopted a more aggressive posture in the early summer of 1981 when it concentrated military forces close to the areas controlled by the NDF. Major sweeps of the southeastern border area were carried out by the army in July and September, and another month of heavy combat extended from late October to late November. Although the fighting during these months was intermittent, many of the battles were fierce and the casualties, among civilians as well as combatants, were high. No high-level political discussions between the Salih regime and the NDF took place over most of 1981, and the NDF claimed that the regime had refused to meet and that it had broken ceasefires arranged by third parties in July and August.[3] Although the regime did not reply in public to these charges, it said in private that the NDF had raised its political demands so unrealistically as to make negotiations fruitless.

The protracted and sometimes heavy fighting, beginning with the YAR's campaign in December 1980, had a severely chilling effect on relations between the two Yemens during the first two-thirds of 1981. Although the two heads of state met under Syrian auspices at the Islamic Summit in Mecca in January, contacts thereafter were infrequent and at a low level. The recurrent fighting and the breakdown of talks between the YAR and the NDF had strengthened the hand of the militant, pro-NDF faction in the PDRY regime, and Salih Muslih Qasim, a strong backer of the NDF, was appointed minister of defense in early 1981. Pressure from this militant faction probably contributed to the absence of any new initiatives by Chairman Muhammad. For its part, the regime in Sanaa showed little interest in efforts to improve relations with the PDRY so long as the latter failed to reduce drastically its political and military support of the NDF.

In a marked turnabout, the heads of state of the two Yemens held three summit meetings during the last third of 1981. This development was the result of a growing realization in both regimes that relations had eroded seriously and that the escalating fighting between the YAR and the NDF threatened to bring the armed forces of the two Yemens into direct conflict. In addition, the regional situation was creating renewed pressure for Arab solidarity at a time when both Yemens needed new regional development aid. Chairman Muhammad travelled to the YAR in September, and during their discussions the two heads of state reaffirmed the agreement of June 1980 under which each regime pledged not to support military, political, or propaganda activity directed against the other regime. Upon returning to Aden, however, Chairman Muhammad was unable to persuade his political colleagues in the PDRY to endorse his acceptance of President Salih's uncompromising terms on the NDF. Fighting between the forces of the YAR and the NDF again intensified shortly after the failure of this latest diplomatic initiative.

The second summit occurred in Kuwait under the sponsorship of the Emir of Kuwait on 23 November 1981, on the eve of the Fez Arab Summit. The talks, which included leaders of the NDF, resulted in a new ceasefire agreement. Then, a week later, just after the Fez Arab Summit, President Salih became the first YAR president to travel to Aden. During this visit, on 2 December, the two heads of state concluded a broad economic and political cooperation agreement. The accord provided for the creation of the Supreme Yemeni Council, consisting of the two heads of state and charged with carrying out unification, and for the creation of a ministerial committee and a secretariat to execute joint projects and initiatives. The agreement also called for joint defense coordination, free passage of people and goods over the borders, and demilitarization of the border areas. Most important, the agreement again reaffirmed the June 1980 pledge by each regime not to support dissidents against the other regime.[4]

The Saudi Connection Strained and Other Relations Reordered. Many observers in late 1978 and early 1979 thought that President Salih's background and connections made him a natural ally of Saudi Arabia. Moreover, the coup attempt in October 1978 and the border fight in February–March 1979 convinced many that the vulnerable Salih, if he were to survive, had no place to go other than deeper into the arms of the Saudis. By the spring of 1979, American officials in Sanaa thought President Salih's survival unlikely. Nevertheless, they took solace in the belief that the border fight and the recently accelerated Saudi-funded transfer of U.S. arms, including F-5E fighters and heavy tanks, would cement Yemeni-Saudi ties and lead to the expulsion of Soviet military advisers from the YAR, a goal long sought by the United States and its Saudi ally. Moreover, there was Abdullah al-Asnaj—longtime adviser to Yemeni presidents, close friend of the Saudis, and bitter enemy of the Marxist rulers of his native Aden—still serving an inexperienced President Salih as foreign minister. Muhammad Khamis, another Yemeni with strong Saudi ties, remained head of the powerful and feared Central Organization of National Security, a post he had held under three presidents since 1975.

This scenario of a closer-than-ever patron-client relationship between the YAR and Saudi Arabia was belied by events almost as quickly as it was propounded. Foreign Minister al-Asnaj was excluded from the reshuffled cabinet in late March 1979; Muhammad Khamis' appointment as minister of the interior in the reshuffle caused many to wonder—rightly, it turned out—whether he was really being eased out of his position of power at national security. However, the bold and surprising stroke that decisively contradicted this scenario was the conclusion of a major arms deal between the YAR and the Soviet Union in the late summer of 1979. The new arms, said to be worth $600 million and to include MIG-21 planes and heavy tanks, began to arrive by ship in September. Instead of leaving the YAR, the Soviet military advisers there were soon joined by others.

The YAR's sudden turn to the Soviet Union for new arms constituted a Yemeni assertion of partial independence from Saudi Arabia and was the direct result of the Saudi's insensitive handling of both the transfer of U.S. arms and the diplomatic situation after the border fight and the unification agreement. The new $300 million triangular YAR-Saudi-U.S. arms deal, long in the making and accelerated with great show by the Carter administration during the border fight, did not result in the political gains that arms transfers are supposed to yield. The Saudis, who insisted on controlling the arms they had paid for, tried to make the piecemeal transfer of those arms as well as a positive reply to a YAR request for supplementary arms conditional on the YAR taking a more militant stance toward the NDF and the PDRY. They tried to impose this condition at the very time that the Salih regime decided to seek a resolution of differences with its fellow Yemenis. The Saudis' heavy-handed dealings with the YAR during this crisis period were almost as damaging and humiliating to President Salih as the army's poor showing in the border fight. Under strong domestic political pressure, President Salih needed to shore up his position quickly with the military and with other nationalistic elements in the country. The surest way to do this was to stand up to the Saudis by turning to the Soviet Union for arms, even if this cost him the support of some tribal leaders and conservatives.

The Soviet arms deal of 1979 ushered in two years of cool and sometimes strained relations between the YAR and Saudi Arabia. Given the former's great dependence on the latter for financial aid, the extent to which the YAR downgraded, neglected, and took risks with its Saudi connection during this period is quite remarkable. Relations deteriorated, and trust and understanding broke down. The Saudis remained very fearful that the Salih regime might choose or be forced to move to the left in its ongoing negotiations with the PDRY and the NDF. Many Yemenis were angered by Saudi Arabia's deep involvement in the tribally-based Islamic Front, regarding it as another instance of Saudi meddling in Yemeni affairs, and by Saudi Arabia's indifference toward the rampant smuggling across their common border in the north and northeast of the YAR. Saudi Arabia was rumored to have threatened to suspend—or to have actually delayed— budget support for the YAR, and border clashes between Yemeni and Saudi forces were also rumored.

This strain in relations was never admitted publicly and was rarely evident on the surface. From the outset, the YAR made a real effort to play down any political significance in its turn to the Soviet Union for arms, insisting that this move—like the earlier turn to the United States—was merely part of a continuing policy of "diversification of sources of arms." Nevertheless, the Salih regime felt compelled by November 1979 to publicly deny the existence of any problems with Saudi Arabia, and both parties felt the need repeatedly to issue similar denials throughout the first quarter of 1980. Despite the denials, there persisted rumors of various differences and grievances throughout these months. Without naming the Saudis, the YAR also issued statements asserting that it was not "in the pocket of any Arab state" and criticizing rich Arab countries that try to buy and subvert the poor Arab countries.[5] The strain did not lead to a rupture, however, and Saudi Arabia agreed during meetings in the spring to the usual high levels of development aid and budget subsidies for the YAR in fiscal 1980/1981. Except for President Salih's visit to Saudi Arabia in August, high-level contacts between the two neighbors dropped off in the late spring, but so did the rumors and denials of problems, and this situation prevailed for the rest of 1980.

The same pattern of relations was repeated in 1981. Rumors and denials of serious problems, among them border clashes and a cutoff or delay of funds to the YAR, circulated in the early months of the year. Prominent Yemenis complained openly and bitterly about the failure of the Saudis to curtail the smuggling that was cutting government revenues and hurting legitimate importers. The most sensational occurrence was the arrest in March of ex-Foreign Minister al-Asnaj on charges of treason based on his private contacts with an unnamed "Arab country," understood to be Saudi Arabia. This dramatic event came a month after the unsolved murder of Muhammad Khamis, the former head of national security. Nevertheless, a flurry of high-level meetings in April resulted in Saudi Arabia again confirming its annual aid and subsidies to the YAR. As in the previous year, rumors and contacts both fell off late in the spring.

Beyond its effect on the Saudi connection, the diplomacy surrounding the cessation of the border fight in 1979 served to increase and to shift the focus of the YAR's regional relations. The passivity if not paralysis of the Saudis during this crisis allowed other Arab states, most notably Iraq and Kuwait, to take leading roles in seeking an "Arab solution" to conflict between the two Yemens. The formerly hostile regime in Baghdad took a friendly interest in the YAR, and this was expressed most clearly in its agreement in 1979 to finance development activities for $300 million over the next five years. Some Yemenis hoped that Iraq would replace Saudi Arabia as the YAR's chief benefactor, an unlikelihood soon rendered impossible by the costs of Iraq's long war with Iran and OPEC's oil price and production crisis. Nevertheless, Iraq did assume second place among the YAR's Arab donors in 1979. With the growing regional polarization in the early 1980s, the YAR's strong ties with Iraq led to a cooling of relations between the YAR and Iraq's regional enemies, particularly Syria, Libya, and Iran. In an effort to avoid having to take sides, especially between alternative sources of development aid, the YAR spoke frequently of its commitment to common Arab positions and its opposition to Arab blocs and regional alliances involving the great powers.

Alarmist statements by Saudi Arabia and the Carter administration notwithstanding, the southwest corner of the Arabian Peninsula did not become a new battlefield in the global struggle between the United States and the Soviet Union. Nevertheless, the position and prestige of the great powers in the YAR did change somewhat with the events of 1979. The Salih regime had not appreciated the transparent use of the Yemeni border fight by the Carter administration to demonstrate to both the Saudis and domestic American critics its decisiveness by accelerating the arms transfer amid much publicity. Nor had the regime been pleased by the United States' persistent deferring to the Saudis on Yemeni affairs and its refusal to deal with the YAR on an unmediated state-to-state basis, a pattern made crystal clear at the time of the arms transfer and the YAR's request for supplemental arms. As a consequence, relations between the United States and the YAR soured in mid-1979 and thereafter were at best only proper. Throughout the early 1980s, the United States was criticized in the YAR for its subordination of Yemeni interests to those of the Saudis, its strong support of Israel, and the quality as well as the quantity of its military and economic aid programs. These criticisms were not stronger probably because Yemenis gradually lowered their high expectations with regard to the United States.

After the 1979 arms deal, which clearly reaffirmed the Soviet military presence, relations between the YAR and the Soviet Union improved steadily but undramatically. The Soviets appreciated both the restraint in the YAR's criticism of their intervention in Afghanistan and the YAR's decision not to push for inclusion in the new Saudi-sponsored Gulf Cooperation Council; in response, they extended a modest amount of new development aid and probably urged restraint upon the PDRY and the NDF. Relations reached a high point with the visit of President Salih to Moscow in October 1981 and with the Soviet Union's rather reluctant agreement to permit the YAR to defer repayment of loans made for the purchase of Soviet arms. Nevertheless, closer ties between the YAR and the Soviet Union were compromised by the latter's already very close links with the PDRY and the hostility between the two Yemens.

Domestic Politics: Shoring Up the Center and Extending Support

The most pressing concern of the Salih regime during its first year was the shoring up of its shaky political position in those areas of the country under its control, although this concern was soon eclipsed by the NDF rebellion. The ability of the regime to defy predictions and survive the spring of 1979 was partly a matter of good fortune. President Salih had been lucky to survive the coup attempt in October 1978; having failed, that attempt served him well by flushing out many previously hidden foes. The regime survived the border fight partly because the PDRY and the NDF were not prepared to take advantage of their quick and easy victory and partly because Arab mediators intervened so rapidly and vigorously. Even the hasty agreement in March 1979 to unite with the PDRY, thought then by many to be a grave mistake, served to confuse politics in the YAR; indeed, much of the new talk about imminent political change was abruptly cut short or deflected by the air of unreality introduced by the unification agreement. Finally, many of the disaffected YAR leaders who had become convinced of the need for change were, upon reflection, sobered by the coup attempt and by the border fight. They put aside their brave talk and resumed a wait-and-see attitude by mid-1979, either (or both) because they saw no obvious alternative to President Salih or because they feared that the attendant turmoil and strife would shatter Yemen's new and fragile prosperity.

Although good fortune was a factor, the regime survived 1979 largely because President Salih kept his nerve and used the prevailing confusion and uncertainty to play for time. Although those who led the coup attempt were dealt with mercilessly, he did not resort generally to harsh and repressive methods to root out and eliminate opponents. Nor did he make a transparent bid for instant popularity through a campaign of self-promotion or announcements of grandiose schemes. At the same time, moreover, President Salih did take modest first steps to build support during the months after the coup attempt. Most of these initial steps were ad hoc acts that seemed hastily conceived and thought through only partially; many of them had little or no lasting effect. Nevertheless, the Salih regime did build upon some of these initiatives in a systematic way and with results that were to prove cumulative in the 1980s.

One of the regime's first political initiatives began in late 1978, shortly after the coup attempt, and turned on the elections for the local development associations and the convention of the Confederation of Yemeni Development Associations, the umbrella organization of the LDA movement. The regime publicized these events highly and made a concerted effort to identify President Salih with development in general and the LDA movement in particular. This effort struck some as strange both because the name of the slain al-Hamdi was so closely associated with the LDAs and because President Salih's career provided scant evidence of concern for development. Perhaps for these reasons, and certainly because the border fight was soon to preempt the attention of most Yemenis, this early public relations exercise did little to enhance President Salih's standing.

A major reshuffle of the Abd al-Ghani cabinet was carried out in March 1979, in the wake of the border fight. Several of the changes were clearly made to strengthen and broaden support for the regime among important leaders and groups. The most significant appointment was that of Shaykh Mujahid abu Shuwarib, the protégé of Paramount Shaykh Abdullah ibn Husayn al-Ahmar, as deputy prime minister for internal affairs. Shaykh Mujahid's appointment was the first of a leading tribal figure since President al-Hamdi had expelled him and the other tribalists from the state in 1975, and many saw it as a big step toward the long-predicted reconciliation with the major tribes and the reincorporation of their leaders into the regime. The appointment of two highly regarded technocrats, Dr. Abd al-Karim al-Iryani and Ahmad Ali al-Muhani, was clearly designed to restore the confidence of modernists and nervous businessmen and bankers, although this partially misfired when Dr. al-Iryani declined to rejoin the cabinet from which he had been excluded a year earlier. Another important change in the makeup of the cabinet was the exclusion of Foreign Minister al-Asnaj and his longtime colleague, Muhammad Salim Basindwa, a move welcomed by those who held these two refugees from Aden to be either or both political outsiders and the officials most responsible for stirring up the trouble that propelled the YAR into the border fight. Finally, although the significance of the appointment of Muhammad Khamis as interior minister was unclear at the time, there was much speculation as to whether it marked the end of his control of the Central Organization for National Security.

The cabinet reshuffle was closely followed by a major shakeup in the military command. The shakeup was the second in six months—the first having come in the wake of the October coup attempt—and was a direct consequence of the poor performance of the army during the border fight. A third shakeup occurred in June 1979 and involved the dismissal of several high-ranking officers, this time amid rumors of a plot against the regime. Throughout this period, President Salih paid close attention to the loyalties and interests of the officers' corps. Seeking both to strengthen the weakened armed forces and to increase his support within the corps, he introduced military conscription and, more important, concluded the large arms deal with the Soviet Union in the fall of 1979. Staffing remained a continuing concern, and by mid-1980 observers were noting the number of relatives and other members of the Sanhan tribe that President Salih had placed in key positions in the uniformed services. In addition, some of the military politicians who had played leading roles in the republic prior to the al-Hamdi era—those identified as the Septembrists because of their role in the 1962 Revolution—were rehabilitated and appointed to high posts.

Another set of actions designed to build support and legitimacy was taken in May 1979 and pertained to the consultative organs of the state. President Salih signed a decree amending the laws governing the People's

Constituent Assembly, the appointed, quasi-legislative body created a year earlier by President al-Ghashmi. The major changes increased the nominal powers of the PCA and increased its size from 99 to 159 members. On the same day, President Salih created the fifteen member Advisory Council to the President. Among the notables appointed to this body were two who had been conspicuously absent from the government since early in the al-Hamdi era, Paramount Shaykh Abdullah ibn Husayn al-Ahmar and Dr. Hasan Makki. Together, the creation of the Advisory Council and the enlargement of the PCA provided President Salih with new positions that he could use as rewards in his effort to co-opt into the regime a broader array of politicians and notables. Finally, President Salih took the occasion of the announcement of these changes to declare that "free, direct, and public elections" for a permanent legislature to replace the PCA would be held in February 1980.

The Salih regime took other political initiatives, including a stream of prominent appointments, during the second half of 1979. The promised legislative elections figured prominently in government statements over these months, and they seemed to move closer to fruition when, in July, a special committee for their preparation was set up with much publicity. By far, the most daring political move began in June when President Salih initiated protracted talks with the NDF. Although the government dismissed recurrent rumors that its expansion to include NDF ministers was imminent, it did assert that members of unspecified "opposition groups" would be allowed to take part as individuals in the upcoming elections.

The negotiations with the NDF did not result in a political accord and the elections promised for February 1980 were not held. President Salih had to announce early in the year that more preparation and improved security were needed before the again-promised elections could be held.[6] As the regime could not risk elections that an untamed NDF might discredit or disrupt, the failure of the two parties to reach agreement had made the postponement inevitable. The promise of elections on a specific date in the very near future had been a serious miscalculation, a tactical error, on the part of President Salih. The promise made sense only if he thought that the NDF would be won over or neutralized before the elections were held, and he probably did begin talks under the mistaken belief that this could be achieved. If so, this bid for a quick political fix failed, and the need to postpone the promised elections was a setback and an embarrassment for the Salih regime. Many viewed it as confirmation that the creation of the Advisory Council, the enlargement of the PCA, and other actions taken in 1979 had done little to strengthen President Salih's position. At best, they said, these actions had bought him a little time and temporarily co-opted some notables. Though many regarded his ability to survive 1979 as no small feat, most regarded his prospects in early 1980 as not much better than they had been a year earlier.

In retrospect, however, it is apparent that the breakdown in talks with the NDF and the postponement of elections in early 1980 overlapped with the modest beginnings of a more elaborate, systematic, and prolonged effort both to reconstitute the political system and to increase the support and legitimacy of the Salih regime. The first public indication of this new initiative came in February when it was announced that President Salih had received the first draft of what came to be known as the National Pact. The claim made for the pact was that it laid out the values and beliefs—the ends and means—in terms of which the Islamic people of Yemen should organize and act in their effort to achieve economic and social development as well as national integration and unity. President Salih said in March that it would serve the nation as "a guide for sound and comprehensive national action."[7] Later he was to describe it as "a theory of political action."[8]

The idea of a national pact has an important place in the modern political lore of Yemen, and the pact proposed under President Salih recalled a similarly named statement of political principles framed on the eve of the ill-fated 1948 Revolution. Its origins obscure, the new proposal to formulate a national pact may have come up in the discussions held nightly by President Salih and his advisers during the month of Ramadan in August 1979. In any case, the new National Pact and, more important, the process by which it was discussed, revised, and approved were to play a central role in the ambitious effort at consensus building and political reconstitution that began in early 1980.

The next and most innovative building block in this new effort was put into place in May with the creation of the National Dialogue Committee, a body consisting of a broad array of prominent Yemenis under the chairmanship of the secretary general of the Supreme Correction Committee. In announcing its formation, President Salih charged the National Dialogue Committee (NDC) with conducting a dialogue with the various national elements over the coming months. He said that the NDC was both to use the draft National Pact as a working paper and to prepare and distribute with the draft a political questionnaire as a part of the process of dialogue; it was then to use the results of the public discussions as the basis for revising the pact. President Salih on this same occasion announced plans to convene a general people's congress for the purpose of adopting the final version of the pact. With the pact to guide all national forces, he said, it would then be possible to hold free and open elections for a new national legislature.

In proposing to hold the General People's Congress (GPC) as a prelude to legislative elections, President Salih was merely reviving a proposal first made by President al-Hamdi in 1977 and then reiterated by President al-Ghashmi in 1978. The element added in President Salih's proposal was the elaborate process by which he would move the Yemeni polity from where it was in 1980 to the actual holding of such a congress—that is, a national dialogue based on the National Pact and under the supervision of the National Dialogue Committee. This structured process provided for considerable activity, ceremony, and popular participation. More important, its several steps provided the flexibility required by a future made uncertain by the NDF rebellion. By making it protracted and open-ended, the regime gave itself the freedom to advance or retard—to highlight or neglect—the process as political circumstances might warrant. The National Dialogue Committee met frequently during the second half of 1980 and its meetings and other activities were well publicized. The president and his spokesmen frequently reminded the people that the purpose of the National Pact and the efforts of the NDC was the political unity of all Yemenis and, in thinly veiled allusions to the NDF, stressed that all who subscribed to the pact were free to participate in its revision and in the elections to be held after its adoption. In early December, the NDC announced completion of the first phase of its work and then appointed several subcommittees, directing them to carry the draft pact and the questionnaire to meetings with the people in the various parts of the country. Under the auspices of these subcommittees, local popular conferences were held at many locations over the first four months of 1981. In March, the regime's spokesman described this much-publicized process as a "plebiscite" in which the opinion of 5 percent of the total population was being canvassed.

The plebiscite completed, President Salih directed the NDC in May to make prompt use of the results to revise the pact so that the General People's Congress and the legislative elections could be held as soon as possible. This work was carried out during the remaining months of 1981, again with considerable publicity. On the occasion of 26 September Revolution Day, President Salih spelled out once more the relationship among the components of his plan for political renovation. The decree has been issued, he said, "to organize general elections . . . for a national legislative assembly. . . . The plebiscite we conducted . . . is a basic and important step toward holding these elections. We shall work to see the elections take place after the General People's Congress has been held. We have called on the congress to look into the final draft of the National Pact, in light of which democratic measures will be implemented."[9] A government decree issued in October authorized the convening of the GPC on an unspecified date in 1982 and stated that it would consist of one thousand delegates, seven hundred chosen locally by the people and three hundred appointed by the regime.

Despite the escalation in conflict with the NDF in 1981, the theme of the national dialogue remained reconcilitation and unity based on the principles of the National Pact and the 1962 Revolution. Public statements continued to allude to the day when opposition elements would choose to join the dialogue and be welcomed back into the political fold. The theme of national reconciliation was further emphasized when, on Revolution Day, President Salih invited ex-presidents Abdullah al-Sallal and Abd al-Rahman al-Iryani to return from exile. Both accepted and were welcomed back by the Salih regime in October 1981. With their return, only the NDF leaders and a handful of other politicians remained outside the system defined by the ongoing dialogue on the National Pact. To tie up one of the remaining loose ends, the regime referred increasingly to the 1970 Constitution as the legal framework within which the new legislature—the new Consultative Council—would be elected after the GPC had met and done its work.

The Government Revitalized

By 1980, the Salih regime's preoccupation with the politics of survival had resulted in a marked deterioration of the government's ability to perform even moderately well its modest role in either day-to-day socioeconomic affairs or longer-term development activities. The government was not attending to its business, and many needed decisions and actions were not being made and taken.

The perception that the government was not doing its job, coupled with growing fears about the worsening security situation, spawned a sense of foreboding within the business and foreign development communities in the YAR. Moreover, a mood of discontent and even anger gradually eroded and replaced the heady optimism and expansive thinking of the second half of the 1970s. Many Yemenis began to express disillusionment with the pace and results of development, laying blame for this on the government as well as on foreign donors, companies, and experts. Donors and companies were accused of profiting at Yemen's expense, arrogantly doing whatever they wanted to do and failing to deliver on promises. The well-paid "foreign experts" were singled out for special criticism, and were charged with being insulting, inexpert, and uninterested in Yemen's problems. Yemeni contractors complained that foreigners were crowding them out and driving them into bankruptcy, and Yemeni merchants complained that uncontrolled smuggling was wiping out their import trade. Acting on these feelings, Yemenis in increasing numbers ceased to invest new capital in Yemen. Instead, they sent or kept it abroad.

For their part, foreign donors and companies were having second thoughts about Yemen as a place to get things done and to turn a profit. Donors complained that public agencies, including the once-respected Central Planning Organization, were not making prompt decisions and facilitating project work. Consequently, some donors began to question the government's commitment to development and spoke of cutting or even ending their aid programs. Some of the foreign banks complained about punitive regulations, low deposits, and uncollectible loans, and many foreign contractors complained about labor and customs difficulties and about the failure of government clients to pay their bills on time. A few companies threatened to seek legal redress of their claims against public and private clients. By 1980, many of the companies working in the YAR were choosing not to bid on new government contracts. Several had already withdrawn from the YAR, and others, including more than one bank, were talking openly about this option.

Although the changing economic climate did not go unnoticed by the Salih regime, it was the hard figures on the growing balance-of-payments deficit and the decline in workers' remittances projected for 1979/1980 that finally brought home to the political leadership that a financial and economic crisis was imminent. Given the size of the growing deficit, it was projected that foreign exchange reserves built up over the past few years would be exhausted in another year or two. The rise in deficits and the declines in remittances were closely tied together as it was the massive inflow of remittance money that had financed the rapidly increasing import of consumer and capital goods after 1974. The significance of the declining remittances was not lost on the Salih regime: The remittances had fueled the prosperity that was the key to domestic political support and apathy.

The loss of momentum and looming shortfalls in the First Five-Year Plan also provided rather clear indications of impending trouble. By early 1980, government officials were acutely aware that the continued flow of generous amounts of external aid depended upon salvaging as much as possible of the plan during its last year and, more important, upon preparing and promoting the next plan. Again, the relationship between domestic political quietism and the prosperity sustained in part by externally supported development activities did not escape the Salih regime.

In an early move to address these problems, the Abd al-Ghani government asked the International Monetary Fund in mid-1980 for help in reviewing government spending and the payments situation for the next eighteen months. At about the same time, it began drawing funds from the Arab Monetary Fund, an organization that the YAR had only recently joined. By mid-1980, the government also had held preliminary discussions with the World Bank on the preparation of the Second Five-Year Plan.

The event that most clearly signalled the concern of the Salih regime was the unexpected appointment of Dr. Abd al-Karim al-Iryani as prime minister in October 1980. Dr. al-Iryani's appointment was well received, especially among Yemeni modernists and within the development community, and was accorded symbolic as well as practical significance. American educated and from a great qadi family, he had been a close adviser to his uncle, President Abd al-Rahman al-Iryani. Moreover, as minister of development and founding chairman of the Central Planning Organization, he had come to be regarded by many in the mid-1970s as Yemen's "Mr. Development." His reputation made easier the removal of Prime Minister Abd al-Ghani who had held that post for nearly six years. Though criticized increasingly for indecisiveness, Abd al-Aziz Abd al-Ghani was a technocrat who represented the modernists and was closely identified with development. His replacement by almost anyone other than his friend and colleague Dr. al-Iryani would have been seen by many as another sign of the regime's neglect and ignorance of development.

Nevertheless, even among the new prime minister's strongest admirers, there was skepticism as to what the political leadership would permit him to do and what he could do under existing conditions even if given a relatively free hand. Many of the skeptics judged Yemen's problems to be too intractable to yield to the efforts of any one man or group of men in government. They also pointed to the uninspired composition of the new cabinet and judged the caliber of cabinet members to be below the modest standard set in the YAR since the mid-1970s. It as alleged that the only colleague freely chosen by Dr. al-Iryani was Fuad Qaid Muhammad, the new CPO chairman and minister of development, and that the other ministers had been dictated by President Salih who felt compelled to appoint the favorites of the leaders of an ill-assorted array of groups.

During much of the first year of the al-Iryani government, the doubters could also point to the absence of dramatic accomplishments as confirmation of their initial judgements. The high politics of the struggle with the NDF and relations with the PDRY and the Saudis picked up in 1981, and the statements and actions of President Salih and other political-military leaders upstaged those of the prime minister and the technocrats in his cabinet. Rumors and reports on these weighty and dramatic matters prevailed over those on routine government operations and even development affairs.

Moreover, Prime Minister al-Iryani's early efforts were by their very nature neither dramatic nor visible. The Office of the Prime Minister, little changed since the early years of the 1962 Revolution, needed to be reorganized and restaffed in order to increase the prime minister's capacity to set policy and to monitor government activities. As a consequence, Prime Minister al-Iryani initially devoted much time to the effective operation of his office. In addition, to give himself and his staff the time needed to do their executive tasks, he tried to drastically limit access to his office and to insist that requests be taken to the proper office farther down the government hierarchy, an effort that ran against the strong "diwan mentality" in Yemeni governance. Another little-noted indication of Prime Minister al-Iryani's concern about the low capabilities of the government was the creation of the Ministry of Civil Service and Administrative Reform. Finally, high on the new prime minister's agenda was the revitalization of the CPO and its restoration to the pivotal place it had occupied in the development process in the mid-1970s. He knew better than most that the capabilities of the CPO had declined in the late 1970s and that other agencies involved in development had found ways to bypass its procedures for the selection and implementation of projects. In an effort to address these problems, the CPO was reorganized and tasks reassigned among the departments in the early months of the new government. The attempt to reassert the CPO's authority involved giving it greater financial control as the paymaster of the development process. It was thought that this would lead to the more timely payment of development bills as well as greater supervision and accountability of development activities.

Although skepticism persisted over the regime's willingness and ability to address major economic problems, the outline of the new economic management and planning team was apparent by mid-1981. At its apex was the prime minister, working closely with the new CPO chairman and with ex-prime minister Abd al-Ghani, now second vice president. Below them were able technocrats in charge of key financial institutions and at least a few of the technical ministries and special authorities. Most important, however, was the evolving relationship of trust and respect between President Salih and this core in the government. The president listened to the top technocrats and deferred to their judgement on most matters concerning development and government operations; he allowed them considerable freedom to make decisions and usually gave them the political backing required to act on those decisions. By late 1981, observers were beginning to discern a mutually beneficial relationship between the political-military leadership, headed by President Salih, and the government headed by Prime Minister al-Iryani.

President Salih had made clear what he regarded as the priority task of the new government when, on the occasion of the swearing-in ceremony in October 1980, he called for a review of progress on the First Five-Year Plan. The al-Iryani government acted promptly on this directive, the CPO assisting each ministry and authority to assess the status of projects under the plan, identify problems, and devise corrective measures where possible. This exercise was undertaken in light of the need to begin immediately on the preparation of the Second Five-Year Plan for 1982–1986. The Supreme Committee for the Second Development Plan, chaired by President Salih and consisting of Second Vice President Abd al-Ghani, the prime minister, and the heads of the major banking institutions, technical ministries, and authorities, was formed at the beginning of 1981. A thirty-member technical committee was set up shortly thereafter to assist the Supreme Committee. Work on the new plan began immediately and the tempo of activity increased sharply over the rest of 1981. A major discussion document on the targets and strategy of the new plan was available by late summer. Prime Minister al-Iryani indicated in early December that the broad outlines of the plan had been adopted by the Supreme Committee and that no major changes were expected.

From the outset, preparation of the Second Five-Year Plan was orchestrated with one eye on the international development community and potential donors. On the same day that the Supreme Committee for the Second Development Plan was formed, President Salih appointed Dr. Muhammad Said al-Attar as adviser to the president on the plan. Dr. al-Attar, the founder of the Yemen Bank for Reconstruction and Development in the mid-1960s and for several years an assistant secretary-general of the United Nations and the head of the UN's Economic Commission for Western Asia, was the Yemeni best positioned internationally to promote and to enhance the status of the YAR's new planning exercise. Throughout 1981, official announcements and statements by the president, prime minister, Dr. al-Attar, and others began to prepare the Yemeni public and the international development community for the new plan well before its first draft was completed. Indeed, the main theme leading up to and during the 26 September Revolution Day celebrations was Yemeni development and the Second Five-Year Plan. In late 1981, the government announced its intentions to promote the plan through an international development conference, one similar to that held in 1977 to launch the first plan. By this time, the government was already giving potential donors previews of those components of the plan on which interest in collaboration had been expressed.

The preparation and initial promotion of the plan were parallelled by a public relations campaign to restore the confidence and good will of the companies and development agencies already operating in the YAR. The foreign banks were assured that their needs would be given greater attention and that they would be given a major role in the financing of projects under the new plan. Leaders of the Yemeni private sector were told that they could expect to have a big say in plan activities and that government help would be available for companies wishing to invest in new industry, especially housing, building materials, and food processing. An effort was also made to resolve the backlog of disputes between foreign contractors and government clients over delayed payments, and assurances were given that new procedures would prevent such disputes in the future. Finally, both foreign donors and companies were exposed to the revived businesslike and cooperative mood at the CPO. This campaign to restore confidence and allay fears was quite successful, and, although in agreement that the past couple of years were best forgotten, many of the Yemenis and non-Yemenis involved in the YAR's development were by late 1981 reasonably optimistic about the future and willing to buy into the next stage—provided the security situation did not worsen.

9

Political Pieces Put into Place: 1982–1984

Each of the major concerns of the Salih regime reached a critical point and was handled with some success during the first eight months of 1982. The completion and promotion of the Second Five-Year Plan in late April restored the YAR's credibility with the development community and held out the promise of considerable aid. In early May, the YAR dealt the NDF a stunning military defeat and reached an accord with the PDRY and major NDF elements, ending the rebellion and doing so at little or no cost to its relations with Saudi Arabia and other countries that mattered. Finally, the Salih regime's effort at domestic political renovation was brought to its penultimate stage with the holding of the General People's Congress, leaving to the future only the promised legislative elections.

From the perspective of the mid-1980s, it may have appeared that the items on the YAR's political agenda simply came up and fell into place as if preordained. Instead, they came together when and in the way they did through foresight, orchestration, and nerve—and a bit of luck. By no means smooth and easy, the process was fitful and often required much pushing and hauling to get desired results. And the several parts of the process were contingent upon each other. The Second International Conference for Yemeni Development, aimed primarily at potential aid donors, had to be planned and announced in advance—and held on schedule. Unfortunately, in early April 1982, during the weeks between the sending of invitations and the convening of the conference, fighting between the YAR and the NDF resumed on a scale that threatened to involve the forces of the PDRY, thereby raising questions about the security situation and undermining the very purpose of the conference. The General People's Congress was not planned for sometime in mid-1982 on the happy assumption that a resolution of the NDF rebellion would precede it. This is what happened, however, and this fortuitous turn of events endowed the GPC with a national significance that it would not have otherwise had.

The NDF and the PDRY

Despite the three summit meetings and the new ceasefire in late 1981, the dynamics of inter-Yemeni affairs at the beginning of 1982 were little changed from those of the previous two years. Simply put, the NDF remained unwilling to end its rebellion on terms deemed acceptable to the Salih regime, and the PDRY remained either unwilling or unable to persuade the NDF to do so. Because of renewed polarization in the Arab world, Chairman Muhammad was being pushed hard by the militant faction of his regime and its Libyan and Syrian allies to continue active support for the NDF. Similarly, the regime in Sanaa was under increasing pressure from domestic elements and its Saudi benefactors to seek a military solution to the rebellion, pressure felt most strongly because of the need for generous Saudi funding of the Second Five-Year Plan.

This all too familiar stalemate was not to persist for long into 1982, and it was the Salih regime that acted to change the political-military equation. In early 1982, President Salih and his advisers concluded that the status quo would inevitably lead to a renewal of the war of attrition and that this was no longer a tolerable alternative to an ending of the rebellion in the near future; they also concluded that they could not rely on Chairman Muhammad and his moderate colleagues for much help in securing its end. Consequently, the Salih regime took the decision to use increased military pressure to force the NDF to come to terms, even at the risk of worsened relations and armed conflict with the PDRY. The leaders in Sanaa were well aware of the risks involved. Since the border fight in 1979, the regime had required that its forces operate so as to minimize the chance of engagement with those of the PDRY. Accordingly, NDF units had been able to operate freely over the border from bases provided by the PDRY. Whenever the YAR put pressure on their forward positions, the NDF fighters withdrew over the border, secure in the belief that YAR units would not pursue them for fear of encounters with PDRY forces. To wage a more vigorous military campaign against the NDF meant that YAR forces would have to occupy and secure their borderlands and probably fire across the border if not actually cross it in hot pursuit of NDF units. Clearly, this would greatly increase the likelihood of armed conflict with the PDRY.[1]

Events in early 1982 suggested that the YAR was prepared to step up military operations against the NDF. YAR officials were expressing off the record their belief that the regime in Aden could no longer control the NDF because of the direct aid the latter was getting from Libya and Syria, and that, accordingly, the YAR would have to take matters into its own hands. In addition, high-level contacts with Saudi Arabia increased noticeably and there was talk about new Saudi arms aid and a new Saudi-funded U.S. training program. Great Britain acknowledged in February that the YAR had approached it about supplying military advisers.

In February, the skirmishes that had punctuated the ceasefire over the two prior months gave way to heavier fighting, and by early March major battles between YAR and NDF forces were raging near the border and in the interior of the YAR. In one instance, NDF units laid siege to the border town of Juban and its isolated garrison; in response, the YAR sent its airforce into action for the first time in several months. Due to the nearness of the heavy fighting, the PDRY mobilized its forces on its side of the border in late March, and PDRY regulars were reportedly manning howitzers supplied to the NDF by Libya and Syria. The result was a situation disturbingly reminiscent of that prior to the conflict between the two Yemens in 1979. Although most of the PDRY troops were redeployed in early April to help the many victims of severe floods, the causes of the tensions remained. Adding to the tensions, YAR security forces in mid-March began a roundup of suspected NDF members in the cities, and the searches and arrests continued for some weeks. This crackdown seemed to close more tightly than ever the door to a negotiated political settlement.[2]

Two events during this period further convinced the Salih regime of the need for increased military action: the NDF's use of SAM missiles to shoot down two YAR planes in mid-March and the capture of the besieged Juban garrison in early April. Although of little military significance, the fall of Juban raised the credibility and morale of the NDF; more important, it occurred only days before the international development conference convened in Sanaa, at a time when the Salih regime was trying to show the world that it had the security situation well in hand. The use of the SAM missiles indicated to the YAR regime that Chairman Muhammad, whatever his inclinations, could control neither the flow of outside arms to the NDF nor the faction within his own regime that favored full backing of the rebellion, an interpretation supported by reports from Aden of sharp conflict within the PDRY political command over the missile incident. The anger and impatience of the regime in Sanaa is evident in an unusually frank statement by Prime Minister al-Iryani: "The preponderant and most active opposition force is . . . a 100% Marxist-Leninist party. . . . What use is there in denying it? Everybody knows that this party has established its headquarters in Aden, that the arms it receives pass through South Yemen, and that its guerrillas carry out most of their movements on the other side of the border."[3]

Despite efforts by Arab mediators to arrange another ceasefire in early April, fighting soon resumed and tensions again rose in the border area. That the combat did not escalate sharply during these weeks was largely the result of the Salih regime's wish to contain the fighting at the time of the development conference. In late April, the conference over, the YAR launched the offensive expected ever since the fall of Juban. Continuing into late May, the campaign involved fighting as fierce or fiercer than that during the 1979 border war. YAR forces won a decisive victory over the NDF fighters, taking Juban and the NDF's main supply route north from the PDRY. At this point, the main force of NDF guerrillas seemed faced with the prospect of total defeat or expulsion from the YAR—unless PDRY forces joined in the fighting.

Clearly, by early May, the possibility of a military confrontation between the two Yemens was greater than at any time since 1979. Faced with this prospect, one that both regimes and most of the other Arab states wished to avoid, the leaders of the YAR and the PDRY held yet another summit. The meeting convened in Taiz on 5 May 1982 and lasted for three days. On this occasion, a concession by President Salih, coupled with his demonstrated readiness to take risks in an attempt to crush the NDF forces, opened the way to a political settlement. He agreed to proclaim a general amnesty for NDF members and to incorporate into the political system those who accepted the terms of the amnesty. In return, Chairman Muhammad again agreed to carry out his promise to end PDRY support for the NDF rebellion. President Salih's explicit pledge of amnesty and political incorporation gave the PDRY chairman what he needed to prevail over the more militant faction in his regime. As the leaders of the two Yemens were striking their bargain, several of the NDF leaders and their armed forces broke ranks and came to terms with the regime in Sanaa.

During the weeks following this latest summit, pressures were strong on both Yemeni leaders to undo or back off once again from their agreement. There remained elements in the YAR, probably still encouraged by the Saudis, for whom the idea of an amnesty or anything less than a crushing defeat of the NDF was anathema; some wanted to destroy once and for all the left in the YAR, to settle old scores with the PDRY, and even to purge the Arabian Peninsula of Marxism by overthrowing the PDRY regime. On the other side, there were those in Aden and elsewhere who saw the NDF as the proper vehicle of the unification of the two Yemens, the radicalization of the YAR, and the advancement of the revolution on the Arabian Peninsula. Finally, there were elements within the NDF itself, notably those close to Sultan Ahmad Umar, who were not ready to give up the struggle and to take their political chances inside the YAR regime. Based upon experience since 1979, the various opponents of the compromise adopted at the summit had reason to hope that circumstance or uncertainties would cause either or both regimes to have second thoughts about implementing an agreement with which neither of them was fully comfortable.

Help for those who supported the fragile agreement came from an unexpected source in early June 1982. The invasion of Lebanon by Israel provided the leaders of the two Yemens with a rationale for putting aside lingering doubts and breaking with the past. They quickly turned their attentions and those of their followers to the events unfolding in Lebanon. Amidst much emotion, the two Yemens separately sent groups of volunteers to fight, and in the wake of the Israeli victory, they launched a joint diplomatic initiative calling for an Arab summit to deal with the new situation. To this end, they went together to Saudi Arabia and Syria in early August and followed this with the dispatch of YAR-PDRY ministerial delegations to all Arab capitals. In another joint initiative, they informed Yasir Arafat of their willingness to absorb Palestinian fighters, an offer that was accepted and acted on when the Palestinian Liberation Organization

(PLO) evacuated Beirut in August. In the meantime, the new ceasefire between the YAR and the NDF held, the promised amnesty was proclaimed, and a number of NDF leaders began taking part in the ongoing political dialogue in Sanaa. Little was said by or about the NDF and the Yemeni People's Unity Party in the ensuing months, though both organizations remained in existence.

Completion and Promotion of the Second Five-Year Plan

The details of the draft Second Five-Year Plan were completed in early 1982 against the backdrop of continuing political-military uncertainties. The government announced that the Second International Conference for Yemeni Development would be held on 17-20 April and extended invitations to a broad array of potential aid donors and development experts. The public relations and diplomatic effort to promote the plan had begun in 1981, and President Salih had set the tone of the campaign with his 26 September Revolution Day speech: the YAR would maintain over the next five years the same high rate of development but emphasis would gradually shift from infrastructure projects to productive import-substitution industry and agribusiness; external aid of $560 million per year would be sought to achieve 7 percent annual growth in gross domestic product. This optimistic development theme was elaborated upon in many statements and interviews in late 1981 and early 1982 by the president, prime minister, and Adviser to the Plan al-Attar.

The keystone of the Salih regime's development diplomacy was continued generous project funding as well as budgetary support from Saudi Arabia, the YAR's biggest and only irreplaceable benefactor. The securing of the kind of Saudi commitment that would reassure lesser donors required that the Salih regime mend relations frayed over the previous two years, and this crucial task was also begun before the end of 1981. President Salih headed a large delegation to Saudi Arabia in early November; the YAR foreign minister was there for talks in the middle of the month, as was the chief of staff in December. In early 1982, the YAR made the point of publicly announcing that Prince Sultan, the senior member of the Saudi royal family long responsible for Yemeni affairs, had been personally invited to the development conference, and in early March President Salih paid another visit to Saudi Arabia. On 7 April, ten days before the scheduled opening of the conference, Prince Sultan led a large ministerial delegation to Sanaa. Statements after the visit indicated that the Saudis were prepared to support the Second Five-Year Plan at a high level of funding. The keystone of the YAR's development diplomacy was in place.

The Salih regime also paid special attention during these months to its relations with Iraq, since 1979 a major source of development financing. Vice President Abd al-Ghani visited Baghdad in mid-December 1981. The Iraqi-Yemeni Joint Commission on Economic and Technical Cooperation met in Sanaa in late December and the Sanaa branch of the Radfidain

Bank of Iraq was opened at about the same time. Both events were seen as endorsements of the YAR's development effort and as harbingers of increased Iraqi aid in the future.

The YAR's diplomacy during this period did not focus only on the fine points of development economics. Politics was at or just below the surface, and the Salih regime had to tiptoe through a minefield of regional conflicts. At the risk of straining relations with Syria and Libya, the YAR went out of its way to proclaim often its support for Iraq in its year-old war with Iran; going beyond mere words, it expelled the Iranian charge d'affaire for subversive activities. Above all, politics were a big part of the environment of negotiations with Saudi Arabia and the lesser Gulf states. The Saudis directly urged the Salih regime to pursue a tougher policy with the PDRY and the NDF; they were also rumored to be encouraging the northern tribalists to pressure the regime to seek a military solution to the rebellion as well as urging the other Gulf states to withhold generous support for the Second Five-Year Plan if the YAR pursued very close ties with the PDRY. It was in this political context that President Salih set out in late February on a nine-day, seven-state tour of the Gulf states, Iraq, and Jordan for the purpose of securing support for the new development plan.

The Second International Conference for Yemeni Development was held as scheduled on 17–20 April, despite rumors of a worsening security situation and preparations for a major battle with the NDF. The conference, with its seminars, presentations, and opportunities for informal discussion, served well the goals of restoring the YAR's credibility with the international development community and promoting the Second Five-Year Plan. The draft plan was greeted warmly, if with some reservations, by the many potential donors and development experts who attended. Prime Minister al-Iryani expressed satisfaction with its reception, noting that none of the criticism was new or fundamental. Even the cynics, who called the plan a "wish list" and viewed the conference as an exercise in matchmaking between donors and projects, conceded that the plan was coherent. The World Bank, which had provided technical assistance for both the preparation of the plan and the conference, strongly endorsed the YAR's development efforts during and after the conference and judged the plan to be very ambitious but probably within the YAR's demonstrated capabilities. "We believe that Yemen is unique among all the members . . . which have borrowed from IDA," said World Bank Senior Vice President Ernest Stern, "[and that it] . . . is one of the countries, perhaps the principal country, where the World Bank looks with great pride and joy at its association."[4]

The attempt at multiple matchmaking quickly yielded results. Before the conference ended, it was announced that the Abu Dhabi Fund had agreed to finance the Marib Dam irrigation scheme and other development projects. Prime Minister al-Iryani's followup visits to the several Gulf states in late May confirmed financing for a number of projects, including that of a major electrification project by the Kuwait Fund. Agreements with Holland, West Germany, and the United States were also concluded during the weeks in which attention was focused on the new plan.

The National Dialogue and the General People's Congress

Preoccupied with more immediate problems, the Salih regime did little during the first half of 1982 to advance its effort to restructure politics around the National Pact. This situation changed in the summer when the regime again had the opportunity to turn to the national dialogue and the holding of the General People's Congress. It was announced that the GPC would be held at the end of August, and the election of seven hundred delegates from all over the country was completed by the National Dialogue Committee in mid-August. The remaining three hundred delegates were appointed by the regime, and among them were some of the former leaders of the NDF, including Yahya al-Shami.

Amidst fanfare and publicity, the GPC convened for several days of meetings on 24 August. In his opening address, President Salih told the delegates that, after completing work on the National Pact, they should go on to the "more profound task of developing the method of national and political action needed to protect the Pact."[5] The revised pact was discussed at length, changed slightly and then approved in the course of the next two days. Turning to their "more profound task," the delegates then decided that the GPC would be made a permanent body, would be elected every four years, and would hold plenary sessions every two years. They also decided to create a standing committee of seventy-five members to act on behalf of the GPC between its sessions. Before adjourning, they elected fifty members of the committee, leaving appointment of the rest to President Salih, who was named chairman of the Standing Committee as well as secretary general of the GPC. In his closing address, President Salih praised the work of the congress, calling it the latest stage in the expansion of free partnership and democracy in Yemen that also included the municipal councils, the local development associations, the Yemeni Students' Union, and the various professional and vocational societies.

The effort of the Salih regime to restructure politics and to foster a new consensus and basis of legitimacy, beginning with the first draft of the National Pact and culminating in the holding of the GPC, was not carefully conceived and orchestrated. Burdened by unpredictable events and many seemingly more pressing matters, the regime did not often accord this political exercise top priority between 1980 and 1982. At times it seemed to be half forgotten or only an afterthought. Moreover, despite the publicity effort, the limited capacity of the regime to reach the people meant that many Yemenis never heard about the exercise much less even vaguely understood its meaning. Many of those who were aware of it found it crudely contrived and amateurish and derided or dismissed it as a joke, a sham, or even an insult. If it were a sincere effort at democratization or some other worthy goal, some said, then it was not succeeding; if it were not such an effort and was only designed to save President Salih's neck, then it should not succeed. Some viewed the GPC as a fleeting, forgettable political show and the pact as a regressive Islamic hodgepodge designed to appease Yemeni traditionalists and the Saudis. Moreover, many who knew something about the exercise were perplexed by it, in part because it was confusing in its presentation and possibly in the minds of its creators. As of 1982, it was not at all clear whether the National Pact was a supplement or an alternative to the 1970 Constitution and whether the GPC and its Standing Committee were the embryo of a new political party or movement.

Nevertheless, this effort at political construction had an importance and a promise for the future that was easily underestimated in 1982. Repeated often over a three-year period, the litany of ideas in the pact began to occupy the consciousness of many politically aware Yemenis. By 1983, critics of the regime and those who were cynical about this exercise found themselves—often to their embarrassment and annoyance—talking politics in the terms spelled out in the national dialogue on the pact. These vague and unexceptional ideas pertaining to the means and ends of government began to channel and constrain political discourse and even political action. Furthermore, the timely end of the NDF rebellion endowed the GPC and the several steps that preceded it with considerable national significance. The slow, fitful advance of this exercise meant that, when circumstances made it possible in 1982, there was an ongoing political process and an embryonic structure into which the regime could safely incorporate elements of the NDF. Stymied on the battlefield, most NDF leaders took their places as merely one among several groups in a political process largely defined and managed by the regime. The two dialogues, the quasi-secret one between the Salih regime and the NDF and the public one involving the regime and the rest of the nation, converged finally in a major move toward national reconciliation. Designed to treat a wound first opened in the 1960s, the process was at least the promising beginning of what might develop into an important and lasting change in Yemeni political life.

Economic Troubles and Political Order: 1983–1984

"The economy is in big trouble and politics—at home and abroad—are in better shape than ever before." So had assessed a young Yemeni modernist at the beginning of 1983. By the end of that year, the economy of the YAR was in even bigger trouble and its politics, if not getting better, still seemed to be in good shape.

The Economic Crisis and the Government's Response

The chief accomplishments of the al-Iryani government during its first eighteen months had been the modest revitalization of the system of development administration and the preparation and promotion of the Second Five-Year Plan. During this period, the government had done little to deal with the YAR's other major economic problems: (1) the high and rising balance-of-payments deficit, caused mainly by the runaway growth in private-sector imports and a decline in workers' remittances; and (2) the growing budget deficit, caused by rising current operating expenses and the inability of the state to generate adequate revenues from taxes and fees. These two problems as well as the prospects for external development aid worsened appreciably during the months after the seemingly successful development conference in April 1982, and this worsening was largely a result of international economic forces over which the YAR had no control. The worldwide recession of the early 1980s triggered the production and pricing crisis within OPEC, and this in turn sharply cut the oil revenues of Saudi Arabia and the other Gulf oil states. These states curtailed plans for their own development, and this led to less demand for Yemeni workers and a further decline in workers' remittances to the YAR. In addition, the effects of the recession and the Iraq-Iran war on the YAR's benefactors led to cuts or delays in external funding for its development activities, including some of the commitments made only months before at the development conference.

As early as mid-1982, as counterpoint to the many announcements of projects planned or underway, there began to be heard in the YAR talk about the possible need to scale down or delay certain projects. Prime Minister al-Iryani acknowledged in the fall that international aid was becoming scarce and that aid targets of the new plan would not be met. The prediction of a slower rate of development made the large balance-of-payments and budget deficits causes for greater concern than previously because their eventual reduction was predicated on rapid development throughout the rest of the 1980s. Nevertheless, the acknowledgement of these problems was accompanied by a mood of confidence, by a belief that they could be coped with if not solved. The government said it could and would adjust the development plan to the funds available, and it also talked about the issuance of government bonds to attract local funds to cover some development costs and the adoption of a budget for 1983 that would reduce the deficit by curtailing expenditures and increasing revenues. The government also sought to encourage local investments and bank deposits by assuring the public that it had no plans to discourage imports by means of exchange controls or a devaluation of the Yemeni rial.

The event that tipped assessments of the YAR's economic and development prospects from hopeful to quite grim was the devastating earthquake that rocked the central highlands in December 1982. In addition to taking some 1,500 lives, this disaster levelled entire villages, rendering 50,000 dwellings uninhabitable and leaving 400,000 homeless. The tasks of relief and reconstruction promised to tax the YAR's limited and already stretched financial and administrative resources. In early 1983, an international commission put reconstruction costs at $2 billion, money that for the most part could only come from the benefactors on which the YAR was counting for development funds and budget subsidies. Despite assertions by the government that funds sought for reconstruction would be over and above those sought for development, it was apparent that the two efforts would be competing in large part for the same funds in a world rendered by the recession less forthcoming than in previous years. In addition, relief and reconstruction would inevitably make demands on the YAR's own funds, funds which it had earmarked for development and current operations.

The projected costs of earthquake reconstruction, the decline in development aid, and the large deficits combined to force the Salih regime to take corrective measures in early 1983. The al-Iryani government began a broad review of the Second Five-Year Plan in order to bring its goals into line with a reduced level of outside funding. This exercise was carried out by the CPO over several months and involved the assistance of World Bank and IMF experts in the fall of 1983.

The more immediate and almost intractable problems facing the government centered on the budget and balance-of-payments deficits. The government's ability to raise revenue was severely limited by its dependence on import duties, a source that was limited in turn by the government's growing need to curtail imports and by its inability to choke off smuggling across the Saudi border. On the expenditure side, most items in the budget were nondiscretionary, at least in a political sense. The military's large claim on the budget allowed for little change. Monies for such essential services as health and education were already at a minimal level, and other monies were obligated as local-government contributions to ongoing development activities. Simply put, there was little fat in the budget, and the cutting of what little there was could produce big political outcries. Regarding the payments deficit, the government could do little because its control of the levers of the economy was so limited and imperfect: it had little control over either the level and mix of imports because of overland smuggling or money in circulation because only a small portion of the remittances ever entered the banking system. Moreover, if the government did what little it could to affect the payments deficit, it ran the risk that its actions would encourage the flight of local capital and discourage the inflow of remittances, results that could turn the recession into a depression of unknown scope and duration.

The al-Iryani government approached the economically and politically sensitive deficits crisis with caution. Although billed as nonexpansionary, the final government budget for 1983 fixed the deficit and spending at the same high level of the previous year. Despite the likelihood that it would encourage more smuggling, the government in March 1983 raised customs duties on luxury and other durable consumer goods. At the same time, it proceeded with plans to cut smuggling and to collect duties on overland imports.

The sharp drop in the value of the Yemeni rial in mid-1983, triggered by another surge in the payments deficit and a strengthened dollar, led to more vigorous action by the government and to widespread talk about the likelihood of a stringent austerity program. The Central Bank acted in August to shore up the rial by ordering the commercial banks to cease trading in rials at the free market rate; it also issued a new regulation forbidding local moneylenders to export large sums of rials without authorization. More important, the Central Bank announced at the same time that it was temporarily ending its long-established policy of selling on request hard currency to the commercial banks. In effect, this meant that the banks and their commercial clients would have to buy hard currency in the Yemeni market in order to finance imports. As the reserves in the Yemeni market largely consisted of remittance money, and as remittances had fallen off, this meant in turn a drying up of available hard currency to back importers' letters of credit. In a related move, the Central Bank announced a few weeks later that import licenses would be issued only after an importer presented evidence that a commercial bank had agreed in advance to make foreign exchange available for the required letter of credit. Together, the requirement that an importer secure a letter of credit before applying for an import license and the declining supply of hard currency for letters of credit promised to slow the flow of legal private-sector imports. Complementing this was the government's stepped-up effort to control imports by curtailing overland smuggling, a sensitive matter that required the strengthening of customs forces and their checkpoints along the undemarcated border with Saudi Arabia.

Rumors and predictions to the contrary, the al-Iryani government did not introduce such elements of a more sweeping austerity program as import quotas by commodities. Nevertheless, the modest and piecemeal measures that were adopted in the summer and fall of 1983 produced both a decline in imports and an outcry from the interests most directly affected. Bankers, importers, and other businessmen maintained that the restrictions were hurting them unfairly and were producing uncertainties and distortions in the marketplace. The tribalists were angered by the attempt to curtail the smuggling that passed through their domains and from which they derived economic gain. Disinterested observers noted that the austerity measures were unintentionally making smuggling more profitable and scarce hard currency even scarcer by encouraging Yemenis to send or keep it abroad.

Bowing to the mounting pressures, President Salih dismissed the al-Iryani government in late 1983, an event rumored since early summer. The new government, headed by Vice President Abd al-Aziz Abd al-Ghani, was installed on 13 November, and Dr. al-Iryani was placed in charge of earthquake reconstruction. The change was welcomed by many as a harbinger of the removal of the unpopular restrictions imposed to control imports and the currency markets. Indeed, some of the restrictions were modified or abandoned over the next several months. At the same time, however, others were maintained and some new ones were added. The effort to narrow the budget deficit continued, and the 1984 budget called for a decrease in expenditures of 6.5 percent from the level in 1983.

It was apparent by early 1984 that the economic crisis in the YAR had abated to some degree. The data for 1983 indicated that, when compared to 1982, the current accounts deficit and the government budget deficit were reduced by 8 percent and 18 percent respectively. Moreover, current accounts for the last quarter of 1983 showed a surplus for the first time in many quarters. The fact that this change was accounted for by lower imports as well as higher remittances suggested that the austerity measures introduced in the summer had had some positive effect. Although these figures did not provide reason for complacency, they were cause for hope that the YAR was not in a free fall toward financial disaster.

Politics: Minor Challenges and Modest Gains

The economic difficulties in 1983 underscored the importance of the gradual strengthening of the Salih regime over the previous three years. It was the regime's broadened support and increased legitimacy that allowed it to ride out the economic storm despite a clear demonstration of the limited capacity of the state to take effective action. The regime was also favored by a relatively benign external political environment, more like that of the mid-1970s than of the more recent past.

External Relations. Struggling against the tide of worldwide recession, the YAR pursued assiduously its time-tested development diplomacy. It cultivated good relations with its benefactors among the industrialized nations, elevating Italy to a place of prominence for the first time in the republican era and making France its third largest trading partner. Its relations with the superpowers remained peripheral and little changed despite another visit by President Salih to the USSR and the signing of a treaty of friendship between the two countries. The YAR usually stuck to its policy of not taking sides in inter-Arab conflicts and of calling for united Arab stands on regional and global issues, the three main exceptions being its open support of Iraq in the Gulf War, its faint praise of the Saudi-led Gulf Cooperation Council and its mild criticism of the Tripartite Alliance of the PDRY with Ethiopia and Libya.

The deep involvement of the two Yemens in the fate of the PLO as well as the PDRY's rapprochement with Oman and other members of the Gulf Cooperation Council served to lessen potential strains between the YAR and the PDRY. Nevertheless, relations between the Yemens were framed by a polarization in the region that often placed the friends of each Yemen at opposite poles. The months from mid-1982 through mid-1983 were marked by claims that their relations were cooling, allegations based on the failure of the the two heads of state to implement certain accords and to meet semiannually as required by the 1981 agreement that created the Supreme Yemeni Council. More alarming were the rumors that Chairman Muhammad was faced with renewed pressure in Aden, particularly a challenge to his leadership by Deputy Chairman Ali Ahmad Nasir Antar and Defense Minister Salih Muslih Qasim, the militant supporters of former Chairman Ismail who remained in exile in Moscow. These predictions of worsening relations proved false, however. The two heads of state held the first session of the Supreme Yemeni Council in August 1983, and they held the second and third sessions in 1984. Although the results were not dramatic, these meetings reaffirmed the improved inter-Yemeni relations achieved in 1982 and also yielded minor agreements for joint economic and social undertakings.

In addition, they served to reinforce the good personal relationship between President Salih and Chairman Muhammad.

Relations with Saudi Arabia, which had improved in early 1982, were strained during much of 1983. Postponement of the annual spring meetings of the Saudi-Yemeni Joint Coordinating Council, coming at a time when sharply reduced Arab funding led the Salih regime to want a quick end to uncertainty over development aid and budget subsidies from its chief benefactor, was in part a Saudi signal of displeasure with aspects of the Salih regime's austerity program and other policies. The austerity program hurt Yemeni business friends of the Saudis and the campaign against smuggling hurt the tribalists and others, including some Saudis, who benefited from the illicit trade. Moreover, the YAR's crackdown on smuggling involved government actions that touched on Saudi territorial claims along their unmarked common border. The Saudi-Yemeni Joint Coordinating Council finally met and reaffirmed Saudi aid to the YAR in late October, just two weeks before the replacement of the al-Iryani government and the rumors that policies adopted to deal with the economic crisis would be changed. The Saudis were pleased with the new Abd al-Ghani government and especially with the appointment of the conservatives Ahmad Abd al-Malik al-Asbahi and Abd al-Wahid al-Zandani as minister of foreign affairs and minister of education respectively. Indicative of the desire on both sides for good relations, a violent border incident in early 1984 that involved Saudi security forces and Yemeni customs agents was speedily defused. High-level contact and Saudi economic assistance continued throughout 1984, although the Saudi-Yemeni Joint Coordinating Council failed to convene that year for its annual meeting.

Domestic Politics. Contrary to the expectations of many, the three-year effort to organize politics around the National Pact did not end with the closing gavel of the General People's Congress in August 1982. Instead, the process continued and underwent further institutionalization. From the outset, the Salih regime placed great emphasis on the workings and activities of the new seventy-five-member Standing Committee of the GPC. Its quarterly meetings, the first of which was held in late 1982, were held on schedule and were well publicized; its members were always identified in the media as being part of the Standing Committee. The ongoing dialogue reached well beyond the Standing Committee. There appeared in November 1982 a new weekly newspaper, *The Pact*, the official organ of the GPC, and in early 1983 all public and private organizations were required to devote time each Thursday to guided discussions of the National Pact. To facilitate this and other efforts at popular political education, courses were set up to train political guidance officers in the civil service, the military, and the local development associations. The progressives, the NDF returnees among them, were allowed a weekly journal, *Amal*, and had representation on the Standing Committee in the person of a longtime NDF supporter.

The second biennial session of the GPC was held in August 1984, and during these meetings a plan was adopted to greatly expand the electoral process by which the members of the GPC were chosen. Although he referred to it as "a political administration . . . responsible for taking care of political activity and for expressing the popular will," President Salih continued to insist in public that the GPC was not an organ of a political party. Nevertheless, however described, the work of the leaders and cadres of the GPC and its Standing Commitee seemed involved in the consensus-building, guidance, and even control functions of a comprehensive national party or movement. By 1984, Yemeni leaders were admitting openly that the GPC had evolved into precisely this sort of political organization.

President Salih resigned the presidency in May 1983 and, as expected, was promptly voted a new five-year term by the People's Constituent Assembly. This pro forma exercise expressed accurately the wishes of most of the relevant actors in Yemeni politics. In the judgement of many, President Salih had finally earned office on the basis of his performance during at least the last half of his first term. Significantly, the main target of the outcry raised by the austerity measures in 1983 had been the al-Iryani government, not President Salih, and his dismissal of that government allowed him to come through this period of economic discontent quite unscathed. He had at last become a popular leader, widely respected if not loved.

Nevertheless, the widespread endorsement of President Salih did not mean that the regime was free of serious political problems in the mid-1980s. The best measure of something still amiss was the failure to hold the oft-promised elections for a permanent legislative body following the adoption of the National Pact by the GPC. The elections were not held despite frequent declarations of the imminence of what President Salih called "the final stage in the process of democratization." In late 1984, he still had to say that preparations for elections required "final touches."

The regime's reluctance to hold elections was not based on fears that progressive forces, reinforced by the tamed NDF members, would capitalize on dissatisfaction generated by the economic recession and move politics to the left. These elements seemed for the time being politically quiescent. Instead, the concern was that religious fundamentalists and other conservatives, playing on economic as well as other discontents, would carry the elections and push politics to the right. The apparent strength of these elements is partly an aspect of the upsurge in Islamic fundamentalism throughout the Middle East since the 1970s, an upsurge spurred by displeasure with efforts at secular modernization. In the YAR, however, the hand of these elements was strengthened by the extent to which the regime had counted on them as allies and tolerated most of their activities during its struggle with the NDF. Throughout that struggle, moreover, they had had the moral and material backing of Saudi Arabia, backing that did not cease with the end of the NDF rebellion. Most visible had been the military activities of the tribally based Islamic Front. Overlapping these activities were the more widespread and ramified cultural-educational and political activities of the Muslim Brotherhood, an organization whose Yemeni members were reinforced by the many Egyptian, Sudanese, and Syrian members working as teachers and other professionals in the YAR.

The Muslim Brotherhood and kindred groups had made very strong showings in the early 1980s in the elections to the local development associations, the municipal councils, and—most important—the GPC itself. Their influence on the Ministry of Education and the educational establishment remained considerable and their ability to block "secular" innovation was demonstrated by their successful opposition to the issuance of fixed-interest government bonds on the grounds that the Koran prohibits interest charges. Although the discontents that led to the change in governments in 1983 were primarily economic, the awarding of the Ministries of Foreign Affairs and Education in the new government to religious conservatives acknowledged the strength of these elements. Although a modernist himself, Prime Minister Abd al-Ghani was welcomed by them as a person who would be less likely than Dr. al-Iryani to push policies that they strongly opposed.

The Salih regime did not regard the Muslim Brotherhood and its allies as an imminent threat to its existence. Instead, the regime was concerned that a legislature in which these groups were strongly represented would institutionalize limits on the government's freedom of maneuver, much as the tribalists through their domination of the Consultative Council had constrained governments under President Abd al-Rahman al-Iryani in the early 1970s. The regime also veiwed the religious and conservative elements as a vehicle through which Saudi Arabia could continue to exert inordinate influence over the course of events in Yemen, much as it has used its patronage of the tribes for this purpose. The Salih regime wanted a legislature that shared its goals of national strength and development and was prepared to allow it to debate freely the means to achieve these goals. However, a legislature opposed to these goals was unacceptable—hence the delay on elections.

Many Yemenis regarded the upsurge of the religious elements as temporary and pointed to the past weakness and limited esteem of the religious leadership in Yemen as compared to some other Islamic countries. They also noted that in recent decades these leaders had been identified with the imamate and Saudi Arabia, identifications that did not sit well with the republican and nationalist mood of contemporary Yemen. Some thought that the Muslim Brotherhood and its allies were vulnerable because they were no longer needed to counter the NDF, that they overestimated and would soon overreach their power and that President Salih was merely waiting for this to occur to provide the justification to put them in their place. The dismissal of the conservative ministers of foreign affairs and education in late 1984 and the return of Dr. al-Iryani as deputy prime minister and foreign minister may have marked the beginning of this readjustment.

10
Yemen and Petroleum: The Mid-1980s and Beyond

Change and variety notwithstanding, politics and social life in North Yemen in the twentieth century if not the whole of the past millennium were constrained by an environment of severe economic scarcity. Rarely did this environment allow for anything but variations on the themes of deprivation and dependence. Imams Yahya and Ahmad secured considerable independence for North Yemen at the price of nationwide deprivation, and even the lot of the ruling family, other great sayyid clans, and top qadi families was not all that enviable. The civil war and overlapping drought made deprivation a prominent feature of much of the first decade of the republican era after the 1962 Revolution. Similarly, dependence, first upon Nasir's Egypt and then upon the Kingdom of Saudi Arabia, has been characteristic of much of the nearly quarter century of republican rule. It is within this context that the regime headed by President Ali Abdullah Salih has operated since mid-1978, still more or less subject to deprivation and dependence. Indeed, it was difficult down to the mid-1980s to separate Yemen and the Yemenis from the presumption of scarcity. Their image in the region and elsewhere was that of the distant country cousins of the richer Arabs, poor and backward, fit to be on the United Nations' list of least developed countries (LDCs). As recently as 1981, Dr. Muhammad Said al-Attar, the high-ranking UN official and veteran of many YAR governments, could title an article on the two Yemens "The Poorest Countries of an Oil-rich Region." Ironically, having given up the austere independence of the imamate in a bid for modernity's promise of prosperity, the YAR seemed to be finding its modern metaphor in the helpless patient living on a life-support machine controlled and operated by others.

Then, in early 1984, an event occurred that promised to change greatly the setting of the YAR's politics—the discovery of oil. This event, coming on the heels of the worldwide recession and the YAR's latest bout with austerity, held out the prospect of a new environment of relative abundance and a sharp decline in dependence and deprivation.

The Search for Oil in Yemen

The Hunt Oil Company of Dallas, Texas, and the government-owned Yemen Oil and Mineral Company signed a twenty-five-year exploration and production-sharing agreement in September 1981, and the newly formed Yemen Hunt Oil Company began exploratory work in a 4,844-square-mile (12,546 square-kilometer) concession in the barren, sparsely populated Marib-Jawf basin, some 125 miles (201 km) east-northeast of Sanaa, at the end of 1982. Little more than a year later, in February 1984, the first well drilled by the Yemen Hunt Oil Company brought in the oil that was officially announced in July of that year. The well, dubbed Alif-1, is located on the eastern end of the concession about 40 miles (64 km) east-northeast of the town of Marib, in the Ramlat al-Sabatayn desert not far from the junction of the undemarcated borders of the YAR, the PDRY, and Saudi Arabia. In a geological formation known as the Safir Dome, the Alif oil field is at an elevation of 3,200 feet (975 meters) in a very wide, flat, and arid wadi. Trapped in a sandstone reservoir, the oil is of excellent quality, light 40° API, and nearly sulphur free.

The speed and ease of Yemen Hunt Oil's effort, and the fast pace of events since the initial strike, stand in marked contrast to the desultory, half-hearted and inconclusive search for oil in North Yemen over the previous sixty years. Nothing came of the first foray in 1923, when two American geologists were allowed to make a hurried survey of part of the coastal plain, the Tihama, on behalf of Standard Franco-Americaine. Of greater historical interest is the episode involving Charles R. Crane, the philanthropic friend of the Arab world and a member of President Wilson's King-Crane Commission to the Near East after World War I, and Karl Twitchell, the Vermont mining engineer who was to play so big a role in the discovery and exploitation of oil in Saudi Arabia. Told of the wonders of Yemen by Charles Moser, who in 1910 had become the third American ever to penetrate the Yemeni highlands, Crane visited Sanaa in the winter of 1926–1927, struck up a warm friendship with Imam Yahya and promised him as a gift to Yemen the services of an American engineer who would make certain physical improvements and study the geology of Yemen for worthwhile minerals. Later in 1927, Twitchell, fresh from work in Ethiopia, was put in touch with Crane, and, as Richard Sanger put it, "thus did Twitchell, the father of economic development in the peninsula, enter the Arabian scene."[1] He worked in Yemen on six expeditions between 1927 and 1932 and toward the end of this period was put by Crane in the service of a new Arab friend, Abd al-Aziz ibn Saud, the impecunious ruler of the newly formed Kingdom of Saudi Arabia. His survey and assessment of the oil prospects of Hasa province opposite Bahrayn Island was the first major step in the sequence that led to the discovery later in the 1930s of Saudi Arabia's fabulous oil reserves.

The oil frenzy in the Gulf area, on the opposite corner of the Arabian Peninsula, served to minimize the interest of the imperial powers in Yemen from the late 1930s through the years just after World War II. In 1937, with Imam Yahya's permission, a geological party in the employ of British oil interests made a hasty survey of a small portion of the northern Tihama coast of Yemen, only to conclude that the prospects for oil were not hopeful. Ten years later, a group of American companies opted to seek a concession in the land between Kuwait and Saudi Arabia, after, as Stephen Longriggs put it, "a glance at Asir and the Yemen."[2] In 1953, Longriggs nicely summed up the consensus on Yemen's dim prospects in his *Oil in the Middle East*:

> Spokesmen of the Government of the Yemen made in these years a number of efforts to interest British or American companies in the oil exploration of the Imamate and, in vague terms, promised favorable treatment; but the little promise revealed by previous exploration (slight as this had been), the unfavorable inland situation of the area of presumed interest east of the main igneous massif, the wildness of the village and tribal population, and the arbitrary and incalculable character of the government itself, were sufficient to deter applicants. There appeared in 1952–53 little immediate likelihood of the Yemen joining the ranks of oil-producing countries.[3]

Despite Longriggs's catalogue of horrors, some oil-related activities did take place in Yemen in the 1950s and the early 1960s in the years after Imam Ahmad succeeded his slain father to the imamate. A U.S. State Department memo dated 22 December 1949, nearly two years after the succession, has Imam Ahmad's chief delegate to the United Nations saying that "his government had recently declared an open-door policy to oil company exploration, preferably by American oil companies."[4] However, it was the German firm of C. Deilmann Bergbau G.m.b.H. that concluded an agreement with Imam Ahmad in 1953 for the carrying out of geophysical and geological exploration over much of North Yemen. An improbable feature of the agreement was the alleged provision by the imamate of 75 percent of the capital required, with the hope of a similar share of the ultimate profits. The German company conducted aerial and other exploration of a coastal area north of al-Hudayda, but the work was cut short by the surprising grant in 1955 of exploration rights over nearly 15,500 square miles (40,150 square km) of substantially the same area to the Yemen Development Corporation, a concern owned mainly by a Texas enterprise. The Germans appealed for arbitration on their prior claim, with results never made public. The Yemen Development Corporation is believed to have carried out some surveys, but it withdrew when faced with the inability to raise funds for exploration and for meeting dead-rent payments. In 1955 another concession covering 10,000 square miles (25,900 square km) was given to the American Overseas Investment Corporation, but no drilling followed from this new initiative. It was also reported at about this time that Russian and Romanian technicians were in Yemen prospecting for oil, and that the Italians and Japanese were interested in looking there as well.

In 1961, more than a year before Imam Ahmad's death and the 1962 Revolution, a concession was granted to the John W. Mecom Company of

Texas over a 10,000-square-mile (25,900 square km) area situated on the Tihama and the adjacent waters of the Red Sea. The agreement provided for a five-year exploration and a thirty-five-year development period. The Mecom company showed more activity than its predecessors, and it drilled, without success, three or four wells to medium depths along the coast at Salif, Zaydiya, and near al-Hudayda. Its efforts, however, were brought to an end by the outbreak of the civil war that followed in the wake of the 1962 Revolution.

The political uncertainties associated with the long civil war caused the search for oil to be put on hold for several years in the newly created YAR. In late 1969, however, the YAR and the Algerian state oil and gas company, Sonotrach, agreed to set up a joint company to explore for oil in a concession covering 5,700 square miles (14,750 square km) of the Tihama, one-third of which was to be offshore and the rest onshore. Sonotrach was to select the exact concession site, put up initial capital of about $1 million, and conduct the actual search. The newly formed company, the Yemen Oil and Mines Industry Co. (Yomico), began exploratory work in the area around al-Hudayda in the second half of 1970. At about the same time, a delegation from Petromin, the state oil concern of Saudi Arabia, visited the YAR and rumors began to circulate that the Saudis were planning to participate in a refinery-petrochemical complex to be built in Yemen, a matter that suprised oil observers in light of the YAR's recent agreement with socialist Algeria. Despite reports that it had found promising signs of oil, Yomico ceased exploration activities in the second half in 1971. In mid-1972, after nearly a year of talks but no other activity, Algeria and the YAR decided to end the operations of Yomico, ostensibly because of the inability of the Yemeni side to meet its financial obligations. The decision may have been prompted by the growing influence in the YAR of Saudi Arabia and the Gulf oil states. In any case, a YAR official said at about this time that Kuwait had agreed to give technical assistance for future oil exploration and to study all offers that might be received from international oil companies.

A delegation from Deutsche Shell of West Germany visited the YAR in mid-1973, and in January of the following year that company signed an agreement with the Yemeni government under which it would prospect for oil offshore between al-Hudayda and the Saudi border. In the spring of 1974 it was reported that the American-Japanese Toyomenka Company had agreed to conduct a geological survey in the YAR's territorial waters to the south of al-Hudayda. The search for oil by Deutsche Shell began in 1976, and late in that year the company announced both that the first well drilled had come in dry and that it planned to begin a second well in the next few months. In May 1977 the company signed a second agreement with the Yemeni government under which it would also explore for oil in the next six months in an onshore strip between al-Hudayda and the Saudi border. Political uncertainties in the late 1970s, produced by the assassinations of Presidents al-Hamdi and al-Ghashmi, the NDF rebellion, and the border fight with the PDRY, led Deutsche Shell to end its exploration activities in the YAR shortly after the turn of the new decade.

This, then, was the meandering stream of history that the Yemen Hunt Oil Company joined in 1981 but with happier results than its predecessors. The announcement of the oil strike in July 1984 reported a flow of over 7,800 barrels per day (b/d) from Alif-1, described as "promising quantities" by Ali Abd al-Rahman al-Bahr, minister of state for petroleum and mineral resources and chairman of the Yemen Oil and Mineral Company (Yominco). Several months later, in December 1984, President Salih took the occasion of the meeting in Sanaa of the Islamic Conference Organization to confirm that the Alif oil field contained oil in "commercial" and "exportable" quantities; he also said that the YAR was going to build a refinery and a pipeline to the Red Sea, and that this construction would take "no more than two years." Indeed, events had moved fast during the several months between the strike at Alif-1 near Marib and President Salih's December announcement. Yemen Hunt Oil Company (YHOC) and Yominco renegotiated their agreement, increasing slightly the size of the Marib-Jawf concession, and the company drilled two more wells in the Alif field, both of which yielded good flows of oil. The company also brought a second drilling rig into the country in order to begin exploration in a second zone at the same time that work proceeded in the Alif field. By late 1984, rumors projecting flows from the Alif field moved upwards to a minimum of 75,000 b/d and a maximin of 300,000 b/d. Based on these rising estimates, the YAR government commissioned the YHOC to study alternatives for the construction of both a domestic refinery and export facilities that would include a pipeline from the oil field to a terminus near Salif on the Red Sea coast north of al-Hudayda.

In the spring of 1985, the YHOC completed its nine-well appraisal and demarcation program in the Alif field and the Hunt Oil Company began both an analysis of these results and a search for outside financing for the field's development. The analysis confirmed the prospects for commercial exploitation, indicating that the Alif field, only one of more than a dozen geological structures that YHOC had earlier identified as likely repositories of hydrocarbons, contained an estimated 500 million barrels of recoverable oil reserves. One informal estimate put the projected flow of the Alif field at a minimum of 200,000 b/d for twenty years, and it was rumored that YHOC's own analysts were basing their calculations and development plans for the Marib-Jawf basin as a whole on the likelihood of a flow of 400,000 b/d. The development costs, which under the concession agreement were to be borne solely by the concessionaire, YHOC, were estimated to be more than a billion dollars, of which roughly a half would go for the pipeline from the oil field to the Red Sea terminus. A portion of the initial development costs were to be met by a South Korean consortium led by Yukong Corporation, formerly the Korea Oil Corporation, to which YHOC had sold a 24.5 percent participating interest in the Alif field portion of the larger Marib-Jawf concession shortly after the initial strike in 1984.

Rather than wait for the technical and financial decisions upon which the development of the Marib-Jawf basin for export purposes depended, YHOC and Yominco agreed in the spring of 1985 that the former should proceed with a $50.3 million program to expedite the exploitation of the Alif field for domestic purposes. Roughly half of these funds were to be used to drill and prepare five production wells, and the remainder was to be used to construct a domestic refinery and the oil-gathering network and separation facilities required to feed crude oil from the production wells to the refinery. It was decided that the domestic refinery, which would cost about $23 million installed, would have an initial capacity of approximately half of the YAR's domestic needs in 1985. It would be sited northeast of Marib in the Alif field, from which motor-grade gasoline, diesel fuel, and fuel oil for power plants and factories would be transported by tank trucks to Sanaa and elsewhere in the northern highlands. In May 1985 the American firm PetroFac was contracted by YHOC to construct a prefabricated refinery in modular form in Texas. It was to be shipped to Yemen in late 1985, erected in the spring of 1986, and ready to come on stream early in the fall of that same year. The $50 million initial exploitation of the Alif field was to be financed by the United States' Overseas Private Investment Corporation (OPIC), the International Finance Corporation (IFC), YHOC's Korean partners in the Alif field, and YHOC itself.

Oil exploration activities in the YAR in the mid-1980s were not limited to those of YHOC in the Marib-Jawf basin. In January 1984, shortly before the strike at Alif-1, British Petroleum (BP) was granted an exploration concession covering an 8,500-square-mile (22,000-square-km) strip of the Tihama coast from the Saudi border to just south of al-Hudayda. Within a few months, BP began a program of seismic shooting and evaluation that was to continue until the end of 1985, at which time it would have to decide whether to go ahead with drilling or to relinquish the concession. In the fall of 1984, the Hunt Oil Company signed its second exploration agreement with Yominco, this time for an offshore concession adjacent to BP's onshore concession. Both BP and Hunt completed extensive seismic work over the course of 1985.

The Exxon Corporation and Yominco concluded an exploration and production-sharing agreement in mid-1985 for a long 8,500-square-mile (22,000-square-km) strip in the central highlands, running from near the northern town of Saada south for about 250 miles (400 km) to near Yarim, a town about 80 miles (130 km) south of Sanaa. The northeastern reaches of this concession adjoin Hunt's in the Marib-Jawf basin. Exxon moved quickly after the YAR gave final approval to the agreement, establishing an office in Sanaa by the last days of 1985 and beginning a program of preliminary seismic testing in the spring of 1986. These tests, designed to develop methods of interpreting seismic data from the unusual geological structure of the Yemeni highlands, will be followed by a couple of years of seismic shooting and evaluation. Though the geology is not typical of oil-bearing areas, signs of gas and the proximity of the Marib-Jawf basin have encouraged people at Exxon.

Another agreement was concluded in the summer of 1985 between Yominco and France's Compagnie Française des Petroles (Total) for an onshore and offshore concession of nearly 3,500 square miles (9,065 square km) on the Tihama south of the BP and Hunt concessions, in the area around the coastal towns of al-Khokha and al-Mukha. It was also reported in 1985 that Agip Overseas of Italy and the United States' Amoco were conducting discussions with Yominco on possible concessions. Clearly, the YAR had become an object of keen interest to many of the major international actors in the field of petroleum exploration and production.

As important as the several new concessions granted in the mid-1980s may prove to be, the event of greatest immediate significance was Exxon's purchase in late 1985 of a 49 percent interest in Hunt Oil Company's concession in the Marib-Jawf basin, including the Alif field. In exchange for access to a known supply of crude oil, Exxon agreed to provide several hundred million dollars of capital in 1986 and 1987 to develop the basin's oil reserves. With Yominco approval, YHOC was named the sole operator of a new Exxon-Hunt joint venture set up to produce and transport oil from the Alif field, explore other prospects in the jointly held concession and build a terminus near Salif and a pipeline from the Marib-Jawf basin to that terminus.

Aided by the infusion of Exxon's capital, YHOC was able to rapidly accelerate petroleum infrastructure development from late 1985 through the summer of 1986. At the beginning of 1986, YHOC awarded a contract to the Houston-based Gulf Interstate Engineering Corporation under which the latter assumed overall responsibility for project management engineering as well as procurement and construction supervision for the oil gathering network and central processing plant at the Alif field, the pipeline down to the coast, and a harbor and loading terminals on the Red Sea. Based on feasibility studies and a survey done in 1985, the decision was made to proceed with the construction of a 270-mile (435-kilometer) pipeline along a southerly arc from the Alif field to Ras Isa near Salif, on the mainland opposite Kamaran Island; the pipeline would cross at right angles the main north-south highway on the Dhamar plain near Maabar, some 50 miles (80 kilometers) south of Sanaa. The project to build a pipeline with an initial capacity of 200,000 b/d was regarded as complex, involving the installation of up to three pumping stations and the laying of the subterranean pipe at some points in basalt rock and at elevations higher than 8000 feet, and was estimated to cost as much as $500 million. In April 1986, YHOC placed an order with a Japanese firm for 78,000 tons of steel pipe for the pipeline; delivery of the pipe, valued at $50 million, began in mid-1986. In the meantime, five consortia prequalified for the contract to lay the pipeline and to build the ancillary facilities required for the export of crude oil. It was anticipated that the large pipeline contract would be awarded by the end of 1986 and that work would be completed early in the spring of 1988.

During this same period, work proceeded apace in the Marib-Jawf basin. Local contractors under the supervision of the Highway Authority completed a new 30-mile (48-kilometer) access road from Marib to the Alif field in early 1986. Drilling in the basin in zones outside the Alif field speeded up, albeit without results as positive as in the initial exploration zone. Most important, the prefabricated refinery ordered for the Alif field was delivered and assembled on site during the winter and spring of 1986. As finally designed, the refinery consists of a distillation unit and a reformer with a total capacity of 12,500 b/d. Its design and output patterned to cater to domestic demand, the refinery will produce 36 percent diesel fuel, 30.5 percent gasoline, and 30 percent fuel oil, as well as 71 million BTUs per hour of fuel gas. When operating at capacity, its output will cover an estimated 36 percent of the YAR's projected domestic demand for these products in the late 1980s. The plant is designed to accommodate overall expansion in the future as well as the addition of capacities to produce liquified petroleum gas and kerosene.

The refinery at the Alif field, the YAR's first, was formally started up by President Salih on 12 April 1986, in the presence of U.S. Vice President George Bush, Ray Hunt, and a high official from Exxon. Commercial operations were set to begin in the fall of 1986, with the facility working up to capacity over the following year. President Salih took the occasion of the opening ceremonies to announce that preliminary study for the possible construction of a second prefabricated, modular refinery was underway. This refinery, if built, would probably be larger than that at Alif and would be sited near Sanaa or on the Red Sea coast.

The unanticipated discovery of oil in the YAR in 1984 necessarily required a major reshaping—and helped to delay implementation—of the imports-based national petroleum products distribution scheme that had been designed and adopted in the early 1980s. In late 1985 Yominco revived and began to revise the nearly $100 million scheme that would still include petroleum import facilities near Salif, a petroleum products pipeline on the coast, and storage tank farms at a number of locations. The revised scheme would drop plans for a pipeline to carry refined products from the Red Sea terminus up to Sanaa and the highlands, a component made unnecessary by the discovery of the Alif field and the building of the refinery near Marib. In mid-1986, a Japanese/French consortium was awarded a $92 million contract to build and manage the distribution scheme, due for completion at the end of 1988.

Yemeni Oil: Current Effects and Implications for the Future

It was clear in 1986 that the YAR was destined to join the ranks of at least the lesser oil-exporting countries, a welcome status that could be attained in 1988 and would extend into the twenty-first century. Given the terms of the production-sharing agreement, Yemen Hunt Oil Company's private projections of a flow of 400,000 b/d from the Marib-Jawf basin promises to add to the annual revenues of the YAR government $2.0 billion if the price of oil is $20/barrel or $1.5 billion if the price is only $15/

barrel. Though modest compared to Saudi oil revenues of $43.7 billion in 1984 (down from a high of $114.0 billion in 1981), this change in the YAR's revenues will have profound consequences and implications for its domestic and external affairs. Indeed, the drama of the YAR in the late 1980s and at least the 1990s will turn on the big effects that will be triggered by a small amount of oil. Most of these highly leveraged effects will be political, and many of them will issue directly or indirectly from the ending of the YAR's economic and financial dependence on Saudi Arabia.

Domestic Effects and Implications

Annual oil revenues of $1.5 billion would be roughly equal to the sum of all worker remittances and external aid—loans, grants, and subsidies—received during the peak year for these inflows in the late 1970s. As a consequence, the exploitation of even modest oil reserves means that the YAR will be able to meet its own domestic energy needs and to finance the development and greater prosperity of Yemen out of its own resources. The leaders of the YAR will have to an unprecedented degree the freedom to take the destiny of Yemen into their own hands. They will have the material wherewithal to make choices for the YAR and to act on those choices. This big political gain will accrue to the YAR even if the net economic gain is rendered modest by declines in both external aid and the remittances of Yemenis working abroad, declines that will almost inevitably follow the rise in oil revenues as external benefactors judge the YAR to be without great need and as Yemeni workers choose to seek work at home rather than abroad.

A reorientation and reorganization of the government's petroleum resources sector—in recent years the purview of Yominco alone—will inevitably accompany the exploitation of the YAR's oil and gas reserves. This sector will grow rapidly and will become far more important—indeed, will become the engine of the government's economic program—and its focus will shift from the import and distribution of refined products to the search for, recovery, and export of crude oil. Already by 1985, the eve of its expansion, changes were made to revitalize this key government sector and to remove it from the shadow of rumored corruption and mismanagement. The World Bank and other donors committed considerable financing in 1986 to provide the technical support and expertise required to upgrade this part of the public sector.

Of greater importance, the development of these oil resources will tilt the balance of domestic political forces toward the state, the modern sector, and the modernists. Indeed, political forces seemed to be anticipating change and responding to the prospect of oil revenues even before production began. Many Yemenis interpreted the changes in the Abd al-Ghani government in November 1984 as the first tilt against the religious conservatives and other traditionalists who seemed so clearly in the ascendence since the early 1980s. If so, the changes may reflect the new strength and confidence felt by President Salih and his colleagues during the second half of 1984 as a result of the successive confirmations of the certainty and the size of the oil strike. The most important of these changes was the appointment of former Prime Minister Abd al-Karim al-Iryani—the YAR's leading technocrat, a strong nationalist, and a secularist—as foreign minister and deputy prime minister for external affairs. The outgoing foreign minister, the conservative Dr. Ahmad Abd al-Malik al-Asbahi, was moved to the lesser post of minister of social affairs and labor. In another change, Dr. Husayn al-Amri, a young modernist, replaced the religiously connected Dr. Abd al-Wahid al-Zandani as minister of education.

Several important government changes, in organization as well as in personnel, were made in 1985. Early in the year, the Supreme Committee for Petroleum and Mineral Resources was created to set policy and supervise negotiations in this sector. Chaired by Deputy Prime Minister al-Iryani, it brought together the heads of the several ministries and public banking institutions most directly involved in development and economic affairs. The cabinet was reshuffled again in March, and the most noteworthy change was the appointment of Dr. Muhammad Said al-Attar, who had served in top positions in development administration during more than fifteen years with the United Nations, as deputy prime minister for economic affairs, minister of development, and chairman of the Central Planning Organization. It was announced in August that in another organizational change the responsibilities of the minister of state for petroleum and mineral resources would be absorbed into a new Ministry of Oil and Mineral Resources. Under this plan, Yominco would cease to exist and its remaining responsibilities for the distribution and marketing of refined products would revert to the old Yemen Petroleum Company. Later in the fall, Ahmad Ali al-Muhani, a very able, experienced technocrat, was named the first minister of oil and mineral resources. The appointment on the same occasion of Dr. Hasan Makki as a deputy prime minister further strengthened the team of modernists headed by Abd al-Ghani, al-Iryani, and al-Attar. As Deputy Prime Minster al-Iryani put it in late 1985: "If we make a mess of the opportunity afforded by oil, no one will be able to blame President Salih for not putting good people in the top positions. The team now in place consists of the best—the very best—that Yemen has to offer."[5]

Even before these changes in government organization and personnel were effected, the decision was made at the biennial meeting of the General People's Congress in August 1984 to hold nationwide local elections that would greatly expand popular participation and representation in the GPC. This decision provides further indication that the ruling politicians and the technocrats were feeling increasingly secure and confident in their positions. The modernists had proposed and pushed for the expanded elections, whereas the various conservative elements that dominated the first GPC, and even some on the left, had opposed them as not in their political interest. The elections were held throughout the country from 17–20 July 1985, and an estimated 60 percent of all men and women aged eighteen and over participated in the balloting for 17,507 members of local councils for cooperative development (LCCDs). The LCCDs, new local institutions created out of a merger of the old local development associations and new district-level arms of the GPC, have local political and development duties as well as the task of providing the electors who will choose the 1,000 delegates of the new GPC that was scheduled to hold its biennial meeting in August 1986. Completing the circle, the new GPC was charged with electing the twenty-member national administrative board of the Federation of LCCDs, the body that has replaced the old Confederation of Yemeni Development Associations. The July 1985 election of the 17,507 members of the local councils, the first step in this process, was held with much official fanfare and a considerable amount of public enthusiasm. Involving by far the broadest participation ever in Yemeni politics, the elections were generally judged to be quite open and honest. In mid-1986, the LCCDs chose the delegates to the new GPC, which held its biennial meeting in Taiz in August under the banner "Popular Participation on the Road of Democracy, Development, and Yemeni Unity." Quite appropriately, the theme of President Salih's opening speech was the benefits of "organized political activity."[6]

The oil-fueled tilt in the balance of power, as marked by these changes in government and politics since 1984, will produce a gradual reordering of national priorities as well as a reordering of key groups in terms of their social ranking and power. Heretofore, the modernists and their allies could barely hold their own against the religious and other conservative elements, and part of the weakness of the former was the absence of the considerable material resources needed to realize their modern vision. As a result of the discovery of oil, the modern sector and modern goals will be backed for the first time by the funds needed to pursue modernity. Money talks, and, with oil revenues, the arguments of the modernists will no longer be merely academic. They will have the funds to build the modern farms, factories, and secular schools they want, even if the traditionalists and their external patrons prefer mosques and religious schools. Already, the modernists are in a better position to expand the narrow beachhead that they established over the past two decades and to fend off the counterattacks of the traditionalists. This is quite a change from the more embattled situation fostered in the early 1980s by an environment of worldwide recession and renewed domestic austerity. This change was evident in 1986 in discussions on the upcoming Third Five-Year Plan—the YAR's first with oil revenues factored in.

Lessened financial dependence on Saudi Arabia will mean that the leaders of the YAR will be freer to pursue the domestic program they regard as appropriate rather than that which is favored by the Saudi leaders. Inevitably, the clients and surrogates of Saudi Arabia in Yemeni politics will have less influence than before as being "close" to the Saudis will count for less. Having Saudi friends and supporting policies favored by the Saudis will no longer be a major or automatic political asset in the domestic political game—indeed, it may be a liability in many cases.

Finally, the pace of state building and national integration should be hastened by the flow of oil revenues. A state with ample funds of its own will be able to offer the shaykhs of the still largely autonomous tribes inducements and alternatives to Saudi subsidies, thereby speeding up their long-predicted cooptation by the Yemeni state and the more modern sector. The major commitment of the YAR government to the agricultural development of the poor and isolated Wadi Jawf region in the mid-1980s is an example of what will be possible when the oil revenues begin to flow. The process of cooptation appears to be taking place simply in anticipation of oil revenues in the cases of Shaykh Mujahid abu Shuwarib and Shaykh Abdullah ibn Husayn al-Ahmar, the paramount shaykh of the Hashid. More and more, these and other tribal leaders seem to be playing politics by rules not set by traditional tribalism or by the traditional relationship between the tribes and the state.

The resurgence and improved prospects of the state and modern sector do not mean that the tribalists and other traditionalists have been swept into the dustbin of Yemeni history. The religious conservatives still enjoy occasional victories, as they did in 1985 when they caused the regime to remove Dr. Husayn al-Amri as minister of education and to shelve, at least for the present, his plan to absorb the traditionalist Islamic institutes into a unified education system controlled by the Ministry of Education. More important, a significant conservative reaction would be possible, perhaps probable, if the modernists were to stumble badly over the next several years. The discovery of oil has merely given the modernists and technocrats the wherewithal to try to move the YAR toward the realization of their modern vision. They can fail, but now at least they have the chance to try. If they have a few years to advance the process of change, moreover, then the likelihood of a long-term deadlock or regression will be greatly reduced, even if their performance is uneven. Oil puts time on the side of the modern sector and the modernists.

External Effects and Implications

The discovery of a modest amount of oil in the YAR is not going to affect profoundly world politics or even the politics of the Middle East region. However, Yemeni oil will end the YAR's status as poor, backward cousin in the Arab family. It will incline the rest of the region to be less condescending toward the YAR and will allow the YAR to play a more significant role in Arab and Islamic councils if it so chooses. Indeed, the YAR was being promoted by Kuwait in 1986 as host to the next Arab summit meeting. Similarly, as the YAR ceases to be a client of Saudi Arabia, the United States will no longer be able—or even inclined—to defer to the Saudis on matters of primary interest to the Yemenis. As a first indication of this changing relationship, Vice President Bush, during his 1986 visit to the YAR, invited President Salih to come to the United States.

The Arabian Peninsula is the arena in which the YAR, fueled by its own oil, will have an opportunity to play a significantly changed and enhanced role. Oil will most directly affect the YAR's bilateral relations with its two nearest neighbors, the PDRY and Saudi Arabia. Indeed, oil will profoundly affect the trilateral relationship of the YAR, the PDRY, and Saudi Arabia. This, in turn, will have major implications for the politics of both the peninsula as a whole and the lesser states on its periphery.

YAR Oil and the PDRY. The belief that the discovery of oil in the YAR would inevitably color relations between the two Yemens was quickly confirmed when President Salih, in announcing in December 1984 that the YAR was about to join the company of the oil producers, stated explicitly that the oil discovered in the Alif field would be used for the benefit of the citizens of the YAR and would not be shared with the PDRY. He did add, however, that the YAR was conducting "studies" to determine whether joint exploration for oil could be carried out in the two Yemens' "adjoining areas." In what could be viewed as an accommodating stance, the YAR had raised no objections when the Hunt Oil Company earlier informed the government of its desire to communicate to the government in Aden both its belief that the prospects for finding oil in the Shabwa district of the PDRY were excellent and its interest in conducting exploratory work there.

In January 1985 there occurred a short but intense confrontation between the two Yemens in the most sensitive of their "adjoining areas," the borderlands between the Alif field and the Shabwa district. The YAR had quietly moved sizable military forces into the area around Marib and then, in the name of providing necessary security for its nearby oil operations, had seized and fortified a commanding hill close to if not straddling its undemarcated border with the PDRY. The PDRY protested at once and, following suit, placed forces on another prominent hill, one clearly within its territory. Intensive negotiations ensued in the second half of January, involving a trip by President Salih to Aden followed immediately by one by PDRY's Chairman Ali Nasir Muhammad to Taiz. The result was an agreement under which the PDRY accepted the YAR's occupation of the high ground on the basis of the latter country's legitimate security needs but with the understanding that its acceptance of this situation did not constitute an admission that the hill in question was in YAR territory.

This episode demonstrated the ability of the two Yemens to contain and to resolve amicably an oil-related dispute. Though tensions had risen sharply, the problem was settled quickly through summitry before it had a chance to escalate into open conflict, political or military. On this occasion, Arab countries that had been frustrated in earlier years in efforts to keep the two Yemens from fighting with each other commended them for their ability to contain this border incident on their own and for their apparent coming of age diplomatically.

Of course, future conflicts between the two Yemens on oil-related and other matters may not be resolved so easily. Saudi Arabia will almost certainly exploit situations with the potential for serious conflict between the two Yemens, situations similar to the border incident near the oil field in January 1985. The two Yemens are aware of this, and seem to have learned over nearly twenty years and in two border fights that conflict between them tends to work to their disadvantage and to the advantage of their common and often demanding neighbor, Saudi Arabia.

With or without Saudi meddling, however, differences between the two Yemens are certain to arise. Their routine resolution depends a great deal on the efforts of the leaders of the two Yemens to cultivate friendly relations and common interests and to enmesh their governments and peoples in an array of joint, mutually beneficial endeavors, as they did with some success throughout 1985. Relations between the two Yemens remained good, despite the border incident and a government shakeup in the PDRY that involved another political challenge to Chairman Muhammad based on charges by the militant faction of his party that he was deviating from the correct ideological line in both domestic and foreign policies. The two Yemens continued to coordinate, with some difficulty, their positions on the most salient inter-Arab issues, especially Palestinian affairs, and the PDRY made peninsular politics easier for the YAR by pursuing improved relations with Oman and other members of the Gulf Cooperation Council. Building on work done in 1984, the YAR-PDRY committee on joint projects drafted an agreement in early 1985 on the financing of future projects and agreed to study possible cooperation in tourism development, agricultural and fisheries projects, earthquake monitoring, the linkage of their electrical grids, and the timing of their five-year plans. President Salih's statement in December 1984 notwithstanding, major cooperation between the two Yemens on petroleum exploration and development has not occurred and, given the degree to which it is so vital and sensitive an issue of national strength, is not likely to occur. If they cooperate enough in other areas, however, working together on this matter will be unnecessary to preserve the peace.

Nevertheless, relations between the two Yemens will also turn on oil developments in each Yemen. A moderate, reformist YAR blessed with oil and an impoverished Marxist PDRY without oil would produce an unstable asymmetry with the strong likelihood of future conflict. In the interest of good relations—and, indeed, of Yemeni unity—the best situation would be one in which each Yemen found itself in possession of petroleum reserves sufficient to meet its development needs. Fortunately, the prospects for finding ample oil in the PDRY are considered very good. Agip Overseas of Italy made a 3,000 b/d strike offshore near Mukalla in 1982 and the Soviet Union's Technoexport has been drilling without success since early 1984 in the area that many petroleum experts regard as the most promising in the PDRY, the Shabwa district that is part of the same geological formation as the YAR's Marib-Jawf basin. Despite disappointing reports of new dry holes earlier in the year, both the Italian and the Russian teams continued their exploratory drilling in the second half of 1985, and there was talk in Aden of opening Shabwa to other foreign oil companies on a production-sharing basis. In addition, Brazil's Braspetro began drilling on an onshore concession and France's Elf Aquitaine Petroleum began drilling on the onshore portion of a site it shares with Kuwait's Independent Petroleum

Group. The interest of other exploration groups in rights to several other areas in the PDRY has been generated by seismological studies funded by the World Bank and released in 1984. Finally, the old BP refinery and tanker terminus at Little Aden was extensively modernized in 1985.

The relationship between the two Yemens was sorely tested during and for a long time after the bloodbath inside the Yemeni Socialist Party in Aden on 13 January 1986, an event that led to the flight abroad of Chairman Muhammad and the virtual decapitation of the party that in one form or another has ruled the PDRY since the British were ousted in 1967. The open dissent in the Yemeni Socialist party (YSP) in the mid-1980s against Chairman Muhammad's policies of domestic relaxation and friendly relations with the conservative Arab states on the peninsula had been interpreted by YAR leaders, wrongly it seems, as a sign of the strength rather than the weakness and vulnerability of the chairman. They had a sanguine view of the dissent of the militants—led by Deputy Chairman Ali Ahmad Nasir Antar and Defense Minister Salih Muslih Qasim—and even of the return to Aden from Moscow of their spiritual leader, former Chairman Abd al-Fattah Ismail. The YAR government became increasingly concerned only after the Third Party Congress of the YSP in October 1985 failed to resolve major issues between the chairman and his opponents.

Fighting erupted at what amounted to a guns-drawn, showdown meeting of the YSP Politburo on 13 January, with Chairman Muhammad and his supporters trying to get the other side before it got him. When the smoke cleared, he and some of the other "losers" were alive but abroad, whereas nearly all the leaders of the "winning" militant faction—including Ali Antar, Salih Muslih Qasim, and former Chairman Ismail—were dead. By one rough count, fifty of the seventy members of the Central Committee on 13 January were dead, wounded, jailed, missing, or in exile. The fighting was intense and devastating, in terms of human life and property. One assessment—hyperbolic but still saddening—had the South Yemenis doing to Aden in two weeks what it took the Lebanese ten years to do to Beirut. The shootout at the top had quickly spread to and split the armed forces, popular militia, and police, and the use of heavy weaponry was widespread. The fighting spread beyond Aden to several parts of the country and to the general population, threatening to become a full-scale civil war. This was avoided largely because Chairman Muhammad, outside the country and denied media access to the people, was quickly bested by his opponents.

The regime of survivors in Aden in the summer of 1986 included a few militant veteran politicians—most notably Ali Salim al-Baydh and Salim Salih Muhammad—and a larger number of senior and junior technocrats. The political leaders had assumed the top posts in the YSP, whereas the technocrats, including Haidar abu-Bakr al-Attas and Yasin Said Numan, had taken over the top government posts. Al-Attas, who had been prime minister under Chairman Muhammad since early 1985, became chairman and head of state, and Numan became prime minister. The new leadership quickly set about restoring order and services and providing relief at home, while giving their neighbors and foreign benefactors assurances that the policies of the recent past would be continued, prior contracts and agreements honored, and friendly relations encouraged with all. A special effort was made to dispel doubts and renew commitments with the Soviet Union, Western Europe, the Arab oil states, and such international organizations as the World Bank.

During the weeks immediately following the fighting in Aden, many informed North Yemenis argued that the Salih regime did not want to get drawn into any scheme to topple or harass the new PDRY leaders and that it had the power to resist pressures and blandishments to permit or participate in this sort of scheme. They claimed that 1986 was not 1972 or 1979, when the YAR state was too weak to say "no" to the adventurism of the tribalists and the Saudis, and that the Salih regime was single-mindedly concerned with developing the YAR's oil resources and with avoiding all actions that might threaten this development. They said that President Salih was just too smart and too strong to stumble now over this issue.

In fact, the Salih regime did not allow itself to get drawn deeply into efforts to influence the course of events in the PDRY during the two weeks of fighting and the months that followed. Although it did not take or encourage hostile actions, however, the regime in Sanaa maintained only "correct" relations with the new ruling group in Aden. The first official comment on relations with the PDRY did not come until late February, when Prime Minister Abd al-Ghani reaffirmed in a speech the desire for unity of the two Yemens. The main road connecting the two was opened in mid-March, and the PDRY's minister of state for unity affairs came to Sanaa for talks at the beginning of April, the first senior official from Aden to visit the YAR since the leadership change. Contacts between the two Yemens increased and improved slightly over the ensuing months, culminating in a three-day summit meeting between President Salih and Chairman al-Attas in Libya in early July. The summit did little to improve relations further, however, because President Salih continued to make a return to really good relations conditional on a resolution of the political conflict between the regime in Aden and former Chairman Muhammad and his supporters, a matter on which Chairman al-Attar was prepared to give little ground. In the meantime, rumors abounded about the many refugees from the PDRY in the borderlands and about the dangers posed by their continued presence.

As of fall 1986, the YAR continued to profess to want ties with the new rulers in Aden that were as friendly and beneficial as those it had had with Chairman Muhammad. The PDRY said that such relations were in the offing, but it seemed that the Salih regime was waiting for these words to be confirmed by deeds. It wanted to see concrete evidence of a policy of inter-Yemeni and regional détente.

In addition, the Salih regime was not quick to embrace the new leadership in Aden because it doubted whether that leadership would survive as then constituted. It regarded the PDRY as faced with staggering economic problems and considered the new YSP leadership as a very heterogeneous group headed by men of limited ability, experience, and stature. There was a good chance that they would not be able to agree among themselves much less unite and lead the nation. If they could not, then the likelihood of further political change would be greatly increased. As of fall 1986, the YAR chose to watch this unfolding political situation from the sidelines.

YAR Oil and Saudi Arabia. The discovery of oil gives new significance to the oft-ignored facts that, relative to Saudi Arabia, the YAR has the larger population, the greater agricultural potential, and probably a greater degree of sociocultural cohesion and sense of national identity. In coming years, whatever the mix between conflict and cooperation, the relationship between the YAR and Saudi Arabia will be one between equals or near equals rather than between patron and client. As a practical matter, this means that the Saudis will have to temper the demands they make on the YAR and, as important, pay attention to the Yemeni requests that they often felt free to ignore in the past. As of 1986, however, the YAR was still very dependent on Saudi Arabia for subsidies and development aid and will remain so for the next few years. During this period, the YAR will have to resist the temptation to bite the hand that still feeds it. The Saudis are, if anything, in a more difficult position, and the future balance of conflict and cooperation between the two neighbors depends in large part on how the Saudis negotiate the transition to this new, more equal relationship. If they were to try to take advantage of the present situation—that is, to put the Yemenis in their place while they still have the upper hand—they would merely feed hostile feelings that the YAR will have the capacity to act upon in the near future. Now or later, if Saudi Arabia challenges the YAR along their undemarcated border or tries to foster conflict between the two Yemens, then it is more likely that the new relationship between the more-nearly-equal Saudis and Yemenis will be one of conflict. The greater the conflict, moreover, the more likely it will be that the Yemenis' deep-seated anti-Saudi feelings will assert themselves. And the stronger these feelings become, the more likely it is that latent irredentist thinking about land lost to the Saudis through war in 1934—the land of Asir, Najran, and Jizan—will become manifest.

The principal elements in Saudi Arabia's Yemen policy since 1970 have been to keep the YAR dependent on its aid and to keep the two Yemens in a state of noncooperation if not open conflict. The end of YAR dependence in the late 1980s should incline the Saudis to place even greater emphasis than before on the fostering of differences between the YAR and the PDRY. However, the Saudis' inability to capitalize on the border face-off in January 1985 or the aftermath of the bloodbath in Aden in January 1986 suggests that the two Yemens are learning to counter, singly and together, the Saudi Kingdom's divide-and-conquer strategy for dealing with its persistent fears about the two Yemens. Nevertheless, the presence of oil near if not under the place where the undemarcated borders of the three countries meet provides the Saudis—as well as other parties—with ample opportunity for mischief. Some YAR officials saw in Saudi behavior in the summer of 1986 an effort to befriend and support the beleaguered regime in Aden, and, in turn, claimed that the Saudis were motivated by a desire to play the PDRY off against an increasingly independent YAR.

Relations between the YAR and Saudi Arabia since the former's discovery of oil have given only the faintest of hints of possible changes to come. The Saudis were pleased with neither the continuation by the government of Prime Minister Abd al-Ghani of many of the austerity measures initiated in 1983 by the government of Prime Minister al-Iryani nor the return of Dr. al-Iryani as foreign minister and deputy prime minister in November 1984. Nor was the twenty-year friendship treaty with the Soviet Union, signed on the occasion of President Salih's visit to Moscow in October 1984, greeted with enthusiasm by the Saudis. The opening in December 1984 of the annual meeting of the foreign ministers of the Islamic Conference Organization, the first major Islamic event ever hosted by the YAR, was delayed almost a whole day by the late arrival of a key participant, the Saudi foreign minister, who was held up by what he termed "more pressing duties and commitments." This slight and the unusually sparse coverage of the conference in the Saudi media were seen as signals of Saudi irritation with YAR efforts to forge a foreign policy more independent of its chief patron. It was during this conference that President Salih, after informing the world that the YAR was joining the ranks of the oil producers, stated pointedly that the infrastructure required to export oil could be in place in less than the planned two years if the YAR faced "economic pressures." Although the types of pressure that might arise were not specified, diplomats noted that the YAR had from the outset consciously played down the oil discovery for fear that the Saudis might use it as the excuse for sharply decreasing its financial aid. For reasons never made public, the Saudi-Yemeni Joint Coordinating Council did not meet to decide on project support and aid levels until May 1985, more than eighteen months after its last session. Earlier, at the time of the YAR-PDRY border incident in January 1985, President Salih had felt compelled to deny publicly rumors that the Saudis were stirring up trouble near the area where oil had been discovered, suggesting the growing ambiguity in relations between the YAR and Saudi Arabia. Although relations were only lukewarm during the ensuing months, the Saudi-Yemeni Joint Coordinating Council did meet again to discuss assistance in May 1986.

YAR Oil and the Arabian Peninsula. As suggested, the Arabian Peninsula is the larger arena in which a YAR with modest oil resources could play a significant role. Indeed, a stronger YAR that is no longer economically dependent upon Saudi Arabia could have major implications for peninsular politics. The necessity that Saudi Arabia deal with the YAR as an equal will afford new opportunities for the peripheral states to act in various combinations to resist Saudi hegemony. Ministates such as Kuwait and Bahrayn will have in the YAR a new, heavy counterweight to Saudi pressures, one which for the first time would make credible and plausible joint efforts by them to stand up to the sometimes overbearing Saudi Arabia and to hold it at bay. What could result might best be described as an informal or formal mutual protection society of peripheral states. Kuwait's and the United Arab Emirates' financial aid to the YAR in the decade from the mid-1970s to the mid-1980s, as with Kuwait's almost solitary support for the YAR over Saudi objections in the early years of the civil war, was motivated in part by such interests and considerations.

A strong, prosperous, and rapidly developing YAR may serve to accelerate political change on the rest of the Arabian Peninsula. That area's rather anachronistic traditional regimes, particularly that of Saudi Arabia, have had reason for concern over the presence in their midst of two examples of "modern" republicanism. Since the 1960s, however, these traditional regimes have been able to find comfort in the less than clearcut case made by the two Yemens for republicanism in either reformist or radical dress: the two Yemeni republics were also the two poorest of the countries on the peninsula and seemed destined to remain so. If oil allows either or both Yemens to combine republicanism with national strength and development, the situation could change significantly. Republicanism could be advanced passively by example—by the demonstration effect—or it could be actively promoted by either or both of the Yemens. If it had the resources at its disposal, there is little reason to believe that the YAR would be much less inclined than the PDRY to promote the blessings of republicanism elsewhere on the periphery and especially in the Saudi heartland of Arabia. Indeed, successful republicanism on the peninsula, however moderate and restrained, may pose the greatest of all threats to the future of the Saudi Kingdom and its ruling family.

Conclusion

Better times appear to be in the offing for the land and people that for centuries seemed mocked by the name Arabia Felix. Nevertheless, the new power and freedom afforded by the discovery of oil does not guarantee development, greater abundance, and a better life. As the cases of Mexico and Nigeria suggest, new oil wealth can confound even reasonably good national intentions and efforts. Though it creates opportunities, this new freedom is also the freedom to make the mistakes that abort the opportunity for development and beneficial change. It can lead to rampant corruption, cultural impoverishment, yawning inequalities, unmanageable indebtedness, and economic collapse. Oil works its wonders in divers ways.

Furthermore, oil wealth does not mean independence from the outside world, certainly not the kind of independence known a generation ago by the Yemen of Imams Yahya and Ahmad. Though it does mean less financial dependence on Saudi Arabia and several other large donors, it also means that the YAR is likely to be plugged more tightly and in a growing number of ways into the international economic system that is still dominated by the mature industrial states—the United States, the countries of Western Europe, and Japan—the international institutions these states largely control, and the multinational corporations. There are tradeoffs here, in terms of both development and independence, and whether the YAR comes out ahead in the short or long run is by no means certain.

Even if oil does give the YAR much greater power to determine its future, it does not follow that the YAR is about to embark on radically new paths in domestic and external policies. Despite dependence on Saudi Arabia, the leaders of the YAR largely did what they wanted to do in the years since 1970. They compromised and dissembled, but they resisted the Saudis and remained true to themselves and their country to a remarkable degree. As a consequence, it is likely that a YAR bolstered by oil will amount to much more of the same. While not as conservative and strictly Islamic as the Saudis might like, the YAR remains deeply influenced by traditional ideas and institutions and is not likely to be transformed by choice into a secularist Marxist people's republic. Nor is the main street running along the top of Independence Square in Sanaa likely to take the place of Hamra Street in the hedonistic, free-enterprise Beirut of old. Similarly, the YAR is not likely to try either imposing its version of Yemeni unity upon the PDRY or establishing by force of arms the boundaries it might want with Saudi Arabia. A reformist YAR—an Arabia Felix, one hopes—setting a good example for the rest of the Arabian Peninsula, is the greatest likelihood.

In 1976, when asked about the YAR's prospects for oil and development, Dr. Abd al-Karim al-Iryani shot back: "Of course I want Yemen to find oil—after ten years. In the meantime, we must both use our poverty to wring as much aid as we can from the rest of the world and develop the manpower and infrastructure needed to put oil wealth to good use."[7] The YAR got just about the ten years hoped for by Dr. al-Iryani. When reminded in 1986 of his earlier wish, he expressed some satisfaction, noting that efforts at agricultural development, which gained strong momentum only at the end of the 1970s, would probably not have happened had oil been struck in 1964 or 1974, instead of 1984. Dr. al-Iryani is most likely correct in the matter of agricultural development. Perhaps by the year 2000 it will be known whether the YAR made good use generally of this decade of grace and the years just after the discovery of oil.

Postscript
December 1986

The economic and political prospects of the YAR in late 1986 closely corresponded to forecasts made at midyear. Both domains were mixes of pluses and minuses, with the former outweighing the latter by a good margin. In short, the YAR's prospects looked more good than bad.

In the second half of 1986, the near-term economic situation worsened by about as much as longer-term prospects became more clearly positive. New shortfalls in external aid and workers' remittances—primarily effects of the further collapse of oil-borne prosperity in the region—caused a return to large deficits in the government budget and the balance of payments. Indeed, economic fundamentals looked as grim by mid-1986 as they had in 1982–1983, and they promised to remain so throughout 1987. In response, the Abd al-Ghani government in July tried to streamline and consolidate the state's machinery for economic management by merging the Ministry of Economy and Industry and the Ministry of Supply and Commerce into a single ministry, the Ministry of Economy, Supply and Trade. Headed by Muhammad Khadim al-Wajih, the former minister of finance and a very experienced administrator, the new ministry was to place emphasis on its responsibility for foreign trade and on the promotion of foreign investment in the YAR.

Of greater importance, the government attempted to place new restrictions on currency transactions and imports. The government announced in mid-July the adoption of controls on moneychangers in an effort to end the black-market speculation in dollars that had sharply depressed the value of the Yemeni rial, especially since the beginning of 1986. Unlicensed moneychangers were to be closed, and licensed ones were to be subject to new regulations. In another move, procedures for approving applications for import licenses were tightened and a new high-level economic committee was formed to evaluate license applications. By the fall of 1986, businessmen in Sanaa were saying that import licenses were becoming increasingly difficult to obtain and that there was a real import squeeze. The only items getting approval were essential foods, raw materials, spare parts, medical supplies, and goods required to build the oil industry infrastructure.

Evidence that the Salih regime took seriously the economic difficulties can be seen in President Salih's unusual open letter to the government, read on Sanaa radio on 13 October, in which he instructed his ministers to take steps to revitalize the economy. This broad policy statement called for revised pricing policies and a new effort to combat smuggling, as well as measures to encourage the investment of expatriate remittances in Yemen and major emphasis upon many areas of agricultural investment. Earlier, by midyear, the YAR government had decided to bridge the current economic gap by seeking its first large commercial loans, one of $50 million to finance imports for the rest of 1986, including crude oil, and another of $200 million to finance some of the costs of the infrastructure of the new petroleum industry.

Current economic difficulties notwithstanding, major and ongoing development activities proceeded apace during the second half of 1986. Completion of the first stage of the Marib Dam project was marked by much fanfare, and progress was made on projects to extend the national electrical grid, increase the capacity of the cement industry, and develop the agricultural potential of major wadis on the Tihama. Most important, thanks to the joint venture between the Hunt Oil Company and the Exxon Corporation the petroleum age and its fruits became more palpable and less easily dismissed as mirage or wishful thinking. The contract for the 261-mile (420-kilometer) crude oil pipeline from the Alif field down to the Red Sea was awarded in mid-September to a three-company consortium. The laying of the pipe, the delivery of which had begun earlier in the year, was to begin at both ends of the route in December 1986. The contract called for completion of the pipeline in late 1987, thereby making possible the flow of Yemeni oil to the coast in early 1988. Contracts for work on the Red Sea terminus and the offshore section of the pipeline were also let, and their completion was set to coincide with that of the onshore portion. Most certainly, Yemeni oil would be exported—and desperately needed hard currency earned—in 1988.

Drilling activities by the Yemen Hunt Oil Company in the Marib-Jawf basin continued at a rapid rate during the second half of 1986, yielding modest amounts of oil and huge quantities of gas. These gas reserves, though they will require separate development at great cost, hold out the promise of meeting a major part of the YAR's energy needs for many decades to come. Oil exploration outside the Marib-Jawf basin also continued throughout 1986. Offshore Yemen Hunt, the operator which had conducted seismic work in 1985 in Hunt Oil Company's concession off the Red Sea coast, announced intentions to begin drilling its first offshore exploration well near al-Hudayda before the end of 1986. The Exxon Corporation's preliminary seismic tests continued in the northern highlands and France's Compagnie Française des Petroles (Total) started offshore seismic work on its concession south of al-Hudayda in the fall of the year.

Domestic politics were not unaffected by the economic hard times and the restrictive measures adopted to cope with them in the second half of 1986. There was considerable grumbling in Sanaa and elsewhere about the intended and unintended consequences of particular policies and about several of the senior technocrats who served in the government and advised

President Salih. The latter was criticized for being out of touch with the situation in the country and the captive of certain "leftists" and "secularists." Much of this criticism came from religious and traditionalist elements that had been on the defensive since the elections of the local councils of cooperative development (LCCDs) in July and the third biennial session of the General People's Congress (GPC) in late August.

These grumblings notwithstanding, the Salih regime in late 1986 did not seem subject to serious challenge or imminent danger. President Salih appeared to have the continuing support of the military and most important civilian elements. And he continued to attend to political concerns. In his opening and closing addresses before the GPC, the president repeated the theme of the need for and his commitment to "the development of . . . organized political action."[1] This litany of political construction was reiterated by him and by his colleagues during the 26 September Revolution Day celebrations.[2] Only time will tell whether the GPC will fill in this verbal framework with a meaningful, persistent pattern of political thought and action.

External politics in the latter half of 1986 were marked by efforts to squeeze as much economic aid and technical assistance as possible from an external environment then less prosperous and generous than before and by efforts to contain the effects of the January 1986 blood bath in Aden. The deals for the $50 million and the $200 million commercial loans from foreign banks were put together, and a loan from the International Development Agency for petroleum-related road construction was secured. Saudi Arabia and Qatar made new grants in July for reconstruction in the area hit by the 1982 earthquake, and West Germany agreed to generous economic aid on the occasion of Development Minister al-Attar's late-October visit. Good relations between the YAR and Saudi Arabia were cultivated by both sides, and Crown Prince Abdullah's participation in the 26 September Revolution Day celebrations in Sanaa was followed in a week by a three-day visit to Saudi Arabia by President Salih and Foreign Minister al-Iryani.

The Salih regime's major political concern during the second half of 1986 continued to be the containment of the ill effects of the blood bath in Aden in January that had resulted in the overthrow of Ali Nasir Muhammad. The brief summit meeting in Libya in early July between President Salih and the PDRY's new chief of state, Haidar abu-Bakr al-Attas, did little to thaw relations between the two Yemens. The Salih regime refused to accede to the PDRY's apparent wish for close ties until the YAR was relieved of the danger and economic burden of the approximately 20,000 refugees from the January upheaval, a condition that could only be met if the new PDRY regime came to some sort of settlement with ex-President Muhammad and the leaders who had fled with him from the PDRY. In addition, the government in Sanaa seemed to be holding out for clear signs in the form of specific policies that the new leaders in Aden were in control and as committed as ex-President Muhammad to a reasonable, moderate course of domestic and external politics. Admittedly, there were risks involved in the Salih regime's insistence on driving a fairly hard bargain with its counterpart in Aden. Though both sides realized that the armed refugees in camps inside the YAR constituted a time bomb, the prevention of its going off would put both regimes to the test. In late 1986, both regimes still seemed to be meeting this test successfully.

Notes

Chapter 1

1. Paul Dresch, "Tribal Relations and Political History in Upper Yemen," in B. R. Pridham, ed., *Contemporary Yemen: Politics and Historical Background* (New York: St. Martin's Press, 1984), p. 154.
2. R. B. Sergeant, "Perilous Politics in Two Yemeni States," *Geographical Magazine* 51 (August 1979), p. 769.

Chapter 2

1. Richard H. Sanger, *The Arab Peninsula* (Ithaca, N.Y.: Cornell University Press, 1954), p. 242.
2. Robin Bidwell, *The Two Yemens* (Boulder, Colo.: Westview Press, 1983), p. 59.
3. Harold Ingrams, *The Yemen: Imams, Rulers and Revolution* (London: John Murray, 1963), p. 32.
4. Ibid., p. 33.
5. Hugh Scott, *In the High Yemen* (London: John Murray, 1942), p. 171.
6. Harry Hoogstraal, "Yemen Opens the Door to Progress," *The National Geographic Magazine* 101 (February 1952), p. 220.
7. Muhammad Anaam Ghaleb, *Government Organizations as a Barrier to Economic Development in Yemen* (Sanaa, YAR: National Institute of Public Administration, 1979), and Muhammad Said al-Attar, *Le Sous-Developpement Economique et Social du Yemen* (Algiers: Editions Tiers-monde, 1964).
8. Bidwell, *The Two Yemens*, p. 129.
9. Fred Halliday, *Arabia Without Sultans* (New York: Vintage Books), pp. 128–129.
10. Talk with Muhammad Abd al-Aziz Sallam, Sanaa, 1978.
11. Edgar O'Ballance, *The War in the Yemen* (Hamden, Conn.: Archon Books, 1971), p. 145.
12. Halliday, *Arabia Without Sultans*, p. 128.

Chapter 3

1. Although his proper title was chairman of the Republican Council, Qadi al-Iryani was usually referred to in English as President al-Iryani.
2. Robert W. Stookey, "Social Structure and Politics in the Yemen Arab Republic," *Middle East Journal* 28, no. 3 (1974), p. 249.
3. Stookey, "Social Structure and Politics," p. 251.
4. Talk with Muhammad Abdullah al-Shami, Sanaa, 1976.
5. This apt label is used by Halliday, *Arabia Without Sultans*, p. 126.
6. Stookey, "Social Structure and Politics," p. 252.

7. Talk with Muhammad Anaam Ghaleb, dean, the National Institute of Public Administration, Sanaa, 1976.
8. Halliday, *Arabia Without Sultans*, p. 144.
9. Talk with Husayn al-Hubayshi, legal adviser to the president, Sanaa, 1978.
10. Talk with Ahmad Abdu Said, minister of state, Taiz, 1976.
11. Reported in the *Arab Report and Record (ARR)*, 16-31 August 1971, p. 453.
12. Discussions with several individuals in Sanaa in 1976 and 1978.

Chapter 4

1. United Nations Development Program, *Background Paper for a Country Program for the Yemen Arab Republic* (Sanaa, March 1973, mimeo.), p. 13.

Chapter 5

1. Yemenis and others commonly referred to al-Hamdi in English as "president," despite the fact that the position allowing him to act as head of state was that of chairman of the Command Council.
2. Reported in the *ARR*, 1-15 June 1974, p. 234.
3. Reported in the *ARR*, 16-30 June 1974, p. 262.
4. Talk with Muhammad Abdullah al-Shami, Sanaa, 1976.
5. Talk with Dr. Abd al-Karim al-Iryani, minister of development and chairman of the Central Planning Organization, Sanaa, early 1976.
6. Reported in the *ARR*, 16-31 January 1975, p. 90.
7. For a brief account of an informal discussion in 1976 that reveals some of the differences between modernists who opposed political construction and those who favored it, a discussion in which the author participated with, among others, Michael Hudson, a former UAR prime minister and a future one, see Michael Hudson, *Arab Politics: The Search for Legitimacy* (New Haven, Conn.: Yale University Press, 1977), pp. 349-350.

Chapter 6

1. Reported in the *ARR*, 16-31 January 1977, p. 62.
2. Reported in the *ARR*, 1-15 August 1975, p. 452.
3. Talk with Muhammad Abdullah al-Shami, Sanaa, 1976.

Chapter 7

1. Confidential discussion, Sanaa, 1977.
2. Confidential discussion, Sanaa, 1981.
3. Confidential discussion, Sanaa, 1978.
4. Talk with Dr. Abd al-Karim al-Iryani, Sanaa, 1978.

Chapter 8

1. Confidential discussion, Sanaa, 1980.
2. Reported in *Foreign Broadcast Information Service, Middle East and Africa, Daily Report* (FBIS), 28 January 1981.
3. Reported in *FBIS*, 12 December 1981; and in the *Middle East Economic Digest* (MEED), 11-17 December 1981, p. 68, and 15-21 January 1982, p. 41.
4. Reported in *FBIS*, 9 September 1981.
5. Reported in *FBIS*, 3 April 1980.

Notes

6. Reported in FBIS, 25 March 1980.
7. Reported in FBIS, 25 March 1980.
8. Reported in FBIS, 2 June 1981.
9. Interview in MEED, 2-8 October 1981, p. 43.

Chapter 9

1. Reported in MEED, 30 April-6 May 1982, pp. 43-44.
2. Reported in MEED, 19-25 March 1982, p. 55; and in FBIS, 15 and 18 March 1982.
3. Reported in FBIS, 10 May 1982.
4. Interview in MEED, 26 November-2 December 1982, p. 86.
5. Reported in FBIS, 26 August 1982.

Chapter 10

1. Sanger, *The Arab Peninsula*, p. 244.
2. Stephen Longriggs, *Oil in the Middle East* (London: Oxford University Press, 1953), p. 214.
3. Ibid., p. 235.
4. Ibrahim al-Rashid, *Yemen Enters the Modern World: Secret U.S. Documents on the Rise of the Second Power on the Arabian Peninsula* (Chapel Hill, N.C.: Documentary Publications, 1984), p. 222.
5. Talk with Deputy Prime Minister al-Iryani, New York, November 1985.
6. Reported in FBIS, 27 August 1986.
7. Talk with Dr. Abd al-Karim al-Iryani, Sanaa, 1976.

Postscript

1. Reported in FBIS, 27 August 1986.
2. Reported in FBIS, 26 September 1986.

Bibliographical Essay

The best political history of Yemen during the two millennia prior to the twentieth century as well as this century down to the demise of the al-Iryani regime in 1974 remains Robert W. Stookey, *Yemen: The Politics of the Yemen Arab Republic* (Boulder, Colo.: Westview Press, 1978). A good, differently focused supplement to this is Robert W. Stookey, "Social Structure and Politics in the Yemen Arab Republic," *Middle East Journal* 28, no. 3 (1974), pp. 248-60; and 28, no. 4 (1974), pp. 409-18.

Three books that deal with politics and social life under the Zaydi imamate at various times in the twentieth century are fascinating reading in part because of the extent to which the Yemen and Yemeni imamate in 1962 was so unchanged from earlier decades. They are Ameen Rihani, *Arabian Peak and Desert: Travels in al-Yemen* (Boston and New York: Houghton Mifflin Co., 1930); Hugh Scott, *In the High Yemen* (London: John Murray, 1942); and Harold Ingrams, *The Yemen: Imams, Rulers and Revolutions* (London: John Murray, 1963). Still worth reading to get a sense of the remarkable continuity in the imamate is the earliest western account of Yemen, first published in 1792, Carsten Niebuhr, *Travels through Arabia and Other Countries in the East*, translated by Robert Heron, two vols. (Beirut: Librairie du Liban, n. d.). Some fascinating material on the imamate in the twentieth century can be culled from two recent collections. They are Ibrahim al-Rashid, ed., *Yemen Enters the Modern World: Secret U. S. Documents on the Rise of the Second Power on the Arabian Peninsula* (Chapel Hill, N.C.: Documentary Publications, 1984); and Ibrahim al-Rashid, ed., *Yemen Under the Rule of Imam Ahmad* (Chapel Hill, N.C.: Documentary Publications, 1985).

Books on the politics of the YAR since the 1962 Revolution tend to become very thin and unsure of themselves on the period from the early 1970s forward. Though it stops in the mid-1960s, in the midst of the civil war, still useful is Manfred W. Wenner, *Modern Yemen: 1918-1966* (Baltimore, Md.: Johns Hopkins University Press, 1968). For a politically radical treatment that puts the politics of the YAR in the context of the struggle for radical change on the Arabian Peninsula as a whole, see Fred Halliday, *Arabia Without Sultans* (New York: Vintage Books, 1975). Halliday updates his story in two good essays in "The Contest for Arabia," *Middle East Research and Information Project (MERIP) Reports* 15, no. 2 (February 1985).

A book that is good on the last decades of the imamate but rather confused and confusing on the period from 1970 to 1980 is J. E. Peterson, *Yemen: The Search for a Modern State* (Baltimore, Md.: Johns Hopkins University Press, 1982). Although weaker than it should be on the 1970s and early 1980s, a book that has the decided virtue of treating the two Yemens in relation to one another is Robin Bidwell, *The Two Yemens* (Boulder, Colo.: Westview Press, 1983). A long chapter that evokes well the YAR in 1978 is found in Jonathan Raban, *Arabia: A Journey Through the Labyrinth* (New York: Simon and Schuster, 1979).

A symposium at the University of Exeter, U. K., resulted in two volumes of very current essays on the two Yemens, and some of them are excellent. The volumes are B. R. Pridham, ed., *Contemporary Yemen: Politics and Historical Background* (New York: St. Martin's Press, 1984) and B. R. Pridham, ed., *Economy, Society and Culture in Contemporary Yemen* (London: Croom Helm, 1985). To learn just about all there is to know about Sanaa and much about Yemen in general, see the monumental R. B. Sergeant and Ronald Lewcock, eds., *Sana: An Arabian Islamic City* (London: The World of Islam Festival Trust, 1983).

The World Bank remains the source of the best studies of economics and development in the YAR. See *Yemen Arab Republic: Development of a Traditional Economy* (Washington, D.C.: The World Bank, January 1979). For a World Bank assessment since the discovery of oil, see *Yemen Arab Republic: Current Position and Prospects* (Washington, D.C.: The World Bank, June 1985).

The two Yemens have not been well covered by the newspapers and the news magazines. Perhaps the best sources for news reporting and feature articles are the *New York Times*, the *International Herald Tribune*, the *Times* (London), and *Le Monde*. Useful material occasionally appears in the *Christian Science Monitor*, the *Washington Post*, and the *Wall Street Journal*.

Among the general news magazines, the *Economist* (London) provides the most regular coverage of the two Yemens. The *MERIP Reports*, published monthly by the Middle East Research and Information Project, P.O. Box 1247, New York, NY 10025, occasionally contains excellent features on the two Yemens. Without question, the best sources for weekly chronologies of events and timely features are *Arab Report and Record* (ARR), 1967–1979, London, and the *Middle East Economic Digest* (MEED), London. (The ARR was absorbed by MEED in the late 1970s, and the latter continues to provide good coverage.) For radio coverage of the Yemens, see the *Foreign Broadcast Information Service, Daily Report, Middle East and Africa* (Washington, D.C.: U.S. Government) and *Summary of World Broadcasts, Middle East and Africa* (London: The BBC).

Index

Abd al-Alim, Abdullah, 59, 61, 80, 90-92, 95
Abd al-Ghani, Abd al-Aziz, 38, 40, 46, 59, 62-67, 71, 80, 84, 92-93, 101-102, 109, 114-116, 122, 128, 130, 132, 141-142, 148, 150, 153
Abdullah, Crown Prince, 155
Abu Dhabi (and Abu Dhabi Fund), 56, 64, 81, 123, 151
abu Luhum, Ali, 51, 60
abu Luhum, Sinan, 31, 50-51, 58-60, 77, 88. *See also* abu Luhum, Ali
abu Shuwarib, Mujahid, 50-51, 60, 109, 144
Aden (city and colony), 4, 9, 12, 15, 19-21, 27, 78, 83, 101, 120, 147-148
Aden, Gulf of, 1, 4. *See also* Indian Ocean and the monsoons
Aden Protectorates, 12, 17, 20, 27
Advisory Council to the President, 110
Afghanistan, similarities to, 7-9, 15, 20
civil war and Soviet intervention, 96, 107
African influence (racial and cultural), 7, 9, 11
Agip Overseas (Italy), 139, 146
Agriculture, Ministry of, 65
Agriculture, 5-6, 11-12, 15, 17, 26, 35, 67, 122, 153-154
Ahmad, Imam, 16-22, 133, 135, 151
al-Ahmar, Abdullah ibn Husayn, 31, 49-51, 54, 58-61, 64, 71, 76-77, 79, 84, 86, 109-110, 144
Aid and assistance (economic and technical), 20, 27, 35, 40, 44-45, 48-49, 66, 78-81, 83-84, 86, 89, 96, 98, 105-107, 113-114, 118, 122-123, 125-127, 130, 141, 149, 153, 155

al-Aini, Muhsin, 34, 36-37, 40, 43-44, 46, 50, 57-59, 64, 78, 88
Akhdam (servant) caste, 11. *See also* African influence
Algeria, 136
Alif-1 oil well and Alif field, 134, 137-140, 145, 154
Amal (journal), 130
American Overseas Investment Corporation, 135
Amoco (United States), 139
Amran, 7, 90
al-Amri, Hasan, 34-35, 37-39, 42, 67
al-Amri, Dr. Husayn, 142, 144
ANM. *See* Arab Nationalist Movement
Antar, Ali Ahmad Nasir, 129, 147
Arabian Peninsula, xiv, 1, 4, 15, 81-82, 107, 121, 144, 150-152
Arab-Israeli (Egyptian-Israeli) conflict and peace. *See* Israel
Arab League and Arab summits, 45, 92, 95, 97, 104, 108, 121, 144
Arab Monetary Fund, 114
Arab Nationalist Movement (ANM), 21, 26-27, 29-30, 62
Arab Socialist Union, 73-74
Arab world or region, 1, 14, 19, 21, 27, 82, 96, 106-107, 119, 129, 133, 144
Arafat, Yasir, 121. *See also* Palestinians
Arhab, 61
al-Arishi, Abd al-Karim, 92-93, 102
Armed forces, 17-18, 25, 30, 32, 37-38, 51, 53, 56-57, 63, 77, 80, 90, 95-97, 103, 127
officers' political role, 22, 34, 36-38, 43, 57-60, 62-64, 86-87, 90-93, 95-99, 101, 109, 116, 127, 155
reform and reequipment, 18, 20, 25, 32, 51, 56, 63-64, 86-87, 109
staff officers, 34, 37, 57-60, 88, 92

163

See also Arms and military aid; Security forces and police
Arms and military aid, 20, 51, 58, 63–64, 78, 90, 104–107, 109, 119. See also Armed forces, reform and reequipment
al-Asbahi, Ahmad Abd al-Malik, 130, 142
Asir, 12, 17, 135, 149
al-Asnaj, Abdullah, 78–79, 83, 105–106, 109
al-Attar, Muhammad Said, 21, 24–25, 38, 116, 122, 133, 142, 155
al-Attas, Haidar, abu-Bakr, 147, 155
al-Awadi, Ahmad Abd al-Rabbou, 50

Baath party, 21, 58–59, 62, 79, 100
Bab al-Mandab Straits, 1. See also Aden, Gulf of; Red Sea; Suez Canal
al-Bahr, Ali Abd al-Rahman, 137
Bahrayn, 134, 150
Bakil tribes and confederation, 10, 18, 23, 50, 59
Balance of payments, 35, 37, 44–45, 66, 113–114, 125–128, 153
Banking, domestic and foreign. See Central Bank
Basindwa, Muhammad Salim, 109
al-Baydh, Ali Salim, 147
al-Baydha, 7
Bayt al-Faqi, 7
Beirut. See Lebanon
Bidwell, Robin, 16, 22
Border troubles, fights, and wars
  with the PDRY, 43–44, 53–54, 80, 82–83, 95–99, 102–108, 119–120, 136–137, 145–146, 148–150, 156
  with Saudi Arabia, 17, 106, 128, 130, 145, 149–150
BP. See British Petroleum
Braspetro (Brazil), 146
British Petroleum (BP), 138–139, 147
Budget Office, 41, 47, 49. See also Finance Ministry
Budgets, budgetary process, and budget deficits, 18, 34, 41, 44, 47, 49, 55, 114, 125–129, 153. See also Budget Office
Bureaucracy. See Civil service and administrative reform

Bush, George, xiii, 140, 144

Cairo Unification Agreement (1972), 54, 96, 100. See also Unity and unification
C. Deilmann Bergban G.m.b.H. (West Germany), 135
Census and census taking, 1, 39, 41, 49
Center-periphery issues, 6–7, 10, 17–19, 23, 32, 51–53, 55, 61, 64, 99, 144
Central Bank, 40, 45–46, 62–63, 66–67, 113, 117, 127–128
Central Organization for National Security, 63, 105, 109
Central Planning Organization (CPO), 38–42, 47–49, 63, 65–67, 113–117, 127, 142. See also Technical Office
China, People's Republic of, 20–21, 37, 45
Civil service and administrative reform, 18, 24–25, 38–39, 41, 50, 53, 63, 65–66, 69, 71–72, 115, 125, 141–142, 153–154. See also Civil Service and Administrative Reform, Ministry of; Corruption and inefficiency; Diwan and "diwan mentality"; National Institute of Public Administration
Civil Service and Administrative Reform, Ministry of, 115
Civil war (1962–1970), 22–27, 29–32, 34–35, 39, 80, 96, 133, 136, 151
Climate and geography, 1–6, 12
Colonialism. See Imperialism
Command Council, 57–58, 60, 64, 68, 80, 88, 91–92, 97
Commando and paratroop brigade, 25, 30, 59, 61, 90
Communist party (Yemeni), 21. See also Popular Democratic Union
Compagnie Française des Petroles (Total), 139, 154
Confederation of Yemeni Development Associations (CYDA), 57–58, 68–70, 91, 108, 111–113, 143, 178
Conservatives, 22, 26, 28–30, 49–53, 58, 60, 66, 70–71, 73, 88–89, 97, 99–101, 105, 124–125, 131–132, 141–143, 155

Constitutions and constitutional issues, 21, 33, 60, 77, 91, 96–97, 124–125. *See also* 1970 Constitution
Consultative Council, 33–34, 36–37, 49, 53, 55–60, 62, 68, 72, 91, 97, 113, 132
Cooperatives and cooperative movement. *See* Confederation of Yemeni Development Associations; Local council for cooperative development; Local development association
Correction Movement, 69–70, 72–73, 76. *See also* Higher (or Supreme) Correction Committee; 13 June Correction Movement
Corruption and inefficiency, 53, 55, 58, 66, 69
Coups and assassinations, 21–22, 37–38, 43–44, 86–87, 95, 101, 108, 135–136, 147
  1955 coup, 21
  See also 1948 Revolution
CPO. *See* Central Planning Organization
Crane, Charles R., 134
Culture of Yemen, 7–14. *See also* Islam, forms and sociocultural role of
Currency Board, 40
Customs duties. *See* Imports, exports, and import-export duties and controls
CYDA. *See* Confederation of Yemeni Development Associations

Damash, Ahmad, 69, 77–78
Deficits. *See* Balance of payments; Budgets, budgetary process, and budget deficits
Dependence and independence (Yemen's), 15–16, 24, 31, 105, 133, 140–141, 143, 149–152
Deutsche Shell (West Germany), 136–137
Development, Minister of, 47, 62, 114–115, 142, 155. *See also* Central Planning Organization
Development and change (socioeconomic and cultural), xiv, 5–7, 15–16, 24, 26, 43, 45, 53, 62–63, 65–67, 71–72, 75, 86–87, 89, 94, 113–117, 122–123, 126–127, 141, 143, 148, 151–154
Development conferences, international, 67, 86, 89, 116, 118, 120, 122–123, 126
Development plans and planning, 38–39, 41–42, 47–49, 55, 67, 86, 114, 116–119, 122–123, 125–127, 143
Dhamar (province and town), 7, 139
Dhufar and Dhufar rebellion. *See* Oman
Diwan and "diwan mentality," 12, 19, 115
Djibouti (city and country), 1, 19, 24, 83
Drought (late 1960s–early 1970s), 4, 35, 133

Earthquake (Dhamar province, 1982), 126
  relief and reconstruction, 126–128, 155
Economic aid. *See* Aid and assistance
Economic crises (of the 1980s), 125–129, 153–154
Economic development. *See* Development and change
Economics and Industry, Ministry of, 25, 38, 65, 153
Economy, Supply and Trade, Ministry of, 153
Education, Ministry of, 62, 65–66, 130, 132, 142, 144
Education and training, 20–21, 24, 41, 66. *See also* Education, Ministry of; National Institute of Public Administration; Sanaa University
Egypt, 20–29, 31, 41, 45, 51, 73–74, 76, 79, 96–98, 132–133
Elections and electoral activities, 33, 36–37, 60, 68–70, 77, 108, 110–112, 124, 131–132, 142–143, 155
Electoral commission or committee, 68, 110
Elf Aquitaine Petroleum (France), 146
Emigration and emigrants (workers and students), 6–7, 9, 19–21, 24–25, 31, 39, 66, 84, 126
Empty Quarter, 1, 6, 18. *See also* Ramlat al-Sabatayn

Eritrean rebellion, 83
Ethiopia, 1, 7, 11, 19, 82–84, 129
  Eritrean rebellion, 83
Europe, Eastern. *See* Socialist camp
Europe, Western. *See* Western nations and Japan (industrial nations)
Exchange rates and controls. *See* Money and currency
External relations and foreign policy
  during the al-Hamdi and al-Ghashmi eras, 58–59, 64–66, 78–87, 90, 92, 137
  under the imams, 12, 14–16, 20–21, 134–136
  during the al-Iryani era, 28, 34, 37, 39–40, 43–46, 51, 53–54, 56, 136
  oil as an influence on, 133, 141, 144–152, 156
  during the Salih era, 94–96, 98–107, 113–114, 116–123, 125–126, 129–132
  during the al-Sallal era, 22–27
Exxon Corporation, xiii, 138–140, 154

Famous Forty, 20–22, 24, 34, 36
Federation of LCCDs, 143
Finance Ministry, 39, 47, 55, 65–66. *See also* Budget Office; Treasury Ministry
Financial crisis (late 1960s–early 1970s), 35–39, 43–45
First Five-Year Development Plan, 67, 86, 89, 114, 116
FLOSY. *See* Front for the Liberation of Occupied South Yemen
Foreign Affairs, Ministry of, 57, 78, 130, 132, 142
Foreign investors, lenders, and donors, 20–21, 27, 36–37, 39–40, 45–46, 48–49, 66–67, 113–114, 116–118, 122–123, 126–127, 154–155. *See also* Open door policy
Foreign policy. *See* External relations and foreign policy
France, xiv, 27, 36, 82, 129, 146
Free Yemenis, 21, 37
Front for the Liberation of Occupied South Yemen (FLOSY), 30, 78

al-Gadr, Naji bin Ali, 23
Gas reserves, 154

GCC. *See* Gulf Cooperation Council
General People's Congress (GPC), 76–77, 91, 111–113, 118, 124–125, 130–132, 142–143, 155
Geography. *See* Climate and geography
Ghaleb, Muhammad Anaam, 21, 38–41, 48
al-Ghashmi, Ahmad Husayn, 58–59, 88–93, 95–97, 110–111, 138
al-Ghashmi interlude, xv, 88–92
Giants Brigade, 58, 64, 90. *See also* al-Hamdi, Abdullah
Glory Brigade, 51
GPC. *See* General People's Congress
Graduates. *See* Emigration and emigrants; Modernists and modern sector
Great Britain, xiv, 12, 20, 27, 29, 36, 78, 81, 119, 135
Guerrilla acts and rebellion, 29–30, 35, 44, 53, 79–80, 82, 94, 102–103, 119–120, 122, 156
Gulf Arab oil states, 45, 79, 81, 123, 126, 134, 136, 148
Gulf Cooperation Council (GCC), 107, 129, 146
Gulf Interstate Engineering Company (Texas), 139
Gulf of Aden. *See* Aden, Gulf of
Gulf War, 107, 123, 126, 129

Hajja, 7, 50–51, 60
al-Hajri, Abdullah, 43–47, 50, 54, 56, 68, 77
Halliday, Fred, 23, 26, 33
al-Hamdi, Abdullah, 58, 64, 86, 90
al-Hamdi, Ibrahim Muhammad, 44, 57–64, 66–70, 73–91, 93, 95–97, 99–100, 108–109, 111, 138, 158(n1)
al-Hamdi coup, 44, 57–58, 60. *See also* 13 June Correction Movement
al-Hamdi regime and era, xiv–xv, 57–61, 63–64, 66–70, 73–85, 87, 89, 97, 109
Hamid al-Din family, 16–17, 21–23, 29, 133
Hasa province (Saudi Arabia), 134
Hashid tribes and confederation, 10, 18, 59, 97
Higher (or Supreme) Correction Committee, 69, 111. *See also* Correction Movement

Himyarites, 14
Horn of Africa security, 82-84
al-Hubayshi, Husayn, 158(n9)
al-Hudayda (city and province), 6-9, 20, 50-51, 60, 67, 135-138, 154
al-Hudayda incident (March 1968), 30, 32, 51
Hudson, Michael, 158(ch.5 n7)
Hunt, Ray, 140
Hunt Oil Company, xiii, 134, 137, 145, 154. *See also* Yemen Hunt Oil Company; Offshore Yemen Hunt

Ibb (town and province), 57, 95, 102
Ideology and political ideas, 8-10, 12-14, 16-17, 21, 28, 30-31, 33, 62-63, 70-75, 77, 86, 96-97, 111, 113-115, 117, 124-125, 132, 143-144, 149, 152. *See also* Nationalism and national identity
IFC. *See* International Finance Corporation
Imam and imamate, xiv, 8-9, 11-12, 15-22, 25, 97, 132. *See also* Ahmad, Imam; Hamid al-Din family; Yahya, Imam
IMF. *See* International Monetary Fund
Imperialism, 12, 14-17, 19-21, 135. *See also* Ottoman occupation and legacy
Imports, exports, and import-export duties and controls, 15, 24, 35, 37, 44, 66, 106, 114, 125-130, 153-154. *See also* Smuggling
Independent Petroleum Group (Kuwait), 146-147
Indian Ocean and the monsoons, 4
Industry and industrialization, 24-26, 67, 69, 86, 117, 122. *See also* Western nations and Japan (industrial nations)
Infrastructure (physical and economic), 6-7, 20-21, 46, 67, 71, 122, 153-154
Ingrams, Harold, 17
Institution building. *See* State building
Interior, Ministry of, 60, 105, 109
International Finance Corporation (IFC), 138
International Monetary Fund (IMF), 39-41, 46-47, 65-66, 81, 114, 127

Iran, 20, 96, 107, 123, 129
Iraq, 58, 64, 79, 96, 98, 106-107, 122-123, 129
Iraq-Iran War. *See* Gulf War
Iraqi-Yemeni Joint Commission on Economic and Technical Cooperation, 122
al-Iryani, Abd al-Karim, 48, 55, 62-63, 66-67, 89, 109, 114-116, 120, 122-123, 125-128, 130, 132, 142, 150, 152, 155, 158(n5)
al-Iryani, Abd al-Rahman, 21, 26, 28-29, 32-33, 37-38, 48, 54-55, 57-58, 112, 114, 132, 157(n1)
al-Iryani regime and era, xiv, 28-35, 38, 43, 49-54, 57-58, 60, 62-64, 67, 69, 72, 74, 78, 80, 87-88, 97
Islam, forms and sociocultural role of, 8-11, 15, 28-29, 111, 131-132, 152. *See also* Muslim Brotherhood; Religious leaders; Shafais; Zaydis
Islamic Conference Organization and other Islamic meetings, 36, 103, 137, 150
Islamic Front, 101-103, 106, 131
Ismail, Abd al-Fattah, 92, 96, 101, 129, 147
Ismailis. *See* Islam, forms and sociocultural role of
Israel, 28, 81, 83, 96-98, 107, 121
Italy, 129, 135, 146

Japan, 135, 139, 151-152
Jawf (wadi), 6, 144. *See also* Marib-Jawf basin
Jews (Yemeni), 8
Jizan, 12, 17, 149
John W. Mecom Company (Texas), 135-136
Jordan, 56, 64, 97, 123
Juban, 120
al-Junayd, Muhammad Ahmad, 47, 49, 55, 66
June 1980 Agreement, 102, 104, 121
Justice, Ministry of, 56

Kamaran Island, 139
Kennedy, John F., 27, 87
Khamis, Muhammad, 63, 105-106
Khamr, 77
Khartoum Agreement, 28

Kingdom of Saudi Arabia. *See* Saudi Arabia
Kissinger, Henry, 81
Korea Oil Corporation. *See* Yukong Corporation
al-Kuhhali, Mujahid, 90-91, 95
al-Kurshumi, Abdullah, 21, 36, 40-41
Kuwait, 40-42, 65, 81, 96, 98, 104, 106-107, 123, 136, 144, 146-147, 150-151
Kuwait Fund. *See* Kuwait

Labor and trade unions. *See* Political parties and pressure groups
Labor party, 62
Land and land tenure. *See* Agriculture
LCCD. *See* Local council for cooperative development
LDA. *See* Local development association
Lebanon, xiii, 6, 27, 75, 121-122, 147
Legal Office, 39, 56
Legal system and judicial reform, 18, 38, 55-56, 63-65
Legitimacy and support, xv, 8-9, 17, 59-60, 68, 77, 90-91, 94, 96-97, 100-111, 114, 116-118, 122, 125, 129-131, 155
Libya, 76, 95, 100, 107, 119-120, 123, 129, 155
Local council for cooperative development (LCCD), 142-143, 155
Local development association (LDA), 67, 69-70, 72-73, 76, 108, 124, 132, 143
Longriggs, Stephen, 135
Luhumis (abu Luhum family). *See* abu Luhum, Ali; abu Luhum, Sinan

Maabar, 139
Makki, Hasan, 44, 54-57, 63, 110, 142
Marib
  dam, 6, 123, 154
  town and province, 6-7, 55, 134, 140, 145
  See also Marib-Jawf basin
Marib-Jawf basin, 134, 137-140, 145-146, 154. *See also* Jawf (wadi); Marib
al-Matari, Ali Ahmad, 58, 60

Merchants and businessmen, 9, 19, 24, 29, 67, 109, 113, 128, 130, 153
Military. *See* Armed forces
Military actions, 17, 23, 34, 53, 61, 77, 95, 102-103, 118-120, 145
Military assistance. *See* Arms and military aid
Modernists and modern sector, 19-20, 24-25, 28-29, 31, 35, 38-39, 41, 45-46, 48-49, 52-54, 57, 59, 62-63, 65-67, 71-74, 88, 97, 99, 109, 114-115, 141-143, 155
Modernization. *See* Development and change
Money and currency, 24, 35, 44, 126-128, 153-154
Moser, Charles, 134
Muhammad (al-Hasani), Ali Nasir, 101-104, 119-121, 129-130, 145-148, 155-156
Muhammad, Fuad Qaid, 115
Muhammad, Salim Salih, 147
al-Muhani, Ahmad Ali, 109, 142
Municipal councils, 124, 132
Muslih, Yahya, 100
Muslim Brotherhood (Ikhwan), 21, 71, 131-132
al-Mutawakkal, Yahya, 60
Muzayyin class, 11

Nahm tribe, 50. *See also* abu Luhum, Sinan
Najran, 12, 17, 149
al-Nasir (Nasser), Gamal Abd, 20-21, 23, 26-27, 73, 76, 87
Nasirites, 62, 73, 76, 95
Nasser, Gamal Abdul. *See* al-Nasir, Gamal Abd
National Council, 33, 36
National Democratic Front (NDF), 62, 70, 73-74, 76, 80, 82, 95-96, 98-108, 110, 112, 115, 118-123, 125, 130-132
National dialogue, 111-112, 124-125, 130
National Dialogue Committee (NDC), 111-112, 124
National Institute of Public Administration (NIPA), 41, 65, 67
Nationalism and national identity, xiv, 8-9, 12-14, 16-17, 21, 26-29, 31,

62, 72-73, 75, 86, 98, 105, 111, 132, 149. *See also* Ideology and political ideas
National Liberation Front (NLF), 29-30, 43, 73, 78, 92
National Pact, 111-112, 124-125, 130-131
National reconciliation (1970), 29, 34, 36
National Tobacco and Matches Company, 25
National Yemeni Union, 54, 57, 68
NDC. *See* National Dialogue Committee
NDF. *See* National Democratic Front
Netherlands Bank, 36-37
1948 Revolution, 21, 111. *See also* Coups and assassinations
1970 Constitution, 33, 37, 57-58, 68, 91, 97, 113, 125. *See also* Constitutions and constitutional issues
1962 Revolution, xiv, 22-26, 50, 65, 109, 112, 133, 136
NIPA. *See* National Institute of Public Administration
NLF. *See* National Liberation Front
Non-aligned Nations, Sri Lanka Conference of, 82
Numan, Ahmad Muhammad, 21, 26, 37-38, 41-44
Numan, Yasin Said, 147

O'Ballance, Edgar, 25
Offshore Yemen Hunt, 154. *See also* Hunt Oil Company
Ogadan rebellion, 83
Oil. *See* Petroleum
Oil and Mineral Resources, Ministry of, 142
Oman, 12, 79, 82, 129, 146
OPEC. *See* Organization of Petroleum Exporting Countries
Open door policy, 45, 67, 78-79, 81, 129, 135, 153. *See also* Foreign investors, lenders and donors
OPIC. *See* Overseas Private Investment Corporation
Organization of Petroleum Exporting Countries (OPEC), 81, 107, 126

Organization of Yemeni Resisters, 44, 62
Ottoman occupation and legacy, 12, 14, 16-19, 21
Overseas Private Investment Corporation (OPIC), 138

The Pact (GPC newspaper), 130
Palestine Liberation Organization (PLO). *See* Palestinians
Palestinians, 14, 121-122, 129, 146
Partisans (political party activists), 21, 26-27, 29-31, 61-62, 72-74, 76, 79-80, 99, 125, 131, 142, 155
Party of God (of al-Zubayri), 26
PCA. *See* People's Constituent Assembly
PDRY. *See* People's Democratic Republic of Yemen
Peasant leagues, 29-30
People's Constituent Assembly (PCA), 91-93, 97, 109-110, 131
People's Democratic Republic of Yemen (PDRY), xiii, 1, 4, 8, 12, 72-73, 78, 81, 83, 92, 94, 100-101, 103-104, 107, 120-121, 129, 134, 146-149, 151
  and YAR-PDRY relations, 12, 29, 43-44, 53-54, 61, 73, 78-80, 82-84, 86-87, 90, 92, 94-96, 98-106, 115, 118-121, 129-130, 136-137, 145-149, 151-152, 155-156
Periphery. *See* Center-periphery issues
Petro Fac, 138
Petroleum
  discovery and development, xiii-xv, 6, 133-134, 137-140, 154
  exploration, 134-139, 154
  exploration and development in the PDRY, 146-147
  implications, domestic and external, 140-152
Petromin (Saudi Arabia), 136
Pipeline, export and domestic oil, 137, 139-140, 154
Plans and planning. *See* Development plans and planning
PLO. *See* Palestinians
Police. *See* Security forces and police
Political construction, xiv-xv, 15, 26, 33, 54, 59, 67-74, 76-77, 88-89,

94, 110–113, 118, 124–125, 130–131, 142–143, 155. *See also* Political parties and pressure groups
Political development. *See* Political construction
Political infrastructure. *See* Political construction; Political parties and pressure groups
Political parties and pressure groups, 19, 21, 26–27, 33, 61, 68, 71–73, 89, 99, 120, 125, 130–131, 155
Politicization and political expansion. *See* Political construction; Political infrastructure; Political parties and pressure groups
Politics and domestic political life, xiv, 19, 21, 26–27, 43–44, 57–59, 68, 75, 77–79, 86, 88–89, 92–101, 105, 108, 113, 115, 118, 124–125, 129–131, 142–144, 151–152, 154–155
Popular Democratic Union, 62. *See also* Communist party (Yemeni)
Popular Resistance Forces (PRF), 29–30, 44
Popular Revolutionary Organization, 26
President (or other head of state), Office of the, 25, 33, 65, 91–92, 97, 131, 157(n1), 158(n1). *See also* Command Council; Presidential Council; Republican Council
Presidential Council, 91–92. *See also* President, Office of the
PRF. *See* Popular Resistance Forces
Prime Minister and Council of Ministers, Offices of the, 25, 39, 65, 115
Private sector. *See* Industry and industrialization
Progressives and others on the political left. *See* Partisans
Protectorates. *See* Aden Protectorates
Protest and opposition, 21, 26–27, 30, 38, 43–44, 60–61, 66, 77, 88–91, 96, 101, 128, 131–132, 144, 154–155
Public administration. *See* Civil service and administrative reform
Purges and government reshuffles, 19, 26–27, 30, 44, 88, 90, 105, 109, 128, 132, 142, 147, 153

al-Qaddafi, Muammar, 76, 95. *See also* Libya
Qadi class, 11, 18–19, 29, 114, 133
Qasim, Salih Muslih, 103, 129, 147
Qat, 5, 11–12, 93
Qataba, 83
Qatar, 155

Radaa, 5
Radfidain Bank (Iraq), 122–123
Ramlat al-Sabatayn, 134. *See also* Empty Quarter
Ras Isa. *See* Salif
Reconciliation (1970), national. *See* National reconciliation (1971)
Red Sea, 1, 4–5, 15–16, 82–84, 136–140, 154. *See also* Bab al-Mandab Straits; Suez Canal
Red Sea security issue, 82–84, 129
Refinery, petroleum products, 136–138, 140
Religious leaders, 8, 16, 19, 66, 131–132, 141–143, 155
Remittances, workers', 7, 44, 66–67, 84, 86, 96, 113–114, 125–129, 141, 153–154. *See also* Emigration and emigrants
Repression (political harassment, imprisonment, execution, etc.), 17, 22, 26–27, 30, 44, 61, 68, 88, 90–91, 95, 108, 120
Republican Council, 29, 33, 38, 50, 157(n1)
Republicanism and republicans, 21–31, 35, 54, 97, 99, 151. *See also* Republican tribalists and other conservative republicans
Republican tribalists and other conservative republicans, 28–32
Reserves, the, 51, 57, 60
Revenues. *See* Taxes and tax collection
Revolution. *See* 1948 Revolution; 1962 Revolution
Revolutionary Democratic Party, 30, 43, 62
Roads and highways. *See* Infrastructure
Royalists (in civil war), 22–23, 29–32, 35, 50, 54
al-Rub al-Khali. *See* Empty Quarter
Rubaya Ali, Salim, 83, 92, 95

Saada, 7, 34, 77, 138
Safir dome, 134
Said, Ahmad Abdu, 158(n10)
Said, Hayl, 67
Salif, 136, 139-140, 154. *See also*
  Pipeline, export and domestic oil
Salih, Ali Abdullah, 91-112, 115-116,
  119, 121-124, 128-132, 137, 140-
  146, 148, 150, 153-155
Salih regime and era, xv, 94-116, 118-
  125, 127, 129-133, 141-156
al-Sallal, Abdullah, 22, 26-27, 33, 112
al-Sallal regime and era, xiv, 22-28, 97
Sallam, Muhammad Abd al-Aziz, 24
Samarra Pass, 5, 8
SAM missiles, 120
Sanaa, 4-7, 16, 29-30, 34, 67, 83-84,
  86, 88, 134, 138
Sanaa mutiny, 30, 32-33, 61-62, 99
Sanaa University, 41, 67
Sanger, Richard, 134, 157(n1)
Sanhan tribe, 97, 109
Saud, King Abd al-Aziz ibn, 134
Saudi Arabia, xiv, 1, 4, 28, 107, 126,
  134
  YAR-Saudi relations, 14, 17, 20, 23,
  27, 32, 35-37, 43-45, 50-51, 53-
  54, 58-61, 64, 66, 72-73, 75, 77-
  85, 87-90, 94, 97-101, 104-107,
  115, 118-119, 121-125, 128-132,
  133, 136, 141, 143-145, 149-152,
  155
Saudi-Yemeni Joint Coordinating
  Council, 80, 84, 130, 150
Sayyid caste, 11, 18-19, 22, 29, 133
Scott, Hugh, 18
Second Five-Year Development Plan,
  114, 116-119, 122-123, 125-127
Sectarian differences and conflict, 8-9,
  12, 17, 27, 30, 75, 91
Security forces and police, 50, 63,
  105-106, 109, 120
Septembrist Grouping, 100
Septembrists, 22, 78, 109. *See also*
  Septembrist Grouping
Sergeant, Robert, 12
Settlement pattern. *See* Social
  organization and settlement
  patterns
Shabwa, 145-146

Shafais (and Shafaism), 8-9, 12, 17, 19,
  24-25, 27, 29-30, 59, 75-76, 78,
  91
al-Shami, Ahmad, 29
al-Shami, Muhammad Abdullah,
  157(n4), 158(n4)
al-Shami, Yahya, 102-103, 124
al-Shayba, Ali, 93
Shii Islam (Shiites). *See* Zaydis
Siege of Sanaa, 29-30, 34, 99
Six-Day War (June 1967), 28, 45
Smuggling, 106, 113, 127-128, 130, 153
Social Affairs, Labor and Youth,
  Ministry of, 55
Social (sociocultural) change. *See*
  Development and change
Socialist camp, 23, 27, 45, 73, 83, 100,
  135. *See also* Soviet Union
Social organization and settlement
  patterns, 6-12
Somalia, 82-84. *See also* Ogadan
  rebellion
Sonotrach. *See* Algeria
Southern Uplands Rural Development
  Project, 67
South Yemen. *See* People's Democratic
  Republic of Yemen
Soviet Union (USSR), 20-21, 23, 27,
  37, 41, 45, 51, 64, 73, 80, 82-83,
  94, 100, 104-107, 109, 129, 135,
  146, 148
Standard Franco-Americaine, 134
Standing Committee of the GPC, 124-
  125, 130-131
State building, xiv, 12, 15, 18-19, 25-
  26, 38, 43-46, 48, 53, 55-56, 62-
  67, 71, 98-99, 144, 151
Statistical yearbooks, 39, 49
Stookey, Robert, 28-29, 32
Subsidies (tribal and government
  budget), 19, 23, 36, 44, 66, 78,
  106, 130, 144, 149
Sudan, 19, 65, 84, 132
Suez Canal, 83
Sultan (of Saudi royal family), Prince,
  84, 87, 122
Summit meetings, Arab. *See* Arab
  League and Arab summits
Summit meetings, Yemeni, 54, 83, 96,
  99-102, 104, 119, 121, 145, 155
Sunni Islam (Sunnites). *See* Shafais

Supply and Commerce, Ministry of, 55, 153
Supreme Committee (Council) for Petroleum and Mineral Resources, 142
Supreme Committee for the Second Development Plan, 116
Supreme Yemeni Council, 104, 129
Syria, 20, 79, 96, 100, 103, 107, 119-121, 123, 132

Taiz (city and province), 5-6, 9, 26-27, 50, 67, 69, 84, 91, 95, 97, 121
Taiz summit of Red Sea security (1977), 84. See also Red Sea security issue
Tariq, Abdullah, 31
Taxes and tax collection, 17-18, 65-66, 125-127, 140-141
Technical assistance. See Aid and assistance
Technical Office, 38-41, 47-48
Technocrats. See Modernists and modern sector
Technoexport (Soviet Union), 146
Third Five-Year Development Plan, 143
Third force, the, 26
13 June Correction Movement, 58, 88. See also Correction Movement; al-Hamdi regime and era
13 June Movement, 95, 100
Three Years' Development Program, 48-49, 55, 67
Tihama, 5-7, 9, 11, 17, 134-136, 138-139. See also Tihama Development Authority
Tihama Development Authority, 46, 67
Total. See Compagnie Française des Petroles
Toyomenko Company, 136
Traditionalists. See Conservatives
Treasury Ministry, 39, 41, 47, 55
"Triangle" (of Sanaa, Taiz, and al-Hudayda), 6-7, 20-21, 23, 103
Tribal irregulars and rebellions, 10, 18, 22-23, 31-32, 37, 51, 60-61, 68, 75, 77, 95, 102-103
Tribes, tribalism and tribal shaykhs, 9-12, 17-19, 22-23, 29, 31-33, 36-37, 49-54, 58-64, 70-73, 77-80, 84, 86, 88-91, 94-95, 97-101, 105, 109, 123, 128, 130, 132, 144, 148
Tripartite Alliance, 129
Turbah, 7
Turks. See Ottoman occupation and legacy
26 September Revolution Day, 86, 102, 112, 116, 122, 155
Twitchell, Karl, 134

Ulema. See Religious leaders
Umar, Sultan Ahmad, 101-102, 221
United Arab Emirates. See Abu Dhabi
United Arab Republic (UAR). See Egypt
United Arab States, 20
United Nations, 41, 45, 49-50, 65, 81, 116, 133
United Nations' Development Program (UNDP). See United Nations
United States of America, 19-21, 23, 27, 45, 51, 60, 64, 80-83, 90, 94, 104-107, 114, 119, 123, 129, 134-136, 144, 151-152
Unity and unification (of the two Yemens), 12, 54, 73, 80, 82-83, 96-97, 99-101, 105, 108, 121, 146
USSR. See Soviet Union

Wadi Zabid Project, 46, 48, 67
al-Wajih, Muhammad Khadim, 153
Weber, Max (and patrimonial political systems), 16
Western nations and Japan (industrial nations), 14, 19-20, 23, 45, 51, 78-79, 81, 123, 129, 148, 151-152
West Germany, 45, 81, 123, 155
World Bank/International Development Agency (IDA), 39-42, 45, 47-48, 81, 114, 123, 127, 147-148, 155

Yahya, Imam, 16-21, 133-134, 151
Yarim, 138
YBRD. See Yemen Bank for Reconstruction and Development
Yemen Bank for Reconstruction and Development (YBRD), 24-25, 38, 40, 46
Yemen Development Corporation (Texas), 135
Yemen Foreign Trade Company, 25

Yemen Hunt Oil Company (YHOC), 134, 137–140, 154. *See also* Hunt Oil Company.
Yemeni People's Unity Party, 100, 120, 122
Yemeni Socialist Party, 147–149
Yemeni Unionists, 21
Yemen Oil and Mineral Company (Yominco), 134, 137–142. *See also* Yemen Petroleum Company
Yemen Oil and Mines Industry Company (Yomico), 136
Yemen Petroleum Company, 25, 142. *See also* Yemen Oil and Mineral Company

Yemen Pharmaceutical Company, 25
YHOC. *See* Yemen Hunt Oil Company
Yomico. *See* Yemen Oil and Mines Industry Company
Yominco. *See* Yemen Oil and Mineral Company
Yukong Corporation (Korea), 137–138

Zabid, 7
al-Zandani, Abd al-Wahid, 130, 142
Zaydis (and Zaydism), 8–12, 16–17, 27, 29–30, 75, 78, 91
al-Zubayri, Muhammad, 21, 26

For Product Safety Concerns and Information please contact our EU
representative GPSR@taylorandfrancis.com
Taylor & Francis Verlag GmbH, Kaufingerstraße 24, 80331 München, Germany

www.ingramcontent.com/pod-product-compliance
Lightning Source LLC
Chambersburg PA
CBHW070402240426
43661CB00056B/2503